Japanese Fashion

Japanese Fashion
A Cultural History

Toby Slade

Oxford • New York

English edition
First published in 2009 by
Berg
Editorial offices:
First Floor, Angel Court, 81 St Clements Street, Oxford OX4 1AW, UK
175 Fifth Avenue, New York, NY 10010, USA

Berg is the imprint of Oxford International Publishers Ltd.

Library of Congress Cataloging-in-Publication Data

A catalogue record for this book is available from the Library of Congress.

British Library Cataloguing-in-Publication Data

A catalogue record for this book is available from the British Library.

ISBN 978 1 84788 253 0 (Cloth)
978 1 84788 252 3 (Paper)

Typeset by Apex CoVantage, LLC, Madison, WI, USA.
Printed in Great Britain by the MPG Books Group, Bodmin and King's Lynn

www.bergpublishers.com

Contents

Acknowledgements

Firstly it is important to acknowledge that without government funding, research of this nature could not take place, and it is therefore necessary to credit both the University of Sydney Postgraduate Award Scheme and the Japanese Government (Monbukagakusho) Scholarship Scheme as the instruments of policy that made this research possible. The opportunity to continue my studies at the University of Sydney and the opportunity to research in Japan were invaluable both in terms of this particular research and in terms of life experience. The institutions which gave me those opportunities will always command my respect and loyalty.

In this vein it is also necessary to express my ongoing gratitude to the other patrons of this research, my mother and father, who always supported and funded my education and who never needed to see a return on their investment other than my happiness. For that gift too, I am forever grateful.

When I first chose art history as a major I imagined that I would finish with a consummate knowledge of Italian or Spanish painting, and I never imagined that I would come to be interested in either fashion or Japan. For this change in interest and perspective I must acknowledge the inspirational lectures on clothing and style of Michael Carter, which established for me the importance of art objects of the everyday, and roused my ongoing interest in them. Further, for turning my perspective eastwards I must thank John Clark, whose expansive knowledge and insights were an inspiration to study and research within Japan and Asia generally.

In Japan I would like to thank Omuka Toshiharu, whose support, advice and introductions made what could have been an extremely difficult experience far more accessible and enjoyable.

Finally, for assistance with Japanese language, research and a million other little things about Japan, I would like to thank Kito Sakiko and Kamijo Wakako. And for tireless editing and advice I would like to thank Anne Slade.

–1–

Introduction: Modernity, Fashion and Japan

The central intellectual concerns of this book are twofold: firstly the importance and meaning of sartorial modernity in Japan, and secondly what this particular geographically limited experience of modernity implies for our understanding of fashion in general. Far from being a hit-and-miss sideshow in the great circus of human thought, clothing fashions operate in such a way as to echo the larger mechanisms of aesthetic change and are indeed central to the processes and legacy of modernity. This book hopes to demonstrate that there are other modernities, and different fashion histories beyond the canon of European and American dress narratives, which dominate nearly all interpretations of the practices, styles, institutions and hermeneutic structures of clothing in the modern age. The question of whether the aesthetic needs of modern life are grown out of one cultural tradition or whether they are found by all cultural traditions under certain circumstances of developmental consciousness is still open, and whatever hierarchies can be concluded from the answer are still of social importance. Even the questions raised by a notion of developmental consciousness—that certain technological, intellectual and social conditions combine to engender a fundamentally different state of consciousness in modernity than had existed before—are not settled questions.[1] The question of social relations ontologically preceding individual consciousness is repeated within fashion theory and is especially important to questions of clothing fashions in a period of great changes in social relations such as modernity.[2]

To look seriously at art objects of the everyday, such as clothes—their discourse and practices, their meaning-bearing forms and their codes of internal and external interpretation—is an essential, and often neglected, component of any study of modern aesthetics. Insofar as clothing and the processes by which tastes, styles and connotations of it transform—that is to say fashion—can serve as representations of modernity, and indeed as a model for how the dynamics of a modern consciousness operate, then any humble conclusions about clothing fashion may have wider application. The Japanese example is examined here for the particular reason that it runs contrary to traditional fashion theory explanations of the sequence and causality of sartorial modernity. And the accuracy of those explanations of modernity is vital for any representation of a condition of *post*modernity and necessary to test, for better or for worse, the validity of our current theories of postmodern fashion.

One of the limitations of this book is that it originally intended to be a calibration of the canon of fashion theory within the context of Japanese modernity, not an authoritative history of Japanese clothing in the modern era. However, in the absence of such an authoritative text, it had to establish a working model of that history before it could achieve its original aims. Most of the work is therefore devoted to establishing the sartorial history of Japan, and it is not until Chapter 5 that a detailed analysis of that history is attempted within the framework of conventional fashion theory. Also, many of the conceptual tools mentioned along the way are not examined closely until that final chapter.

It is a constant issue throughout the book that Eurocentric models fit the Japanese modern experience imperfectly. The use of theoretical constructs from Western philosophy, when related to the Japanese, context bring up many potential difficulties in applying what may be culturally specific tools to a different cultural context. Being aware of this, one of the intentions of the book is to reposition theories of fashion to account for clothing behaviour in contexts outside these theories' origin. It aims to find what is universal in the clothing of modernity and what is culturally specific.

Most of the discourses referred to throughout the book are naturally from the perspective of fashion theory, and their more specific meanings in this context are not defined until the final chapter, for the very reason that this book intends to redefine them in terms of a particular sartorial history which it first must establish. A key term used throughout is the idea of Kantian veracity—a tendency in all modernities towards reductionism and essentialism—which is applied to fashion modernity by Anne Hollander in her definition of the suit.[3] This is examined more closely in Chapter 3. Another key discourse which is specific to fashion theory is formed by the ongoing questions of the governing dynamics of fashion and change characterized divergently by either historical drivers, material possibility or *Zeitgeist* explanations. The particular framing of this larger debate, around which the whole discipline of fashion revolves, was characterized by Michael Carter, and the present text can also be read as a contribution to that debate from a Japanese perspective.[4]

Modernity

Modernity can be a very flexible designation. Commonly intermingled and confused with modernization—the processes of political, industrial, scientific, economic and technological reform and innovation—and modernism—the wave of avant-garde artistic movements that represent and/or respond to the changes in experience and sensibility—modernity generally refers to the way in which modernization infiltrated everyday life. This poses a problem for the study of Japan, as many of the attributes generally associated with modernity and indeed modernism predate the processes of modernization, reversing the notion that one is a prerequisite for the other. This is especially relevant for theories of sartorial modernity and the appearance of a modern fashion system and will be discussed in greater depth later.

Modernity, as a cultural phenomenon, is confined in the Japanese experience to the period after the Meiji Restoration of 1868, and while modernity in Western Europe is often used as a term that is extended backwards from industrialist–capitalist society to the ruptures from preceding social systems leading into the social and cultural changes which took place from the mid-sixteenth century, the particular history of Japanese isolation means that the periodizations that can be made are neater. While the levels of urbanization, literacy and trade in consumer goods were all uniquely high in late Edo Japan, the enforced intellectual isolation makes premature any characterization of that period as one of modernity, despite some modern elements which could be recognized as part of a modern fashion system: mass produced woodblock prints used to advertise clothing, product placement of kimono textiles in kabuki theatre and rapidly changing seasonal styles in urban Edo culture were some of these. Modernity is largely confined, for this book, to the development of consumer culture, and is concerned with the relationship between the processes of production, distribution and consumption that developed between the reopening of Japan in the late 1860s and the full militarization of the late 1930s. Focusing the long history of Japanese clothing on this period is appropriate not just because of the totality of the nation-reshaping events that bookend it—the Meiji Restoration and the Second World War—but also because this era is preeminent in the establishment of a global fashion system into which Japan becomes more and more integrated. This is the period when the words 'Japanese' and 'Fashion' can truly be combined. Nineteenth-century modernity was imperial as much as it was industrial; as much about communications, world trade and high finance as it was about coal mines, factories and technological progress, and it is this globalization, particularly of clothing fashion, that also characterizes the time.

Modernity is something more, however, than the expansion of processes that began with the rise of mercantile and agricultural capitalism or indeed with Commodore Perry's warship-backed insistence that Japan be part of that rise. The term alludes more to a *Zeitgeist* than to a clearly distinct epoch—as for different nations, classes and individuals the parameters of that epoch are highly elastic. Modernity is thus more precise than simply everything since the industrial and French revolutions and something less narrow than a mere politically neutral term for capitalism. It refers to things both intangible and undeniably material: the look and feel of modern life through eyes that were seeing it for the first time. The welcome experience of newness becomes a transformation to which all premodern societies must adjust.

Elizabeth Wilson notes that central to modernity is a paradox: the Enlightenment, the series of intellectual movements in the seventeenth and eighteenth centuries that allowed for advances in technology and reform to social organization—and that Japan evoked in the early Meiji period to inspire the same effect of overturning tradition, obscurantist superstition and baseless, wasteful customs—has as its core values of scientific method and rationality.[5] However, it emerged in tandem with, or as a precursor to, industrial capitalism, which has been theorized as irrational, out of control and unstoppable. The internal logics of modern production and mechanization did not equate to a systematic logic for social betterment. Modernity is defined by reason and science but also by speed, mobility and mutability. While in Europe and revolutionary America the Enlightenment came before these areas' industrial revolutions, for Japan the twin parts of modernity, the two halves of progress, arrived at the same time. This characterization of modernity is almost the opposite of the way Adam Smith envisioned a market economy working: individual vice equating to collective good. If people all acted selfishly, consuming whatever they desired, then this would be to the benefit of the system. The paradox of modernity sketched here is the inverse: rational behaviour equating to systematic irrationality. This illogical state has vexed fashion theorists, notably Thorstein Veblen, who will be discussed in more detail later, as it applies to clothing and the value systems of fashion as an extension of the way in which Marx understood use-value and exchange-value in modern capitalist society as a whole.

Modernity also meant the extension of the logic of industrial, mechanized modernization to other areas of social and economic life. This resulted in the advent of rational bureaucratic structures of domination, actual and virtual—which will be discussed with reference to the way in which the Meiji state used clothing reform as a tool of nation-building and control. It also resulted in the birth of mass leisure pursuits—dance halls, cafés, sports, cinemas, mass holiday destinations and department stores—all of which were the social spaces at which modernity could be performed—and the beginning of mass consumption and the actual modernization of production techniques with the need for masses of factory workers. The adjustment to mass, industrial, urban life was intensified in Japan because of its speed, with Japan starting to develop industrially much later than England, Germany or America, and compounded by the perceived further alienation of modernity, which was seen as foreign, rapidly replacing traditional culture and identity.

Essential to modernity is the idea of reflexivity—the continual reexamination and reevaluation of knowledge in every sphere. Modernity and its central precept of progress brought the end of certainty. Unchallenged sources of authority, whether political, religious or scholastic, were all ousted by modernity. Scientific and technological advances and social and economic reforms created anxiety rather than the reassurance of traditional sources of knowledge. Without adherence to absolutist and, most often arbitrary, Confucian epistemology, the population sought new means of knowledge production and new sources of information. But far from resulting in certainty, this led to continually changing practices and fads—fashions—in ideas and the things that become repositories for those ideas, especially clothing, which is, before almost everything else, the repository for conceptions of individual and collective identity. In modernity, progress was constantly sought, yet constantly questioned, undermined and remodelled. It was this feature of modernity—the reflexivity of continual reappraisal, before most of the trappings of industrial modernization and the physical experience of urban mass culture—that arrived and reordered the aesthetics of Japan.

The large part of that reordering did not, however, conform to modern reasoning but was based in the redefinition of 'Japan-ness' that accompanied the arrival of the new twin others, modernity and 'The West'. The perceived unstoppable trajectory of modern progress that was embraced by Japan also resulted in nostalgia and, if not an overt longing for the past, then at least a formless melancholy and regret that some essence or intangible element had been lost. Modernity everywhere repeatedly clothes itself in reconstructions of the past, and Japan was no different, recreating a national costume and inventing traditions to authenticate this past and to authenticate the very idea of Japan itself.

While individual garments conform to both an engagement with the key concepts of modernity—rational reform—and to an enraged critique of the new economic and social order, fashion as a system is firmly on the side of the irrational. Despite the logic of an extension of the project of modernity to create a scientific and rational dress, clothing fashions instead play host to the other side of modernity. Even as tradition and superstition were consigned to the past, they were resurrected in the culture of modernity, in the sartorial uncanny, where the magical—romantic dress—and the irrationality of arbitrary ornamentation persist despite Enlightenment thought's insistence that they be abolished. Often the clothing most typical of the period of industrialization and modernization is in opposition to the scientific and rational values that industrial society is supposed to produce and constitute. Because Japan entered this process of dialectical sartorial antithesis late, most of its forms were borrowed, but they were equally irrational. Japanese attempts to rationalize indigenous dress also failed in the same way that Dress Reform rationalizations failed in Britain. Fashion operated under its own logic, and indeed it was this logic that infected modernity, rather than 'rational thought' infecting clothing fashion.

The sociological periodization of the beginning of the Meiji period is distinct from that of other modernizing nations in that, unlike the inexorable but gradual transformation to modern society in Western Europe, enforced isolation in Japan acted like a dam holding back the comprehensive reshaping of society until it all burst at once. This meant that while European class structures had had several hundred years to respond to social reorganization—particularly the enrichment of the urban middle classes—in Japan this process was condensed into a much shorter time, and the reactionary cultural products were different. The pecuniary system, identified by Veblen and others, that developed as the leisure classes—mainly reconstituted aristocracies—sought to continually differentiate themselves through conspicuous consumption in modernizing Europe had a long period in which to institute its semiotic vocabulary. It functioned by institutionalized envy and invidious distinction. In Japan, the samurai class, which could have been restyled into a leisure class that consumed without producing, was abolished before such a value system could be instituted. The jump from feudalism to modernity was so quick that the fashion system that developed was less an expression of interclass rivalry than of the other factors that influence dress. This was partly because of an anomaly, namely that any adoption of fashion could be considered nouveau riche—the cardinal sin of aristocratic value systems—and for Japan it was predominantly an imported phenomenon. Thus any claim to legitimation as the ruling class by traditional entitlement could not be reflected through sartorial distinction as it could in aristocratic Europe, where the class changes that engendered a reactionary response were more gradual. The association of modern dress with the victorious side in the civil war that ended in the Meiji Restoration also meant that the meanings associated with the adoption of a fashion system were on a very different plane of signification than the European systems they originally imitated. While far from being the classless society of popular myth, Japan was different from its European model in the sartorial signs that could be used to distinguish class.

The characterization of pre-Meiji Japan as feudal in its class arrangements and intellectual disposition is expedient but not entirely accurate. European feudalism is defined by the debate as to the scope to which the term can be applied. On the one side are those that define feudalism on very narrow terms, arguing that feudal relationships existed only within the medieval nobility itself and were confined to legal and military implications.[6] In contrast to this is the view of feudalism as a type of society with hierarchical relationships between classes:[7] vassals performing military service in exchange for their fiefs, peasants performing physical labour in return for protection. While there is reluctance to classify other societies according to European models, in Japan, the system of land tenure, with the vassal receiving tenure in exchange for an oath of fealty, is very close to the system in parts of medieval Europe.[8] The intellectual confines of the Tokugawa shogunate were also feudally restrictive, in that knowledge production was extremely regulated and the State assumed the supreme role in philosophical authority. For our purposes, the shogunate in the Edo period also regulated the visual manifestations of ideology and class through sumptuary laws whose abolition, with the Meiji Restoration, is often commented upon as an explosion of colour signalling the new age. The term feudalism is useful to delineate the period when class, gender and regional relations were fixed and there was a closed discourse for all semiotic media including clothing.

As Michel Foucault points out, the Enlightenment or Age of Reason had to construct a vision of 'unreason' as being demonic and subhuman, and therefore evil and befouling. By analogy, rationalism in the modern period is, likewise, a construction. The use of the term *bummei kaika* (civilization and enlightenment) by the Japanese state as an expression of public policy implies, of course, that the period before it was uncivilized and unenlightened, when this in many regards was not the case. The reasons for defining, in this situation, clothing of the pre- and post-Restoration eras as inherently enlightened or unenlightened are arbitrary. The argument that indigenous styles were in fact more rational and efficient will be taken up later. What was necessary was signs that demonstrated the worth of change as a value in itself, signs that progress required constant reevaluation of everything and that this would be of benefit, not necessarily just the forms that the reevaluation took along the way. Fashion—a constant reshaping and a requisite freedom of mobility of forms manifested as a socially replicated aesthetic restlessness—is indeed a central value of modernity as it makes possible the reflexivity that replaces arbitrary intellectual authority.

Enlightenment generally implies the use of rationality to establish authoritative ethics, aesthetics and knowledge; yet the Japanese experience often merely substituted the obviously arbitrary for the not so obviously arbitrary. However, it is in the process of continual substitution that the real agenda of modernity lies. Immanuel Kant described enlightenment as man's leaving his self-caused immaturity—the incapacity to use one's own understanding without the guidance of another. This was certainly the intention of the Meiji state, to turn the passive compliance of the populace into active spiritual participation in the realization of national objectives; to reconstitute the people into more than simply objects of rule, so that they could become knowledgeable and self-disciplined subjects in the dual Foucauldian sense—that is subjects who were not only subjected to 'control and dependence' but were also possessed of their own identity, having a 'conscience or self-knowledge'.[9] Once freed to be part of a national process of modern reflexivity in the service of civic progress, the individual identity of the freed person also enters a state of constant reevaluating flux and once within that state of flux expresses it—the self-reflexivity—through following or rejecting, adopting and discarding sartorial fashions.

Enlightened times will enlighten only a small number of people, as Voltaire noted of Enlightenment France, and this was the case also in Meiji Japan.[10] Even by Taishō times, those with an understanding and capacity to engage in modern dress were limited to certain urban elites. Susan Sontag, writing about mainly French attempts to define a new postmodern consciousness said: 'To speak of reality becoming spectacle is a breathtaking provincialism. It universalizes the viewing habits of a small, educated population living in the rich part of the world where news has been converted into entertainment.'[11] The argument seems to be that a new consciousness, which exists within an elite, should not be examined until it is shared by a majority. The same could be argued of the obvious point that most of Japan, living in the countryside, did not in fact experience modernity—change entirely from a feudal understanding of the world to a modern one—until a long time after the urban elites. In terms of making that ultimate self-identification as modern, donning Western-style clothing, the majority of the population waited until well into the twentieth century. But this is to miss the point. Sontag would have us only examine the new modern consciousness in Japan when the last woman in the furthest, poorest village gives away her kimono and puts on a day dress. The change in aesthetic values is elitist at first and its diffusive process is long, but it is an important process nonetheless and an important instrument if we are to calibrate any measurements of aesthetic modernism. Furthermore, the embrace of sartorial modernity is not an exclusionary action by elites but, on the contrary, part of a wider agenda of elite provision of examples for the greater population.

One of the processes of modernity is a universalization of national identity, facilitated mainly through the institution of universal education and the burgeoning mass media. Through deliberate propaganda, such as dissemination through newspapers and the distribution of imperial portraits showing the Emperor wearing modern uniforms, Japan was transformed from a loose abstraction to a far more established and significant idea—from a collection of feudal domains to a unified nation-state—in the minds of the people who inhabited it. This centrally modern process of creating a collective identity through the fabrication and propagation of national mythology was aided by the fact that Japan was far ahead of most nations in literacy and education; indeed, compulsory education was instituted in Japan before it was instituted in the United States and Germany, and newspaper readership and literacy levels in Tokyo have consistently been amongst the highest in the world from very early on. Knowledge about foreign clothing came well before the actual ability, materials and industry to make it, but because it was introduced at the same time as many of the myths of 'authentic' Japanese culture were themselves being introduced, its foreignness was partly mitigated.

Materially and culturally, in Japan as in Europe, the process of embourgeoisement of the bulk of the population began in the nineteenth century but did not really get into full swing until the twentieth. Arno Mayer, in *The Persistence of the Old Regime*, showed that aristocracies continued to dominate the ostensibly bourgeois nineteenth century in Europe.[12] Only with the First World War were old elites levelled, making way for mass society and a people's history. The elusive nineteenth-century bourgeois revolution, then, was less about an amorphous class than about the spread of law and new civic institutions and cultural myths. The embourgeoisement of vast areas of the planet was a distinctly twentieth-century phenomenon. Any bourgeois dress revolution in Japan was retarded by the fact that the material capacity to engage fully in a sartorially modern life was not achieved until well into the twentieth century. But the seeds were planted much earlier through intentional elite provision of models and a proactive agenda aiming at the cultural transformation of Japan.

The experience of modernity—speed, mobility, mutability, mass transport, new employment, early consumerism and access to mass information, visual and written—often occurs before modernity is brought into the home. The change in clothing is also something public long before it becomes something private. Taste becomes a divided phenomenon; public livery in modern style is considered appropriate, but private interiors and dress remain traditional for a much longer period. Japanese identity is obsessively comparative; there is always an *other*. In Meiji Japan, perhaps clothing was the clearest illustration of dialectical materialism: the new experience of the foreign, defining the previously undefined notion of what was Japanese. In the broadest terms, Marxist theory is a way of treating each aspect of a historical moment—its art, its industry, its politics, its clothing—as being implicated in the whole, and understanding that every dominant idea depends on, defines itself against, whatever it suppresses or excludes. Dialectical thinking is a brake on the tendency to assume that things will continue to be the way they are, only more so, because it is a reminder that every paradigm contains the seed of its own undoing, the limit-case that, as it is approached, begins to unravel the whole construct. Most cultural products work in several ways at once, however.

Modern aesthetics, based on Kant's assertion of the autonomy of art—that it should be true only to itself—provides in its logical extension the narrative for the history of modern art, and it is possible to graft a parallel narrative onto the history of clothing. Sartorial reductionism, its reduction to component parts and atomic entities, both actual and motivational, is, for theories of modern dress, a logically parallel application of Clement Greenberg's characterization of modernism as a tendency towards essentialism.[13] This process in Japan was complicated by the fact that to the extent that it was adopted, Western dress was often more complex, ornate and arbitrary than its indigenous predecessor in Japan. Any process of liberation from custom and tradition is one that is also appropriated, in terms of a reductionism or streamlining of dress. The 'we invented the future for you'[14] attitude particularly of American histories of modernity forgets that the hierarchies that such a narrative hopes to engender are paradoxical, as the point of such an aesthetic agenda is to free aesthetics from the service of politics. Issues of appropriation and the stealing of forms, in sartorial as well as other modernist media, is an idea that privileges the nation and nationality as organizing principles of culture. By definition, imitation is form without content, yet what was being manifested in Japan was the same dress forms but with a different content. Any characterization of clothing, as well as other expressions of culture, as a product of national identity rather than of an aesthetic that is in the process of freeing itself from all service to state and religion is one that, perhaps deliberately, misunderstands the modernist aesthetic agenda.

The freedom of the individual and of art that, following Kant, lay at the heart of modernist thinking came to be at odds with what became a recurring product of modernity: the absolutist state. The absolutism of religion and the feudal state, which by definition had to be overthrown as a condition of modernity, was reinstated in the form of Hitler in Germany, Stalin in Russia and to some extent the emperor cult in Japan, which reached its climax during the Second World War. The new absolutism of totalitarianism in its various manifestations was profoundly anti-fashion, preferring uniforms and utopian sartorial visions, and is another reason why this project is limited to the pre–Pacific War period. When there is no provision for reflexivity, none of the reevaluation of knowledge that comes with the absence of epistemological authority, then fashions, in ideas, opinions and clothes, ceases to the extent that the system is dominant. The point should be made here that while the cultural and political conditions of Japanese modernity were sufficient for the emergence of fascism, this was not a necessary and inexorable consequence. The confusion of sequence and causality often enters the discourse of pre–Pacific War Japanese cultural product, but the fact that Japanese fashion had a component of competitive, nationalist and even social-Darwinist motivation did not necessarily mean that ambition would sacrifice the other aspirations of modernity or that it was the only cultural motivation at work.

The Kantian imperative of aesthetic freedom entered the Japanese experience before many of the accompaniments of modernity. Japan experienced modernity before it fully experienced modernization. The locating of modernity in the urban is a common theme; commencing with the Baudelairean notion that the pivotal moment of modernity was located in the flux of the nineteenth-century city. In 'The Painter of Modern Life', Baudelaire famously described the experience of modernity in the Paris of 1863 as incorporating 'the ephemeral, the fugitive, the contingent'.[15] Comparably, Simmel coupled fashion to the fragmentation of modern experience and argued that modern life's neurasthenia—overstimulation and nervous excitement—came with the growth of the metropolis.[16] Simmel discussed the close relationship between art, fashion and consumer culture and equated fashion with the middle classes and with the urban, as well as with the stylization of everyday objects, as in the Jugendstil movement in Germany. Walter Benjamin interpreted the shift in the structure of the experience of modern life as being one of violent jolts and dislocations. Benjamin cited Baudelaire's description of the urban crowd as 'a reservoir of electric energy'; the person who plunges into it is 'a kaleidoscope equipped with consciousness'.[17] Urban encounters with cameras, traffic and advertising are fractured and dislocating, and are experienced as 'a series of shocks and collisions'. Simmel and Benjamin both suggest the idea of rupture with the past in their writing on modernity.

Yet the clear manifestations of Japanese modernity were not contingent on any of these urban experiences. Despite the fact that the city of Edo had had over a million residents since the beginning of the eighteenth century if not before, and the fact that it was certainly no stranger to human traffic, the other conditions for Baudelaire's, Simmel's and Benjamin's modern city were not present until well into the Meiji period, and thus the urban experience cannot be said to have been a requisite condition of Japanese modernity. It can perhaps be argued that the sudden need to engage with the foreign technology, ideas and aesthetics was intellectually as dislocating, violent and alienating as the urban experience would be later. It was not the city that gave birth to the modern fashion system in Japan but the moment of doubt that accompanied the sudden wave of foreign ideas and objects in which those ideas were embodied. The Enlightenment had begun with the replacement of absolutist authority by doubt and with a questioning of every structure. That moment of doubt in the authority of the church and the State led to new means of knowledge production, which are themselves continually questioned, providing not new certainties but constant reappraisal, constant doubt and continually changing fashions, not just in the styling of the objects with which we adorn ourselves and our lives but also in the ideas with which we order our lives and the things in them. This is the crux of modernity; the moment of doubt, both in terms of how to conceptually order existence and in terms of what to wear for it. Japan's long occluded encounter with the outside world was the mainspring of Japanese modernity and its accompanying fashion system because of the uncertainty it generated within the Japanese. The city of neurasthenia was virtual in Japan before it was actual, and thus it affected elites before the greater populace, though the members of this populace weren't too far behind, because of high literacy and newspaper dissemination, even if they lacked the physical resources and social mobility to engage in sartorial modernity at first. The internal interpretive dialectic this provoked was one that put foreignness and modernity together, defined as against the indigenous and traditional, where this was not necessarily the case. Europe and America were also fascinated with Japan and incorporated Japanese styling into their own ongoing discourse of modernity.[18] Yet it was the notion that forms, actual and abstract, can and should be questioned and requestioned and reconstituted not necessarily in the form of the model that started provoking the questioning and began modernity in Japan. The iterative work of forms, particularly ones as cheaply renewable as clothing, is an essential element in the new structures of modernity.

A fashion system—the aesthetic restlessness and desire to constantly restyle the objects and ideas we make—governs even the way we theorize that system. The way we embrace or reject the discourse-altering theories of postmodernity too is governed by a system of fashion. This, in Japan as elsewhere, is the legacy of modernity.

Global Fashions and National Cultures

The extension of the meaning of fashion, from merely the regular annual or seasonal manipulation of appearances through dress to fashion as a metaphor for the dynamics that govern all reorderings of things, thoughts and aesthetics, is a predominant constituent of postmodern understandings of fashion as an organizing principle of contemporary, late-capitalist society. Fashion, to Jean Baudrillard, is as anachronistic and dream-laden as a sailing ship, an astonishing debauchery of efforts to produce a minimum of garments, an *acte gratuit*, an extravagant adventure that cannot be logically justified.[19] Baudrillard maintains that the universal denigration of fashion results from its futility and artificiality, qualities that constitute a taboo in a utilitarian society. 'In our culture, futility plays the role of transgression and fashion is condemned for having within it the force of the pure sign which signifies nothing.'[20] Fashion, as the desire to continually remake appearances, is arbitrary and prodigal, and it is against the principles of utility and efficiency which ostensibly dictate economic choices. The transgressive role of fashion, to create meanings and forms other than those of economic and social progress and an efficient streamlining of the manifestations thereof, continually evokes the past. The co-opting of bygone clothing incarnations into the sartorial structures of the present has, as argued earlier, the role of the uncanny in the modernity of clothing—the resurrection in modernity of what its sartorial reductionism had insisted should be abolished. Baudrillard claims that since, in late capitalism, all the processes of Kantian liberation—aesthetic, economic, sexual, and so on.—have been completed, the form our visual dialectics now takes is one of simulation and constant repetition of those processes.[21] Fashion has perhaps always done this. The enthusiasm for early modernity's borrowings from the forms of ages past was depicted as nostalgia, desire for the tradition and stability of a world gone by. It was reinvented in an image which suits contemporary needs and is commensurate with postmodernism's summoning of forms from struggles already won, dialectics already complete, which it labels parody and pastiche. Both modernity and postmodernity had an impulse to seek stability in arbitrary styles already tried and judged and therefore outside the riskier, destabilizing process of vestimentary innovation. It is a type of exoticism, replacing the appeal of the geo-graphically far away with that of the temporally far away. Resurrecting old forms and investing them with fresh significance and value as emblems of a past whose worth and moment has been newly clarified and acknowledged is an essential, though mainly reactionary, facet of fashion. What fashion may predominantly be, then, is a new way of ordering time and the forms that constitute milestones in it.

To define fashion as a reordering of time is congruous with the earlier conclusion that the essence of modernity was not the nature of the changes it wrought but the institution of change as the paramount value in itself. Certainly, for Japanese moder-nity, the principal change in the disposition of aesthetic sensibilities was the clas-sification of forms into specific temporal abstractions such as traditional, Japanese, civilized, enlightened, modern, Western, and so on, and applying hierarchies to these abstractions. The way in which Japanese society and identity had been formed by the past, and so acquired a sense of continuity and belonging, was challenged by the sudden arrival of modernity from alien sources. The erosion of traditional time, which was seasonal and festival-based, and expressed through dress, is dealt with more thoroughly later. The theme of changing perspectives on time was examined in depth by James Laver as an extension of the not entirely unfamiliar theme of time's dissolution of 'all that is solid' in Western letters.[22] Placing formulations of time at the centre of his elucidation of fashion, Laver cites Charles Darwin, Karl Marx, Henri Bergson, Albert Einstein and Benedetto Croce as representatives of the new 'time-consciousness', while natural evolution, Hegelian dialectics and the theory of relativity are, for Laver, all attempts to register the arrival of this new deity and organizing principle, time.

Laver scrutinized the role of time in modernity, as it became the dominant me-dium of human existence, and the resulting primacy given to the increase in the speed at which all aspects of existence were being lived. For Laver, the loyalties of locality (space) had been replaced by those of time, and temporal loyalties equated to the growing dominance of fashion in social life. In societies where place dominated life, differences between dress styles were indicative of spatial differences, but once time became the chief orchestrator, dress differences came to indicate fashions—differences that gain their significance by being distributed over time. Once traditions became more liquid with the social mobility that accompanied modernity and with general globalization, identity could not be graphed to place so much as it could be to time. In the Japanese experience, the acceptance of change and the values of progress—history in the modern sense—meant that there were very clear temporal markers for identity to accept or reject, and indeed most of the civil war period in Japan before the Restoration was, on one level, a violent manifestation of the difficulty of accepting a new means of identity-framing. Identity based on place, by region within Japan or by the division between Japan and foreign, was slowly replaced with identity based on location in time: modernizing Japan, as distinct from feudal Edo Japan and so on. For Laver, human beings and all their works may be children of time, but this does not mean that history reveals nothing but arbitrariness and confusion; what is revealed is the presence of an all-pervasive influence that places its imprint on every aspect of an age, and it is the presence of such an imprint that constitutes our sense of what an age is like. To closely correlate the sartorial trends of the Meiji, Taishō and early Shōwa periods with the concurrent political and social history is to at least partially accept this approach, rather than that of other fashion historians such as Alfred Kroeber, who insisted that no such correlation can be shown to exist.[23] An analysis of Kroeber in the Japanese context will be pursued later, but it will suffice for this introductory framing of fashion to affirm that our approach is Kantian, in that it assumes a process where styled objects such as dress, can, though not always, echo parallel processes of history, political, economic and social, and in that it assumes there is free will in the sartorial choices that can be made at an individual level. Kroeber presents a determinist view of clothing manifestations—an autonomous, superorganic wave pattern dictates permutations in the shape of dress and is beyond individual influence. Kroeber is fashion's Calvinist, in his assertion of stylistic predestination. It is impossible to incorporate his view into a general theory of fashion without rejecting almost all other theories. The present study of Japanese clothing aesthetics assumes, like Kant, that while there are trends that outlive any individual influence, there is still free will in individual aesthetic choice. While clothing, like many arts, is not, for the most part, sensuously mimetic, its nonsensuous mimesis is still observable. This comes with a reservation, as Marx suggested, that 'men make their own history, but they do not make it just as they please, they do not make it under circumstances chosen by themselves, but under circumstances directly encountered, given and transmitted from the past.'[24] Kroeber's discovery of patterns and wavelengths in dress—independent and autonomous mechanisms over and above both individual consciousness and historical events—supports an aesthetic element to clothing but rejects any other element. The present book has, implicit in its approach to fashion in modern Japan, an assumption of contextual and cultural causality in the forms taken by clothing. While many such approaches—that of Veblen for one—stress a materialist or economic agency behind acts of dress practice, and the few attempts to theorize early modern Japanese clothing refashionings almost exclusively underscore the political workings evinced in the clothing of the period, it is the hope of this book to demonstrate the presence of both political and economic elements and an aesthetic, above and beyond earthly considerations, that is at work in the evolution of the clothing of Japan in the modern period. While many factors influence dress, they do not all operate all the time; nor do they have equivalent outcomes synchronically.

To say that, as Japan became a coherent nation-state, a national character was reflected in the way it rendered the forms of objects, clothing especially, in the sense of a style manifesting an inner essence onto the outer world, is perhaps to place too much emphasis on the ideas out of which the idea of style was born, particularly racial distinctness and innate cultural purity.[25] These were conceptual principles that were warmly embraced by the Japanese; their early understanding of cultural difference was heavily influenced by the ordering of cultures like sideshows at the world fairs, which were one of the elite's first nonindigenous hermeneutics of the globalizing world after the reopening of Japan.[26] The world the Japanese encountered was very much in the grip of the twin ideas of romanticism and nationalism, both of which utilize style as a key concept in their formulation.[27] The manipulation of a concept of style to authenticate communities in the service of establishing the mythical apparatus of a centralized nation-state was utilized by Japan, as it had been in its close model of political modernization, Germany. This concept of style also set the stage for the conceptualizing of the political entity of the State as a work of art, and the imperial system as the legitimate manifestation of a Japanese spirit. The structures of aesthetics were arrogated for use in political economy—the appropriation of conceptual frameworks was not just economic thought subjugating other disciplines but also economic meta-narratives borrowing from, adapting and being influenced by discourses outside of economics. As has been mentioned earlier, however, the infiltration of the concept of style into statecraft was a sufficient but not a necessary condition for the Japanese fascism of the 1930s.

In an enlightened society, one that places authority in reason rather than divinity, style is used to classify the world into its own order, to replace the order previously provided by absolutist religion. The collective subject of the Japanese nation, unified by state-generated symbolism, encounters the problem that an authentic dress style can only be indigenous, while the clothing of modernization is wholly imported and without any Japanese influence. In the struggle of expression and identification between individuality and generality, style is a principle of generality.[28] The more unique something is, the less style plays a role in its impression and interpretation. Thus style has a role in unifying the sartorial actions of people into hermeneutic concord. By virtue of style, the particularity of an individual garment or individual use of garments is subjugated to a general law of form that also applies to other garments; it is relieved of its absolute autonomy. Because it shares its nature or part of its design with others, it points to a common root that lies beyond the individual. Thus the adoption of modern clothing by parts of the Japanese populace was not just the result of the sum of individual choices to wear something new; it can be traced back to a root that lies beyond any individual dress choice and is thus something immaterial—a change in aesthetic consciousness. In the fundamental distinction between art and fine art, that fine art is an expression of genius and has a unified wholeness beyond temporal style, nearly all clothing falls into the category of art, part of a generality governed by style.[29] This is partly because of the division that must exist if clothing is to be considered a practice of art: first it is something designed, then it is something given context and meaning by advertising and the marketplace and then it is something chosen to be worn. The three different stages of creation all influence any conception of what a style, considered as a unity, might be. The problem remains that no governing structure or style of modern clothing in Japan is something that reflects a *Volksgeist*. Because of the gap between what native styles were and what they chose to become, they could never, no matter how creative the state-generated symbolism, be called an authentic manifestation of an inner Japanese spirit. This was, on the whole, left to other forms and cultural practices, though for a time it was reworked in the framing of the return to kimonos in women's dress as an embodiment of national style and an allegorical representation of cultural purity.

The Japanese experience of sartorial modernity, more obviously derivative than elsewhere, fits the newer conceptual model of a fashion system better than it fits a hermeneutic of style. While some certainly claimed an innate Japanese superiority manifested in other contexts, militarily and colonially for instance, to do so sartorially was untenable in a modernizing context. In Japanese literature, to be elegantly dressed in a modern style was to have a sophisticated awareness of the world but never to demonstrate a keener essence.[30] Style is the modality but also the way of thinking about that modality, and members of Japanese elites became acutely aware of how to conform to the styles of modernity. However, this represented an understanding of modernity itself rather than an expression of national *Geist*. A foreignness of sensibility does not permit the real individuality of something to be grasped, only its more general and typical features. The early Japanese experience of foreign clothing in this way remains conscious of style in all dress; the generality of dress form is always more consequential than the individuality of dress forms.

A *Zeitgeist* and its material manifestation in style grant the many forms assumed by dress a content.[31] This is complicated in the Japanese experience by the adoption of forms whose original content is not germane to the cultural particularities they are thrust amongst. The belief that analogical relations exist between the social and political structures of an age and the details of its dress, requires, if the system is to be transplanted, that the forms of those relations be reasonably plastic. Any meaning structure that reflects a *Zeitgeist* is accordingly connotative rather than denotative. Yet since sartorial modernity was a universal experience and a reaction to the same phenomena, albeit in differing contexts, it is reasonable to assume that while the provenances of the modern in dress were unique, the consequences were, to a point, homologous. The many winds of *Zeitgeist* were all blowing in the same direction; toward a fashion system where reductionism is countered with commensurate reactionary forms, such that the system's defining feature becomes fluctuation of form and aesthetic restlessness. According to James Laver, taste, as a set of collective aesthetic dispositions that incline social groups to prefer one form of clothing to another, can be thought of as the presence of *Zeitgeist* in the soul of the individual.[32] Laver combines a social, and hence socially differentiating, element of fashion with a general adherence to a contextual and cultural causality in the form of the *Zeitgeist*. His most famous formulation, called the 'Decay of Chic' or the 'Gap of Appreciation or Stations of Taste' (see Table 1.1), outlines the processes followed not so much by the form of things but by the interpretations and popularity of forms. This hermeneutical distinction is essential to fashion in modernity, as it is the genesis of a liquidity of taste that becomes the catalyst for a liquidity of form.[33]

Roland Barthes effects the paradigm revision that establishes the logical priority of the whole fashion system over its material and immaterial parts. As already outlined in the present work's definition of modernity and fashion as intricately and inextricably interrelated, sartorial modernity was engendered by the totality of social, economic and aesthetic relationships of mutual dependence rather than by its component parts. For Barthes, the entirety of social relations and activities is required for fashion to come into being; it is a system in which the whole and the parts can only be properly explained in terms of the relations that exist between the parts. Consequently, neither are human sartorial activities random, nor do they originate from within the individual, and the nature of a systematic approach means that fashion cannot be regarded as something with a singular identity. Barthes also locates the signifying order in the language that describes fashion not in the objects of fashion themselves. Thus it would be possible to follow Barthes for the Japanese adoption of certain modern clothing forms to be considered aping and not a fashion system at all, fashion being a linguistic phenomenon rather than an aesthetic one. This was certainly the inherent criticism of foreign cartoonists and satirists in early Meiji Tokyo when

Table 1.1. Laver's Decay of Chic[33]

Indecent	10 years before its time
Shameless	5 years before its time
Outré (daring)	1 year before its time
Smart	---------
Dowdy	1 year after its time
Hideous	10 years after its time
Ridiculous	20 years after its time
Amusing	30 years after its time
Quaint	50 years after its time
Charming	70 years after its time
Romantic	100 years after its time

they lampooned early Japanese dress experiments. These sometimes racist caricatures show a failure to understand, however, that the connotations of wearing the same garment in different global and cultural contexts are almost entirely different. The value was in change as a value in itself, not particularly in the use of clothing to signify the same meanings of class, status, masculinity, education, and so on. That being so, the moment there was an engagement with aesthetic change in Japan, a fashion system was operational.

Once there is an imperative to regard the social geographic and temporal dispersion undergone by even just one garment, the benefits of Barthes's signifier/signified distinction are immediately evident. Margaret Maynard has demonstrated how the connotations and meanings of clothing change as they circulate in their new colonial environments.[34] Maynard shows how European settler populations assumed styles of dress that had originated in Europe and had been taken or maintained by expatriate peoples as they manufactured new nations and identities. The original signifieds of the clothing forms changed but they didn't become an empty imitation of their origins; rather they came to signify the new imperatives of the populations wearing them. For colonial dress histories, the idea that a garment originates from a geographical, or social, core and subsequently migrates hither and thither with its original meanings intact has given way to more precise studies of how garments acquire, or do not acquire, certain meanings within freshly and repeatedly defined social groupings. For a study of Japan this is acutely so, as the new dress norms that are adopted are without migratory antecedents and are subsequently arbitrary to an even greater degree.

The link between the form of clothing and its possible meanings is only rarely mimetic. As Barthes states, 'Clothing form has its own rhythm and these changes in form have a relative independence from the general history that supports them. The finite archetypal forms of clothing are dependent on a cyclical history that is clearly not compatible with a linear one.'[35] Yet the period of Japanese clothing history here examined is very much a case where the archetypal forms of clothing take on a linear history and are totally remade by historical events; and modernity, in Japan as elsewhere, was a time when the ideologies of form, such as reductionism, were mimetically manifested in dress. Furthermore, Barthes's linguistic approach limits any aesthetic element in dress, any notion that what might be changing in Japan was what was considered beautiful, beyond the needs of communication. A liquefaction of taste, away from concepts of the classic, is an essential part of modernity's project and certainly something much dwelt on by Japanese writers as part of the melancholy and reactionary counter movement that accompanies progress, as modernity defines it.

The deliquescence of traditional tastes did not mean an abandonment of classical forms; indeed the male suit is the quintessence of sartorial classicism and the epitome of sartorial modernism. It is the dialectic between a classic aesthetic and a fashionable aesthetic that is inherently modern, not simply adherence to the fashionable side of the formulation. The argument that the existence of a classicism in premodern Japanese aesthetics—a stylized, ordered nature, Zen-minimalism that was influential over modernism in general—allowed for an easier acceptance of modern aesthetics in Japan gains credibility when seen dialectically, because one side of the dialectic had already been established. Though the depiction of premodern Japanese aesthetics in this way is simplistic, its application to clothing forms fits within the system outlined. Classic forms put up an inward resistance to fashion but in so doing provide an aesthetic base against which fashion can define itself. For Georg Simmel, classic form has an internal formal coherence that is capable of repelling all attempts made to dismantle it: 'the classic possesses something collective, which does not offer so many points of attack, as it were, from which modification, disturbance and destruction of the balance might emanate.'[36] The minimalism in premodern Japanese aesthetics follows that definition in reducing the opportunities for parody and incoherence to the point at which adhering forms cannot be reduced or reproached. While Simmel characterized this as a limitation of fashion, it is perhaps more useful to think of classic aesthetics as a part of the fashion system, as it is only when tastes desolidify in modernity that what is inherently classic in formation can be recognized.

Simmel adopted an aesthetic perspective in the articulation of social theory and particularly in his discussions of fashion and clothing—terms he rigidly delineated. He recognized an element of the functioning of forms of dress that was not articulated by materialist theories of fashion—an aesthetic element. 'For us, the essence of aesthetic observation and interpretation lies in the fact that the typical is to be found in what is unique, the law-like in what is fortuitous, the essence and significance of things in the superficial and transitory.'[37] His primary formulation of the motivations for fashion and clothing was of a conflict between individuality and generality, group imitation and individual differentiation in which each garment is a momentary resolution of these numerous conflicting forces. But beyond these dual antithetical purposes, there was an element in dress, for Simmel, that was beyond any useful function, earthly or abstract. Even though clothing is inextricably linked to the body and its functioning, and to the self as a means of the fabrication of identity, Simmel maintained that there is a moment in which clothes function as art objects. In early modern Japan this insight is particularly useful, as the elements of imitation and differentiation operate quite differently from the way they do elsewhere.

Aestheticism as an approach may elevate the mundane to the sublime, but it also necessitates an examination of an object's physical configuration, its formal composition and the sensual impact these have upon the perceiver. This is the perspective, certainly, of Japanese literary discussions of Japanese clothing change—that what was occurring involved a certain mental attitude and emotional disposition as well as a distinctive physical transformation. Modernity was a change of consciousness as well as a change in somatic manifestation. The physical forms assumed by clothing merge into and participate in a collective ordering and interpretation of the substance of the world, and this absorption into the general relieves the individual of the burdens of differentiation. 'Being formal', then, becomes an activity that has a precise sartorial correlative, namely absorption by and into a form.

What was achieved quite early by Japanese elites was a near-perfect imitation of American and European clothing, though partly because it was adopted by elites, and partly because the reasons for wearing it are incommensurate with the reasons their models had, what was achieved was an elegance. Elegance in this sense means both a leisure-class exemption from personal contact with industrial processes and, more importantly, an avoidance of individuality in favour of generality and the most abstract configurations. The greater formality in Japanese clothing, in the early Meiji period and even today, is the greater weighting of the imitative and the general or abstract side of the creation of new forms. The extreme fitting-in that is manifest in Japanese sartorial behaviour is an elegance or a formality that is divergent from the vestimentary models. Simmel's fundamental principles of individual sartorial adaptation to the social and individual elevation from it can also, then, be applied to both groups and nations: Japan's clothing structures seek, from the modern period, both to emulate global styles and to differentiate themselves within that emulation. Because the construct works on two or more levels, however, the forms at the individual level tend more to abstraction, because their models have an aura of authenticity and are therefore more immune from the designation of cultural cloneship. Japanese modern clothing styles cannot access the individuality side of the equation, because they are by their nature copies and therefore not unique. Fashion is a set of relations, not a set of contents.

The new aesthetic that developed in Japan was influenced in the direction of abstraction and formality by issues of appropriation, but perhaps more important is the way it was organized temporally. Simmel emphasizes that it is the break with the past that allows fashion to gain its significance and intensity within the social and mental conditions brought about by the arrival of the modern. No aspect of fashion is more redolent of the modern than the temporal structure it exhibits. 'The break with the past which, for more than a century civilized human kind has been labouring unceasingly to bring about, concentrates consciousness more and more upon the present ... so to that degree will it turn to fashion in all fields, and by no means merely with regard to clothing. Indeed, it is almost a sign of the increased power of fashion that it has overstepped the bounds of its original domain, which comprised only externals of dress and has acquired an increasing influence over taste, theoretical convictions, and even the moral foundations of life in their changing forms.'[38] A preference in form for the new over the traditional, an emphasis upon the present as a moment disconnected from any other point in time and a sense that time consists of fleeting moments rather than a continual flow provide the foundation of the new aesthetic consciousness of modernity in Japan. Fashion thrives most readily in the modern metropolis where the money economy has reached a certain level of penetration of daily life, but more importantly, where this corresponds to a high degree of social mobility. The carrier of sartorial modernity was originally the elite, but by the Taishō period it was not so much the financially and politically powerful who symbolized the modern as the urban but not necessarily affluent modern girls and modern boys who were most conscious of a modern aesthetic and performed it. There was a take-up from below as well as the take-up of modern form from the elites above.

What Simmel asserts they are in fact performing are moments of fashion time, the defining feature of which is that every instance appears to be autonomous and replete within itself. 'By reason of this play between the tendency towards universal acceptance and the destruction of its significance, to which this general adoption leads, fashion possesses the peculiar attraction of limitation, the attraction of a simultaneous beginning and end, the charm of newness and simultaneously of transitoriness.'[39] This is similar to Baudrillard's characterization of fashion as an *acte gratuit*— gratuitous and a pure sign. There is not a trace of expediency in fashion—the act of doing it rather than selling it—and in that way it is a superlative aesthetic object, or at least it is for its fashionable moment. Awareness of the momentary nature of fashion gives a fleeting glimpse of fullness, a moment of absolute appropriateness. Kenneth Clark suggested that we can enjoy a purely aesthetic sensation only as long as we can keenly savour the smell of a fresh-cut orange. After that one moment, the fashion object is no longer new and the sensation will be different. Kishida Ryūsei characterized the change in Japanese aesthetics in this way, also asserting that beauty had gone from something contemplative and lasting to an aesthetic contained in a quick glance and a quick glance only.[40] That glance, or that fashion moment, is autonomous and replete, free from expedience and purely without external reason for its creations. Baudelaire had seen this too; that the fashion moment, and it could only ever be a moment, was the embodiment of modern beauty par excellence.

Fashion, however, has only a moment that is purely aesthetic and many others in which it serves as a system of provision, intervening and arbitrating between producers and consumers, using capital and information to effect a profitable reconciliation between the capacity to produce and the desires of consumers. There is a great deal of expediency in this part of fashion, the artificial creation or amplification of the desire to have, consume and wear certain objects. Yet at the heart of most economic decisions of surplus, that is above and beyond subsistence, is not rationality but whim and fancy. Companies and stock markets rise and fall not only because of thrift and efficiency but because of their alignment to shifts in taste and aesthetic impulse. No matter how shrewd the supply side of the provision of clothing, it is always at the mercy of the demand side, which follows the logic of fashion. The market-driven cycle of demand and supply is evolutionary in that its imitations are similar to previously successful forms with small differentiations, of which some will be successful and some will fail to be bought.

Max Weber argued that the provenance of capitalism, and thus modernity, lay in the Protestant work ethic and that its leitmotifs were modernization and rationalization but also, and crucially, ambiguity. Weber's exploration of why the institution of modern capitalism came into being in a particular region (Northern Europe) at a particular time (the seventeenth century), even though the *auri sacra fames* as he puts it—the greed for gold—is as old as the history of man, involved a questioning of the basic assumption of economics, which economics itself rarely broaches—the psychological underpinnings, the reasons for certain behaviours and choices, and the values informing these: happiness, satisfaction, security, and so on.[41] The product of increasingly rational forms of organization, modern society's institutions are governed by systematic rules and impersonal procedures, rather than by custom or religious obligation, and this, for Weber, sets modern society apart from virtually all other world cultures. For capitalism to operate, everyone needs to accept that earning more money, even if one has no particular need for it, is an incontestably good thing. And this is what separates precapitalist societies from capitalist ones: that consumption for its own sake is an incontrovertible aspiration of all and an assumed mainspring of happiness. From this aspect, fashion is a mechanism through which the demonstration of this value can be performed: that any aesthetic restlessness is a product of the need to continually create and expend a material surplus, not an end which, once a surplus becomes available, can be achieved by larger proportions of the population.

The Puritan doctrine of predestination, that there was no way to affect—or even know—one's eternal fate, makes ambiguity a central constituent of the social system such a doctrine begets. Puritans believed—to follow Weber—that the faithful were obligated to live as if they knew themselves to be amongst the elect, through constant, uncomplaining labour. Weber's perspective, incidentally, does not follow the logic of its object, as the actions of the faithful are not predestined but based on free psychological motives. Thus work and capital accretion acquired an ethical dimension, and this was coupled with a deep opposition to sensual pleasure, such that the various ascetic Protestant sects toiled away but didn't spend, thus acquiring capital, which, prudently invested, produced still more capital. Subsequent generations lacked their forebears' spiritual commitment to labour on the one hand, and self-denial on the other, but once the system was instituted, it carried all before it. As Weber put it: 'when asceticism was carried out of monastic cells into everyday life and began to dominate worldly morality, it did its part in building the tremendous cosmos of the modern economic order. This order is now bound to the technical and economic conditions of machine production which today determine the lives of all individuals who are born into this mechanism, not only those directly concerned with economic acquisition, with irresistible force. Perhaps it will so determine them until the last ton of fossilized coal is burnt.'[42]

For all of his insistence on the importance of abstract ideas in the inception of capitalism and modernity, Weber follows Marx in viewing alienation as the essential experience of the modern economic order. The wealthy and the poor, owners and workers, lead economic lives of quiet desperation. And while Marx pictured a liberating crisis at the end of history, Weber pictured a future that is apt to be as unsatisfactory as the present. The fashion system, as a manifestation of the imperative of modern subjectivity to consume, was, by Weberian reasoning, a means of enslavement without any element of redemption. Japanese conceptions of modernity, far from imagining everyday life as a source of negativity and enslavement, as Martin Heidegger, like Weber before him, proposed, saw in the performative, in the present nature of material culture, the promise of liberation from a binding past that still managed to lay claim to the present and the full potential of modern life. The constituent elements of the experience of Japanese modernity—speed, shock, sensation and spectacle—came so soon after the experience of a feudal structure of life that emancipation from confined social structures is greatly stressed by Japanese writers, writers as diverse as Tosaka Jun, who was noted by Harry Harootunian,[43] and, importantly for the situating of clothing in the grander scheme of modernity, Kon Wajirō. Kon's programme of *kongengaku* in Japanese, or *modernologio* in Esperanto, took as its method the study in minute detail of everyday life. In doing, this Kon perhaps preceded the Frankfurt school's Walter Benjamin and Siegfried Kracauer in privileging clothing, consumption and fashion in the analysis of mass society and advanced capitalism, and in explaining new social relationships as mediated by commodities such as clothing. Kon recognized modern culture as based on commodities and consumption rather than custom and value, and this led him to consider the paradox of modernity as both a liberating and an enslaving social force.

Kon theorized that the consumption of commodities formed an integral part of modern life and that patterns of buying were marked by 'a wave of custom transmitted by imitating the upper classes'.[44] Kon is known to have been familiar with the work of Gabriel de Tarde, who perceived this form of mimicry amongst classes in custom and style, and indeed, by applying this to fashion, Kon directly follows the logic of Veblen and other fashion theorists in explaining its mechanisms and motivations through pecuniary competition and conspicuous consumption. Kon follows Tarde in extending the implications of interclass sartorial imitation or mimicry to sealing social solidarity in industrial society and averting class antagonisms and conflict. Kon recognized the power of commodities to stimulate consumption: something primal in the texture or shininess of objects like clothing that impels the desire not just to observe them but to have, to own and incorporate them into ourselves. In this primal aspiration, which was given innumerable new forms by modernity, Kon perceives both the possibility of a tyranny of objects and commodification and a liberation from fettering custom through a new mechanism for expression and the fabrication of the self.

Kon's research focused on quantitative aspects and was concerned with the sheer multiplicity and proliferation of commodities and custom in modern life, and through this, he came to see people and objects in constant interaction, *ugoki tsutsu aru*—in a moving present—as constituting the great narrative of modern life.[45] In Japan, Kon saw the coexistence of three moments of customary and essential sartorial usage, fashion and rationality as stratified layers, constructed atop each other, wrestling with each other within a common social order, yet authorizing different styles of living and competing temporalities. The idea from the Meiji period of the double life, at first meaning simply the wearing of suits for work and public life and indigenous styles for home life, is extended by Kon into a multistrata construct of the fusion of Western and Eastern motifs across the delineated temporalities in which objects are used by people to define themselves. The discourses and practices, meaning-bearing forms and codes of interpretation of clothing were, for Kon, demarcated by the disparate social spaces of modern life. In the household, people learned to identify useful things to consume and assigned one set of meanings to objects, while in the streets and especially in the shops and cafés they learned to assign another set of meanings to the same things. In the streets, consumption was outside the necessary, with the café the epitome of the street experience, where pleasure was derived from the 'height of foolishness' and increased to the extent at which things were wasted.[46] Kon follows Veblen and Marx in this materialist division of exchange value and use value, and he separates them metaphorically between the street and café displays of exchange value and the household's knowledge of use value.

But what makes Kon especially relevant for the examination of fashion is his acknowledgement that beyond the economic analysis of use value there is the possibility of an interpretation of the phenomenon of clothing consumption and display as an expression of social liberation: small replete moments of aesthetic gratification and the manifestation of individual and collective identity. Though the act of consumption of clothing was driven, for Kon, by the desire for imitation (*moho*) of the upper classes, it was not the only force at work. For Kon, fashion was double-edged—even though it was associated with wasteful living and a reproducing cycle of imitation, it seemed also to possess the power to liberate people from the iron grip of tradition, custom and etiquette, through the bestowal of delimited but crucial aesthetic agency. Premodern Japan had been governed by custom, which meant the absence or drastic limitation of subjectivity—in a feudal unconscious composed of habit and tradition. Absolute sources of intellectual, spiritual authority meant that feudal society was un-reflexive and therefore un-self-conscious, and clothing styles were determined by an economy of ceremonial value and distinction. For Kon, feudal society relied on the implementation of abstract principles that referred to an imagery that people internalized to constrain beauty. Utility, which meant for Kon the recognition of what was useful to everyday life, was the principle that should inform all art, not ritual or expenditure. The agenda of Kon's work was to create forms that would avoid alienation and excess, and that would put an end to the unconscious deformation of life. As with Frank Lloyd Wright's architecture, art and clothing were obliged to avoid ornamentation and instead seek their forms from the use value accompanying the rationality of materials and structure. The forms of life, always moving from the concrete to the abstract, must obey the coordinates of time and place.

Kon sits neatly amongst the canonic writers of fashion theory, with flashes of Veblen, Laver and Simmel all discernable, though there is no evidence that Kon had any direct acquaintance with them. His addition to the way fashion was conceived in Taishō Japan, and the way it can be conceived now is most critically his recognition that fashion constituted forces which not only ushered in complex cycles of ensnaring consumption but also provided a catalyst for new means of expression and self-actualization. These could be liberating and beautiful, something which a purely pecuniary or economic explanation of fashion precludes. The social motivations at the crux of capitalism are, for Kon, not just the rational, systematic, sober, scrupulous, efficacious Protestantism, or empty echo of Protestantism, of Weber, but an impetus also for experimentation with novel forms of beauty: not just a market-driven cycle of desire and demand, but also a modern mechanism for the fabrication of the self-readable as valid artistic expression. The two are of course linked: capitalism requires the generation of excess demand, which is rendered through an extension of avant-garde impulses into the value of newness amongst commodities. If fashion is a paradigm of the capitalist processes which inform modern sensibilities, then it is also a vibrant metaphor for modernity itself. With change as the central value, clothes are not only an exchange-value commodity in a consumption cycle of pecuniary competition but also another canvas for avant-garde experimentation into untried forms for purely aesthetic gratification.

Modernity, in so far as it might be interpreted as types of entities causally linked to their environment via adjustments in their structure mediated via the flow of information, could be said to have fashion, that is popularity, biases within that information, as a guiding mechanism.[47] Modernity in clothing fashion is a complex relation of design and wearing practices, temporal and geographic styles, formal and informal institutions, and individual and collective hermeneutic structures, but its recurrent feature is the reinforcement of those features. This is manifest through forces of popularity: fashion is something followed, with only limited variation by individuals being adopted by the collective. Further reinforcement comes from the physical and psychological inflexibility of the system—through institutional structures of training, clothing generation and distribution, through imparted advertising contexts, through the confirmation or disconfirmation of any of these structures via the interpretive judgements, both internal and external, of social groupings, and through the application of judgements of taste based on perceived utility, national authenticity and appropriate balance between individual and collective identity. Perhaps the characterizing feature of the fashion system of modernity, compared to previous systems, is the motility and multiplicity of these information flows, rather than the production and reception of styles in terms of interpretive judgements much more narrowly defined against public criteria, and values having a gendered, pecuniary or class-conventional definition.

Change seen through such a structure has an evolutionary construct—variation tried randomly and gradually, its aesthetic appeal embraced or rejected. Herbert Spencer, writing in the late nineteenth century, used evolution as a key concept in explaining social phenomena, including fashion, where he sees sartorial display as an extension of class and sexual competition. His interpretation balanced the process of increasing differentiation (that is to say specialization of functions) and integration (by which he meant mutual interdependence of the structurally differentiated parts and coordination of their functions).[48] Spencer seems to have arrived at his concept of evolution—as a trend towards increasing differentiation coupled with integration—by giving greater generality to the idea of progress as the product of advancing division of labour, which Adam Smith had used as an economic foundation. To explain fashion as an evolutionary process, through the dual workings of differentiation and integration, is to buy into a hierarchy of creation and to assume that all preceding fashions were nothing more than antecedent rather than replete artistic moments. The way forms change and the fashions they follow are often quite different from the structures of change we try to squeeze them into—evolution, influence, modernization, revolution. These are all modes of change implying arbitrary structures, when the actual structure of fashion change may not yet have an adequate vocabulary.

Fashion is a structure of change, the systematic processes of which are the defining mechanisms in shaping the forms of modernity. Fashion's centrality to modernity in Japan, as elsewhere, had to do with the fact that change, even irrational change, was more rational than no change at all. The consequences of reflexivity were movement, mutability and speed, not any process, force or impetus that was rationally concrete or scientifically definitive. The focus of fashion history has traditionally been on accounting for clothing as a universal but nonbiological phenomenon, constructed as a social given, in that it is a species-wide manifestation. Some universal inner disposition of humanity somehow leads to the contrivance of clothes, and in the possible provenances of this, it is assumed, are also to be found the answers to questions regarding fashion as it operates in modernity. There is a narrative assumption in clothing history—an origin from which the future is determined—and this hermeneutic tendency to subsume preceding forms as prefigurations of moments now surpassed is also characteristic of modernism. Fashion's operations, outcomes and, indeed, satisfactions are quintessentially modern, and conversely, fashion's interpretive and hermeneutic processes are crucial for explaining how modernity works. Features of human behaviour that appear in both modernity and premodernity are clearly group-specific; forms of clothing seem to be closely aligned with group membership; and changes in styles over time are likewise aligned to the internal dynamics of social groups. It is the visible and collective clothing dynamic that is referred to as fashion. Explanations of fashion systems in modernity also focus on collective dress similarities and differences. Veblen, Simmel, Flügel and Laver all produce theories of imitation and differentiation—these two processes, which work concurrently, both collectively and individually, were understood by these thinkers within modernity as the only conceivable solutions to the question of the way in which clothing styles circulate among defined populations. The Japanese example, and the native theorists of it, demonstrate some of the failings of the European and American theorists of fashion meta-narratives. And the capacity for deliberate reinvention, in Japan, negates somewhat Kroeber's theories about superorganic forces dictating fashionable behaviour, though in other contexts Kroeber's ideas remain irrefutably beguiling. Yet particulars of the Japanese experience—modernity before modernization, abstract modernity before industrial and urban modernity, staggered and accelerated development and the cultural extremes that had been the result of political isolation—provide an example that calls into question the hitherto and perhaps Eurocentric configurations of the way fashion operates.

An ordering of things in time that replaces an ordering of things by place remains a general principle of sartorial signification in Japanese modernity. However, this and many other elements that form actual and interpretive elements of an aggregation of the abstraction of fashion do not always function synchronically. Signification is not always the operating principle governing fashion. Signification implies an expediency that any construal of clothing as an art object would by definition deny. Failure to account for an aesthetic moment within fashion was also the shortcoming of structuralist approaches to the problem of the governing dynamics of vestimentary behaviour. Roland Barthes, who introduces a high level of theoretical reflexivity into fashion theory, still relies upon the densely formulated intellectual traditions of modernism, which were originally formulated to explain other phenomena and then reworked, imperfectly, to explain clothing.

The discourses to which fashion has most commonly been affixed have been economic rather than aesthetic. And more recently fashion has been used to bridge these economic discourses—fashion is pecuniary competition—with semiotic ones—fashion is communication—and even biological ones—fashion is evolutionary for the purpose of sexual selection. Economic explanations of fashion, such as the use of noninformative information cascades, are often simplistic. John Maynard Keynes explained this comportment pattern by citing the example of two empty restaurants approached by a couple that makes an arbitrary choice between them. Every subsequent group that approaches the restaurants uses the information that people have chosen one restaurant to reflect the superiority of that restaurant, and they choose the same one, thus resulting in an empty restaurant and a full one. This is an empty explanation of fashionable behaviour, for it assumes that none of the choices made were endowed with real knowledge. Fashion in clothing and restaurants is certainly not merely a result of cascading arbitrary chance. At the base of most economic conjectures are assumptions about happiness, self-actualization and aesthetic choices. The desire for newness merely for newness's sake drives economic acquisitiveness and is, despite the rational edifices built upon it, inherently irrational and inefficient. At the irrational base of economic systems, commodities are not consumed for reasons of efficiency or maximized opportunity costs but for fancy, on a whim and following a culture-wide aesthetic restlessness. If anything, economic discourses have borrowed from aesthetic ones by building systems around commodities which need to be true only to themselves—to have only exchange value—and are thus not about distributing needed goods from limited resources but concerned with circulations of fashion and fashion only.

Fashion is an abstraction for a myriad of sartorial events which cannot possibly be humanly observed as a totality. It can be seen as an amalgam of a population's countless aesthetic choices, manifestations and interactions, the content of which go beyond the individual. The problem with constructing a coherent fashion narrative of Japan, as elsewhere, is that interpretive generalities—recorded in media designed to last rather than in the fleeting fabulousness of cloth—never reveal the true economics of aesthetics, and we must make do with imperfect glimpses. Also the limited vocabulary of fashion means that unsystematic fragments of vestimentary behaviour are absorbed into the normative structure of a clothing language, because they cannot be accounted for in the recording means available.

Simmel said that the essential accomplishment of the mind may be said to be its transformation of the multiplicity of the elements of the world into a series of unities.[49] Patterns can be seen in countless forms and throughout time, and perhaps trying to construct an economics of aesthetics, a key to fashion's innumerable moments, is like Jorge Luis Borges's story of the cartographers who tried to perfect their craft to the point where they produced a map that exactly fitted the area it represented, as if fashion is so large and complicated that the only true equation or general theory that can accommodate all its possibilities or generalize how it works is fashion itself. But it is an uplifting hope that like the librarians in that other Borges story, the story of the library that held every combination of the twenty-six alphabet letters in untold volumes of books, there still exists the chance that one of those combinations in the endless entropy could act as a key to understanding the infinite combinations of which it is but one.

–2–

Japanese Clothes:
Events and Tendencies

From the earliest times, several dominant narratives have run through historical explanations of Japanese clothing: a political narrative, ascribing clothing shifts to government policy and international affairs; a material narrative, ascribing clothing trends to the introduction and availability of various textiles; a class-based narrative, ascribing to clothing the role of representing class relations; and a social narrative, ascribing clothing changes to things such as celebrity, consumption patterns, social values and media influences. An aesthetic narrative needs to be interwoven with these, to take into account the element of creativity and originality in clothing and the extent to which it is a behaviour and a practice independent of the other disciplines which attempt to explain it through their own paradigms.

The very earliest knowledge of Japanese clothing comes from pottery in the Gomon period, before 400 BCE. The Gomon pottery depictions show close-fitting trousers and short upper garments, funnel sleeves and rope-like belts. In the pottery, the clothing seems to have either embroidered or painted curvilinear designs,[1] but this may be more a feature of the style of representation than an accurate picture of the clothes themselves. The clothing of this period is usually assumed to have been made of hemp or similar worsted material. There was, interestingly, no distinction, in the pottery at least, between male and female garments. The very fact that a decorative culture in pottery exists could reasonably suggest that clothing also served this particular aesthetic need, as well as social needs such as distinction of rank and gender, in early civilizations. The role of clothing—practical, social or decorative—in the first human migrations to the Japanese islands is beyond the scope of any evidence currently in our possession, but as many fashion historians have concluded, it was most likely decorative before it was anything else. The fact that there seems to be no sartorial sexual dimorphism does add an interesting twist, but as mentioned before, this may be due to the representation rather than the clothes themselves.

By the Yayoi period, the development of rice cultivation and the movement from hunter–gatherer communities to agrarian societies greatly affected clothing. The Chinese historical account in the *Wei Zhi*—History of the Kingdom of Wei—claims that clothing more appropriate to agriculture was worn: unsewn fabric wrapped around the body and poncho-type garments with head holes cut into them. This account documents the use of pink and scarlet makeup but also claims there was no difference in the deportment of father and son, or women and men.[2] The document is disputed, due to its obvious cultural prejudices, but it seems unlikely that it would have entirely disregarded sartorial distinctions of rank, age and gender, had there been any. Interestingly, there is a commonly held Japanese belief which anecdotally claims this as a utopian period for the same reasons, before the corrupting elements of Chinese materialism began to encourage the use of clothing as a marker of social, gender and age distinction.

During the Yamato period (300 CE to 550 CE) many artifacts were created from which the details of Yamato clothing can be derived. In particular the tomb statues or *haniwa* show a quite different style from that recorded in Chinese accounts of the previous age.[3] The *haniwa* statues are dressed in two-piece outfits: an upper piece with a front opening and close cut sleeves, and loose trousers for men and a pleated skirt for women. Sericulture is believed to have been introduced in this period by Chinese settlers, but the cost of silk would have meant its use would have to have been mediated by rank or class.

During the Asuka (550 CE to 646 CE) and Nara (646 CE to 794 CE) periods, the development of a more unified government meant that Japan was able to send missions to China in order to deliberately introduce cultural innovations to Japan. Along with Buddhism and Confucianism, the government also adopted Chinese systems of codes regulating various ranks and the corresponding sumptuary laws. The laws governed the use of both styles and colours according to social rank. Sewing methods became more sophisticated, and clothing in general became longer and wider. In the court, clothing was divided into formal clothing, court clothing and uniforms, the colours being the main means of differentiation between rank. The higher classes wore clothing that was essentially in an imported Chinese style. Men wore a loose upper garment, slit on both sides, with a stand-up collar and trousers secured with a sash. Women wore a shorter upper garment and a long flowing skirt. Members of other classes still wore clothing similar to that of earlier periods; however, there were some basic developments towards what we would consider more attributes of the kimono: looser styles than earlier, tied with a sash. Women also started wearing a short undergarment and tying their robes from right to left.

Following this period, the Heian Period (794 CE to 1192 CE) saw the establishment of a considerable aristocracy in the capital, Heian-kyo, later Kyoto. The Fujiwara family of courtiers rose in power and influence, and this brought stability and wealth enough for a leisured class, or leisure-only class, to develop. This, coupled with the suspension in 894 CE of communication with China, saw the development of many key garments and the evolution of a more unique Japanese style amongst this very exclusive class. Luxury and sumptuousness were available and valued as they could not have been in previous times.

The Tale of Genji, attributed to Murasaki Shikibu, and written in the early eleventh century at the peak of the Heian period, gives a window into this world and the role and form of the clothing in it. The aristocracy was made up of only about five thousand persons, uninterested in anything but leisure. Their obsessions, as with most aristocracies, were rank and breeding and the means of signalling that rank through the pleasures of distinction; music, poetry and fine clothing. The theme of the novel, and of many of the religious and cultural products of the time, was the evanescence of worldly things. In clothing, this meant attention to seasonal changes and in particular to the matching of colours. Garments had become excessively complicated, in particular the *juni-hito*, literally the twelve layers, but actually consisting of anything from ten to twenty-five layers, reflecting essentially escapist themes such as seasons, virtues or elements of the earth and nature. The overlapping of sleeves was an important element, and sleeves alone would be seen protruding from carriages as a means of fashionable display and sartorial demonstration of one's wit and style.

Other key garments developed during this period. *Kosode*, what is today thought of as the kimono, developed, but essentially as an undergarment. *Hakama*, pleated pants worn over a kimono, also developed in this period, though as an exclusively male garment and associated with martial arts rather than with higher learning as it was later. Men are known to have worn their hair in topknots during this time, while women favoured long straight styles, flowing to the floor.

Aesthetically, the extravagance of the Heian period was as unsustainable as the political system that allowed for it. The following Kamakura period, so named for the new capital near modern Tokyo, saw a reaction to the extreme impracticality of Heian garments for anything but leisure. The Kamakura period marked a transition to a land-based economy and the concentration of military technology in the hands of the samurai class. Minamoto Yoritomo established his *bakufu* (tent government) in Kamakura in such a way as to differentiate it from the court life of Heian. Thus clothing in this period was more appropriate for a military class: simple, frugal and easy to move in. Men's clothing was simplified and contained cords by which sleeves and legs could be drawn up. Women also wore a simplified costume.

As Donald Keene notes, in the reign of Yoshimasa from 1449 to 1473, the influence of Zen Buddhism was brought in and mixed with the more seasonal and ostentatious aesthetics of the Heian period. The taste for ink painting, nō theatre and the tea ceremony gained popularity, as did the permanence and simplicity of rock gardens rather than more ornate seasonal gardens. Although this is a grand simplification, it does help to pinpoint the establishment of the unobtrusive elegance that broadly characterizes classical Japanese aesthetics.[4]

The Ashikaga period was also a period of military rule, in which the luxurious court styles continued to be rejected. The repudiation of decadence is a common theme in Japanese clothing history, but it was further emphasized in this period with the deliberate use of cheaper materials such as linen instead of silk. Family crests also began to be used on garments, probably due to influence from Europe. Heraldry and other means of distinguishing rank were keenly studied in the periods when contact with Europe was not restricted.

An interesting, though not very influential, figure in very early European contacts with Japan was Hasekura Tsunenaga, who from 1613 through 1620 headed a Japanese diplomatic mission to the Vatican. The reasons for his mission, trade with Europe using Spanish silver from Mexico traded through the Philippines, and the Christian faith in Japan, were about to be dropped, and there would not be another embassy to Europe for more than two hundred years. However, Hasekura does represent a religious and commercial flirtation with Europe that had an obvious influence on his clothing and hints at what might have occurred had Japan not opted for two centuries of isolation. At a time when both Europe and Japan were more robed than tailored, Hasekura would not have looked out of place at the Vatican, unlike the late Tokugawa envoys to the world fairs two hundred years later, who looked distinctly out of place as the only people not wearing tailored clothing. From the surviving portraits of Hasekura, his dress seems to have been a hybrid of samurai and Jesuit. Indeed, one portrait shows him in full Jesuit black after his conversion to Christianity in 1615. After colour and motif, collars and sleeves were the elements of his costume he chose to adapt to a more European style. In the 1615 portrait of Hasekura by Claude Deruet in the Borghese Collection in Rome, despite the more elaborate colouring and the Japanese swords, the form of his clothing would not have been very different from that of Paul V, whom he had come to meet. This may, however, be the artist's culturally specific understanding of how to paint clothing, rather than a perfectly accurate record of Hasekura's outfit on the day of his sitting.

Neither Hasekura, nor Japanese Christianity nor any of the European styles they might have brought to Japan were to last very long, and by the time Hasekura returned to Japan, efforts to eradicate Christianity had begun and Japan was moving towards the *sakoku* policy of isolation. This was quite obviously to be a defining policy of the Edo period and, by extension, of its cultural products. While the early influence of globalization informed the scientific revolution and the Enlightenment, Japan's self-imposed seclusion prevented any serious engagement with early intellectual modernity, and its collective consciousness and epistemology remained stubbornly feudal. Hence clothing, as a primary means of self-actualization and expression, also remained feudal. However, certain other factors, social and economic if not intellectual, were also at work forming the unique sartorial conditions of the Edo period and beyond. Primarily, though, the lack of an extended period of enlightenment, by which is meant the process of questioning all forms of knowledge, greatly limited the ruling class's reaction to embourgeoisement in clothing.

The Edo period was one of unprecedented political stability, economic growth and urban expansion. Kyoto remained the centre of aristocratic culture and luxury production, while Edo developed into one of the largest cities in the world, a city in which the critical mass of population and wealth led to a fashionable dress culture. The primary consumers of dress were the samurai, yet the merchant and artisan classes, who benefitted most from the peace and prosperity, were a continuous challenge. The rigid hierarchy of Tokugawa Japan meant that wealth could not be used to improve status directly. Instead, various other strategies of consumption and display were used, stimulating an extensive textile industry. As clothing became a key indicator of rising affluence, and as aesthetic sensibilities were used as a challenge to social order, various sumptuary laws were introduced, regulating the kinds of fabric, techniques and colours to be used by different classes. Although the laws were not consistently enforced, leading to regular shifts between opulence and restraint, they did create various codes of subtlety. New techniques were developed, and the subdued colours and fabrics formed their own aesthetic values, codified as *iki*, or elegant chic, discussed in Chapter 5. The use of restricted colours and fabrics for undergarments and linings was also popular as a subtle means of demonstrating wealth and personal style.

One of the principal reasons for the stability and wealth of the Edo period was the policy of *sankin kōtai* (alternate attendance) that was in effect from 1635 to 1862. Although its details changed throughout the 260 years of Tokugawa rule, in general it required that all the daimyo move periodically between their home provinces and Edo, and when they were not in attendance in Edo to leave members of their families there. The expenditure necessary to maintain lavish residences in two places and to travel between them created financial disincentives to fighting between domains, and also generated an extraordinary amount of economic and cultural activity. Road-building, a travel and inn culture, new trade and the cultivation of tastes for goods from around the country, as well as a massive influx of wealth into Edo itself, made the policy influential in very far-reaching ways. The deprovincialization of the back-waters of Japan began at this point, as the compulsory stay in Edo allowed for a great flow of information and transfer of fashions between centre and periphery.

As with Louis XIV's policy with regard to the palace of Versailles, requiring all the *noblesse de l'épée* (nobility of the sword) to attend on him for six months of every year, the concentration of the ruling classes in Japan created ideal conditions for a culture of competition through fashion and displays of wealth and style. However, unlike the situation at Versailles, certain value systems would not allow decadence to be taken too far. One reason for this was that the concentration of wealth was never as extreme as in France, as the Tokugawa policy on trade was rather free, though Japan was closed to foreign investment. Throughout the Edo period, distribution networks developed and the industrial takeover of household crafts and specializations progressed. Currency stability, banking and insurance were all reasonably mature, and thus trade became a key source of wealth unhindered by excessive tariffs or levies. From comparatively early on, the merchant class flourished economically, while the samurai class, there being little violence to monopolize, was largely parasitic. This was reflected in culture, particularly in the rhetoric concerning work in the Edo period literature.

The fact that work was dignified in Edo literature to a much greater extent than it was in European literature is a sign of the class dynamic. Early modern Japanese writers made work a subject of common knowledge and a source of pride. In many ways, work defined the self and self- and social respect replaced social hierarchies. One possible reason for this, and a common theme of literature, was that the economic integration of a country with so many natural disasters meant that an earthquake in one part of the country could very quickly raise the price of a commodity in another and local disasters could become national famines. Work and thrift were the barriers separating a family from calamity. There are numerous examples of advice literature, concerning time efficiency and the peace of mind gained by saving against future crises. This literature echoed Weber's characterization of predestination in Protestantism. Generations worked hard without consuming in proportion, because they saw as a virtue the acquisition of wealth to stave off future disaster. Thus there was enough capital accumulation for investment and the beginnings of a modern economy.

However, work was more than catastrophe control; the accumulation of wealth was desired, there being less religious prohibition of materialism than in Christianity, and throughout the Edo period an industrious revolution took place, filled with innovation and customs of self-improvement and the recording of mistakes. Prosperity was useful, even with strong class stratification. Family obligations, including those to ancestors and descendants, became more elaborate and imperative. Notions of society—of an abstract social body—expanded, mainly through trade and disaster interdependence, and this led to the notion that sustained good opinion was the key to prosperity. And sustained good opinion required the keeping up of appearances.

The pleasures of consumption itself—of styling oneself—were available in Edo as the distribution of resources slowly shifted, as specialized production required more specialized consumption and as acquisitiveness itself became a stimulus to production and was therefore encouraged. The sumptuary laws were restraints on consumption, but illicit fashions in violation of the laws were common. However, there remained the generally accepted notion that presentation should conform to rank. It was in this concept of civility and conforming that the real agent of consumption, a blossoming fashion system, lay. As notions of civility proliferated, so too did the number of practices and goods required for civility. Bridal dowries, funerals, and festivals all became areas of perceived essential expenditure, and thus fashions in the goods accompanying them thrived. In the desire for thrift and household utility, many new luxuries, such as clothing, books, lacquerware, furniture and tatami matting, were framed as practical, efficient and money-saving even if they were not so in actuality.

Utility and civility became the engines of Edo consumption and fashions. Certain items were considered more and more essential. Things such as tea, poems, letters and gifts were no longer considered to be luxuries but to be essentials. Self-cultivation too became more and more essential and, commodities became objects of virtue: instruments, ink, books, flower arrangements and appropriate clothing were not items of selfish consumption but virtuous expenditure. Consumption became part of the moral economy and this led to classicism in Edo fashions. Things had to be fine and appropriate rather than new and challenging.

However, the rise of the merchant and artisan classes troubled the Edo government, and numerous sumptuary regulations were issued to control the expression of ideas that were deemed a threat to public decorum, safety or morality, or that were subversive to the shogunate. Ostentatious and inappropriate behaviour and display for all classes was codified, though often ineffectually. The earliest sumptuary laws were based on similar practices from China, where manifest consumption was correlated positively with sanctioned social status. The Japanese version of these regulations was called *ken'yakurei* (law regulating expenditures) and was applicable to all classes of society. These regulations did not constitute a distinct body of laws but rather were included in occasional regulatory proclamations issued by the *rōjū* (council of elders) and were disseminated through various intermediaries to the targeted group or class. Although the *chōnin* (townfolk) often complained about repressive measures, the government generally relied more on threats and exhortation than on the imposition of punishment. Only a limited number of cases of arrest for violating sumptuary edicts were recorded in legal documents of the Tokugawa period or in popular literature. Throughout the Edo period, the sumptuary regulations frequently referred to previous edicts, suggesting that many were not considered permanent or practically enforceable, and that compliance among the targeted groups was often a problem. An expression of the time, *mikka hatto* (three-day laws), suggested that violations of sumptuary laws often came after only brief periods of compliance, and that clothing fashions and the means of signalling social subversion through them changed very rapidly.[5]

The sumptuary edicts were intended to have a significant impact on two of the principal areas of social and political life: the content and expression of ideas, and appearance and expenditures. During the Edo period, there appeared various periodic restrictions on content, such as edicts that prohibited publishing about current events, unorthodox theories, rumours, scandals, erotica, government officials or anything relating to the Tokugawa rulers or the Imperial Family. One of the most repressive sets of edicts was the Kansei reforms. The death of shogun Iehuru in 1786 left the shogunate in the hands of his successor, the adolescent Ienari, until 1793, and an effective regency was established by Matsudaira Sadanobu, who held the post of chief councillor. Understandably insecure, he initiated reforms after a series of riots in various cities in the summer of 1787, precipitated by high rice prices following several years of poor harvests and famines. The reforms began with the removal of certain corrupt officials and the institution of specific measures to check inflation and stabilize prices. A later extension of the regulations to publishing, in 1790, decreed that no new books should be published except by special permission. Furthermore, it was specified that current events were not to be depicted in prints, and gorgeous and extravagant works were forbidden. The publication of unorthodox theories was banned, while the publication of erotica, a considerable industry, was to be gradually brought to an end.

The first and most sensational prosecution under these new laws was the punishment of the popular artist Santō Kyōden for three *sharebon* (books of wit and fashion), popular light literature set in the Yoshiwara (pleasure quarters) published in 1791. Though the books did deal with courtesans and some depravity, they were neither political nor pornographic, so the ulterior motive for the application of the laws in this case was most probably that the shogunate was attempting to intimidate writers and publishers.[6]

These same laws also dictated the accepted relationship between class and aesthetics, attempting to prescribe the appearance and the expenditure of wealth appropriate to each class. Merchants in Edo had begun to amass large fortunes and to live in a manner which the samurai believed suitable only for themselves. The sumptuary laws sought to reinforce the distinctions between classes, encourage frugality and maintain a neo-Confucian system of moral conduct. The concern would appear to have been that the morals and discipline of the samurai class should not be undermined by ostentatious displays of wealth amongst their social inferiors. Many regulations proscribed the consumption of goods and services and placed limits on luxurious entertainment.

The government recognized that fashion could be used as a means of crossing over the class boundaries, which were often differentiated by styles of clothing and accessories. The potentially seditious nature of dress and fashion during the Edo period was reflected in a large number of repressive edicts involving clothing, and further, aspects of behaviour and lifestyle. Edo period sumptuary edicts were, in a practical sense, directed at controlling the more visible displays of social status, and they were issued with increasing frequency in the seventeenth century. This is perhaps one of the influences on the development of the more internalized aesthetic of *iki* amongst the merchant classes, stressing details and simplified perfection. Edicts issued as early as 1617 prohibited gold and silver leaf appliqué on courtesans' clothing, while others banned gold thread. In 1649, the first comprehensive list of restrictions for merchants was issued for Edo, which included a ban on gold lacquer decoration, houses with gold or silver leaf trimming, and gold lacquer riding saddles. Also considered too ostentatious were gold and silver clasps on tobacco pouches, which were occasionally forbidden.

A case of flagrant violation of these attempts to regulate sartorial display occurred in 1681, involving the wealthy Edo merchant Ishikawa Rokubei. The Rokubei household had worn particularly magnificent dress in order to view the fifth shogun, Tokugawa Tsunayoshi, when he visited Ueno. Assuming that Rokubei's wife was the wife of a samurai, the shogun inquired after her, but when informed she was only the wife of a merchant, the shogun, believing the couple to have shown scornful disrespect to their social superiors by dressing above their station, had them arrested, their property confiscated and the family banished from the city. Most probably as a result of this incident, in 1683, Tsunayoshi issued more sumptuary regulations in regard to merchant clothing, demanding frugality, which was ironic given that Tsunayoshi himself was famous for wasteful spending and an ostentatious lifestyle. An interesting parallel is Nicolas Fouquet's construction of Vaux-le-Vicomte, with its sumptuous luxuries, which was in 1661 confiscated by Louis XIV because of its obvious challenge to the King's domination of the spectacle of fashion.

An interesting note with regard to Edo period sumptuary laws was that, while they were justified as frugality measures, since expenditures were supposedly appropriate to one's social status, they also prescribed levels of minimum spending. People of every class had to live according to their social position, and failing to do so was regarded as not fulfilling one's social obligations. While the samurai class would have understood frugality as both virtuous and practical, the members of the merchant class would more probably have viewed its imposition as a repressive measure designed to limit their success and protect the parasitic samurai estate at their expense. Culturally, the edicts seem to have been effective, and several practical guides, such as *Chōnin bukoro* (The Townsmen's Bag) by Nishikawa Joken, advised against outdoing one's superiors. Two famous teachers of social and ethical philosophy, Ishida Baigan and Nakazawa Dōni, urged the observance of social position on the grounds of protecting against disorder and maintaining the natural order.[7]

Historians of Japanese prints often cite the edicts that affected print-making, such as the banning of prints with portraits of women in 1800. The edict did not argue that there was anything wrong with the prints but stated that they were to be banned as *medatsu* (conspicuous), suggesting that the government was uncomfortable with any cultural product that was too popular or successful. Art could be tolerated so long as it was not too influential or fashionable. Another example of an edict affecting print-making was the ban, in 1793, on prints with the names of women other than courtesans. The intention appeared to be the maintenance of social distinctions by protecting the reputations of women who, although connected with the floating world, were not actually prostitutes, women such as geisha and teahouse waitresses.

The later edicts were amongst the most repressive, perhaps as the pressures on the traditional class hierarchy became more acute. A ban on prints with theatrical subjects almost shut down the print-making industry in Osaka in 1842, as the government came to fear not just the subversive influence of theatrical satire but even celebrity itself. In one case, enormously popular actor Ichikawa Danjūrō VII was banished from Edo because of his extravagant lifestyle and ostentatious stage productions. The specific charge was that his use of genuine samurai clothing, armour and weapons on stage, instead of props, was a clear infraction of the separation of classes.[8]

An indication of the extent to which Japan had moved towards becoming a mercantile-oriented society in the Edo period can be witnessed in the prominence of the names of merchants, their shops and the merchandise available in them, in Edo period art, fiction and drama. One of the central subjects and a driving force of the bourgeois-oriented arts was the representation of desire in all its multifarious aspects, whether desire for money, merchandise, social status or sex. Any distinction that the samurai class might have wanted to sustain between elite high art and vulgar plebeian advertising was impossible to sustain owing to the latent ascendancy of merchant culture.

Popular Edo artists, writers, and actors, with their proven public appeal, were in constant demand by merchants for advertising purposes. Hayashi Yoshikazu contends that the earliest evidence of this practice is found in the numerous advertising broadsides that were regularly turned out by the most popular writers of the day. Hiraga Gennai's *Hika rakuyō* (1769), for example, contains advertisements for Sōsekikō, a convenient toothpaste in a box. Sometimes entire Edo stories took the form of advertisements. Santō Kyōden, for example, wrote *Onna Masakado shichijin-geshōhin* (1792), in the form of a parody of a legend, for the opening of a cosmetics shop, and Jippensha Ikku's *Irozuri shinsomegata* was composed for the Tokiwaya kimono shop's winter sale.[9]

The frequent depictions of popular kabuki actors endorsing products seen in Edo period woodblock prints suggest that neither actors nor artists were any more averse than authors to capitalizing on their celebrity by placing endorsements for commercial products in their work. As early as 1715 in Edo, this practice had its beginning when famous actors in all three of the major theatres were reported to have begun inserting announcements (*kōjō*) into their performances for a kimono pattern sold by the Echigoya shop in Nihonbashi (much later to become the Mitsukoshi department store). The practice continued, linking this early form of mass media, the theatre, with merchandising for fashionable goods. Many *ukiyo-e* prints by Kunisada, Kuniyoshi and Eisen, to name only a few, depict such popular cosmetics products of the time as Senjōkō ointment and Kumonoue white base cream (*oshiroi*). Also in the prints, famous courtesans are frequently depicted wearing kimonos or carrying umbrellas with the trademarks of well-known brothels or popular shops such as Ebisuya, Matsuzakaya and Echigoya, or drinking the tea or sake sold by certain shops, or dining at particular restaurants. Which goods and places were currently in fashion was, with the aid of such advertising, clearly at least as much a matter of common knowledge among the cognoscenti of the time as of our own. There were also detailed portrayals and appraisals of actual brothels, prostitutes, customs, attitudes and connoisseur products in the theatre, in plays such as *Sukeroku*, performed by Danjūrō II from 1713, which also functioned as advertisements for the myriad particular commercial aspects of the pleasure quarters.[10] These demonstrate the degree to which such things were also discussed as a matter of taste and fashion.

Political factors dominated, or at least placed firm parameters around, what clothing could be worn and what fashions might come into existence in Edo period Japan. Most influentially, the *sakoku* (national seclusion) policy insured that there was virtually no influence from the outside world on the forms of clothing within Japan. However, the policy of *sankin kōtai* (alternate attendance) had the effect of deprovincializing clothing fashions and disseminating them throughout the country. The policy's added economic effects, of centralization, stability and urbanization, established the foundations for the greatly enlarged merchant class and its associated culture. The long-established *mibunsei* (four-class system) further maintained the social order and attempted to limit social mobility through regulations controlling the use of money, the production of goods, migration, intermarriage, the flow of ideas and, of course, clothing.

The general economic trends of the Edo period worked against these attempts to preserve the status quo in class relations. The rise of mercantile culture and values, along with great urbanization and wealth accumulation amongst the merchant class, allowed the values of the mercantile, at the expense of the military, class to extend into taste and fashion systems. The rise of the merchant class allowed for ongoing subversion of the established class rules and for entire sartorial practices to be established as part of that subversion. The practices that were increasingly considered essential for general civility amongst all classes increased the acceptability and volume of consumption for the purposes of self- or family styling. Yet a monopoly on more awe-inspiring visual display was still claimed by the samurai, and thus there were still great limits on the accessible consumption and therefore fashionable behaviour. This in itself helped to establish the particular restrained aesthetic of merchant clothing, in a manner similar to the establishment of the bourgeois sartorial values in Europe which negated both aristocratic excess and working-class meniality.

The monopoly on violence claimed by the samurai class had been extended, over the period of protracted peace and therefore growing redundance of the samurai, to a monopoly on the visual violence of awe-inspiring dress. The fading prestige of the martial aspects of Japanese society and correspondingly also of martial dress as an indication of social importance led to abundant subversion through clothing, aided by the defection of celebrity to the side of commerce, the growing influence of the media amongst a highly literate population and the increasing acceptance of greater consumption for customary purposes and perceived essentials. Yet the intellectual isolation of Japan and the reliance on sumptuary law rather than on economic arrangements to maintain class differentiation meant that there was virtually no trickle-down system of fashion, such as had developed in reaction to the rise of the bourgeoisie in Europe, in the Japanese context when the Meiji Restoration suddenly removed the legal restrictions on dress.

The Meiji Restoration was in many ways a response to modernity, to the rise of industrialism, urbanism and a global economy characterized by legalistic and bureaucratic authority and by gradual cultural homogenization, first forced upon Japan in the form of America's black warships. Japan had to engage immediately with the conditions, as described by Marx, of 'constant revolutionizing of production, uninterrupted disturbance of all social conditions, everlasting uncertainty and agitation . . . All fixed, fast-frozen relations, with their train of ancient and venerable prejudices and opinions, are swept away, all new formed ones become antiquated before they can ossify.'[11] For Marx, modernity's defining characteristic is that change is the new and only constant.

As Louis Menard puts it: 'In premodern societies, the ends of life are given at the beginning of life: people do things in their generation so that the same things will continue to be done in the next generation. Meaning is immanent in all the ordinary customs and practices of existence, since these are inherited from the past, and are therefore worth reproducing. The idea is to make the world go not forward, only around. In modern societies the ends of life are not given at the beginning of life; they are thought to be created or discovered. The reproduction of the customs and practices of the group is no longer the chief purpose of existence. Meaning is no longer immanent in the practices of ordinary life, since those practices are understood by everyone to be contingent and timebound.'[12] Christopher Breward argues that it is this very instability of knowledge, customs and taste that creates the conditions for fashion to exist, and that therefore fashion cannot really exist, or can exist only in a limited sense, in a premodern context.[13]

It may be argued that fashion can exist amongst premodern elites if you follow Hannah Arendt's contention that elites do not really believe in the espistemologies that underpin their regimes.[14] She argues that official ideologies, often with religious foundations, are usually absurd and known to be absurd by the leaders who preach them. Elites are cynics for whom everything is a lie, anyway. They appeal to tradition, custom and nationalism as a means of legitimating their social dominance. Tradition, custom and nationalism are known by elites to be arbitrary, but they are predicated on the assumption that proving that a thing is true is less effective than acting as though it were true. According to this argument, premodern elites already operate under the assumption that knowledge, custom and taste are unstable and therefore already engage in a fashion spectacle.

In Japan, pre-Restoration fashions are mostly to do with patterns and fabrics rather than form, and they conform to socially accepted patterns of life rather than acting as challenges to them. They might be defined as codified newness rather than radical newness. They are also framed as essential customs rather than as something which stands outside of established custom or constitutes something new. While mercantile culture increasingly dominated Japan in the Edo period, rational self-interest was still an inadequate foundation for selfhood. Clothing still functioned as an element of custom and community structure, as part of relations with others and with the stages of life and generation that gave an individual life meaning. Modern social forces, which deracinate, alienate and atomize, were not yet in existence, and therefore the use of clothing as a means of self-actualization and identity expression was not yet important.

The shock of reestablishing communication with the rest of the world, which had been experiencing modernity for some time and had a multitude of forms in which to engage with its conditions, was offset by the fact that the social and economic conditions in Japan were in many ways predisposed to modernity, especially in terms of literacy, urbanization and commerce. This may go some way towards accounting for the enthusiasm for foreign clothing and the obvious pleasure taken in new aesthetic forms and the desire for them upon the reopening of the country.

Sartorial Modernity

Sartorial modernity was not always the coveted dress modality of the modernizing Japanese. The primary shift in tastes that accompanied early economic and social embourgeoisement was a more conservative adoption of samurai tastes, previously inaccessible, financially and legally, to other classes. The ascendancy of finer materials, cotton and silk, amongst the greater populace was the background tendency of much of the Meiji period, and experimentation with tailoring, divided garments, shifting erogenous display, and other facets of modernity in dress were left to an exclusive few. The very fact that choice for the lower classes now existed—they had the opportunity to formulate new identities and express previously dormant aesthetic impulses—was the wellspring of modernity in fashion. The installation of change as an acceptable and preferable value was, in the context of Japan, where in many ways modernity preceded modernization, the central formulation of modernity. The paradox that conservative vestimentary behaviour was actually progressive and an act of modernism, as it denoted a social liquidity in which people were self-actualizing, is a central formulation of modernity in Japanese clothing. At the level of form, however, the modernist project was a limited phenomenon. The application of Kantian aesthetic values to sartorial forms, although instituted in formal, male, occupational dress very early, took a long while to be manifested more widely. This was not the case in the related comportment modifications of hairstyling and cosmetics, whose relative accessibility allowed the early manifestation of naturalism, reductionism and streamlining—all ventures in achieving a Kantian truth in form.

While male Japanese dress adopted the suit briskly, and this, it will be argued, is an exemplary example of modernism, as it balances being true to the body and the clothing without emphasizing either one, women's dress waited a long time before it could assert the same. This is mainly because the imported women's fashions of the 1870s were a profound reaction against modernity and were consequently immoderately ornamental, anatomically perfidious and formally arbitrary. Indigenous women's styles in Japan already fulfilled many of these requirements for the reactionary performance of femininity in early modernity, which was characterized by the full weight of display being transferred to women, and male dress demonstrating seriousness and utility in contrast. It was not until the 1920s that the need for political emancipation, appropriate mobility and aesthetic modernity were finally reflected in female dress. The male adoption of sartorial modernity, by way of the suit, was only half the story, as the phenomenon of the 'double life', mentioned earlier, meant that sartorial modernity was adopted only for public life, while private life, in the home and in the leisure quarters, remained partial to traditional dress forms. The double life was partly to do with the practical consideration of clothing appropriate to furniture and living arrangements. Domestic interior design remained predominantly traditional until the advent in the 1920s of the *bunka seikatsu* (cultured life) and *bunka jūtaku* (cultured houses)—which meant Western-style houses with Western-style furniture.[15] Desks with chairs were introduced for the civil service around 1872, making it practical to wear suits at work, though leisure and home life remained floor-based and thus at variance with fitted garments, difficult-to-remove shoes and the other attributes of Western garb.

The invention of tradition in the Meiji period, which accompanied the general inclination of all classes towards samurai tastes and sartorial practices, will be dealt with in detail later, though it is important to note, in terms of general tendencies, that indigenous styles were far from stationary, and they adapted dialectically to the provocation of imported styles. The refinement and adaptation of 'traditional' clothing forms facilitated the construction of Japanese identity as something both adaptable and modern and, at the same time, unique and uncontaminated. The monarchy was often constructed as the pioneer in this, demonstrating sartorially the military and economic sophistication of Japan, while at other times stressing the importance of continuity and racial and cultural integrity. The invention of dress practice and its authentication as 'traditional' was the primary engine of early Meiji reinvention, once the sumptuary laws were lifted and the newly permitted importation of cheaper fabrics, mainly from China, allowed the bulk of the population to reinvent itself as much closer to samurai styles than before.[16] This realignment of class tastes was not limited to dress but permeated custom, morality and ritual, with the result that while the economic currents moved towards embourgeoisement, the cultural currents moved, at least initially, towards samuraization. The cultural confines of samuraization, as they were codified in the Meiji period, allowed participation in it with limited means; stoicism, abstemiousness and Zen-restraint being key features in the abstract that easily translated into consumption patterns, interior design and conventions of sartorial array.

Thus, in general, sartorially avant-garde practice was at odds with early social trends. The move toward modernity in dress, defined as a Kantian veracity in forms of dress, did not become the predominant trend until the Taishō period, even, by some accounts, until after the Second World War.[17] Modernity was not the dominant tendency and it was not performed by traditionally avant-garde sections of the populace: the adoption of suits was a state-instituted fashion amongst the political and bureaucratic elite, normally a very sartorially conservative group. Later styles were promulgated by the *mobo* and *moga* urban youth, another demographic not considered economically endowed or socially liberated enough to act as a generator of sartorial trends, until after the youthquakes of the 1960s. Top-down formulations of fashion were inapplicable in both cases, with only the Imperial Household as an example of elite provision of vestimentary models, and even that was highly unusual use of a monarchy, as an engine of progressive reform rather than conservative continuity.

The construction of the Rokumeikan, which will be examined in detail later, and its employment as a means of demonstrating cultural sophistication and adaptability through carefully replicated dress and the more formal leisure customs of international diplomacy in the 1870s, was an example of deliberate and politically motivated sartorial modernity. While the point has been made that because early sartorial modernity was merely a political manoeuvre, born of anxiety about the unequal treaty arrangements and put into place as a calculated demonstration of cosmopolitanism, it lacked the validity to be considered a real tendency towards modernity in Japanese culture. Yet, though the Rokumeikan was a failure in its political objective of restoring equality to the treaty arrangements of Japan through charm alone, it was a defining product of the particular experience of early modernity of the Meiji political elite, whose members were fascinated by American and European culture and technology and particularly enthusiastic about a cultural programme which equated modernization with Westernization. As a sartorial event which went against the general tendency of samuraization in early modern Japan, early sartorial modernity can be considered an avant-garde dress experiment, conducted by the educated and newly empowered political elite. Besides early sartorial modernity's limitation to a very small class and, especially in the case of women's dress, its later repudiation, there are also reservations that can be made regarding the concept of the 'double life', in which sartorial modernity was limited to public and formal life but was deliberately prevented from infiltration into other areas like leisure activities or the home. This was perhaps part of a cultural strategy which the Japanese adopted, consciously or unconsciously, to limit the potency of foreign cultural influence, in reaction to the rapidity of the arrival of external cultural ideas. The designation of certain foreign cultural practices as 'play' enables a divide to be maintained between what is Japanese and what is foreign. It permanently positions some customs as nonserious and not real, which prevents them from ever being fully assimilated into authentic Japanese culture. This strategy for maintaining a kind of cultural purity, or a veneer thereof, will be examined more closely later.

The events that ran counter to the general trends, or were decades ahead of where those general trends would eventually lead, and thus avant-garde, were in general performed by groups that can be seen to have been nontypical when compared to sartorial avant-gardes elsewhere. This was partially the result of the unique class arrangements and conceptualizations in Japan, and the swiftness with which these arrangements had to attune themselves to modernity. Also critically significant was the threat to notions of Japanese identity and self-conception posed by the inundation of anomalous forms and superior technologies that came with the reopening of the country, and the rejoinder to this threat. Avant-garde sartorial events were at odds with general tendencies, and further, they were performed by atypical avant-gardes. Civil servants were producing and giving form to a modern nation state, and their clothed appearances were part of that agenda; yet the Taishō period's modern boys' and modern girls' only product was themselves. They were avant-garde in the displaying and the being, not in the production of works; they were existentially modern. Furthermore, and critically for modernity, they were free and responsible sartorial agents who determined their own dress development through acts of will.

There is a clear distinction between the conscious actions of the creators and the wearers of the garments of modern Japan and the long-term trends displayed by clothing, which do not appear to result from these short-term intentions. The implication is that a history of Japanese clothing would have to be very different from a history of singular events that were the outcome of individual intentions and actions. Causality in dress would, like physics, seem to operate differently at the particular and at the universal levels. Though it would perhaps be possible to formulate sartorial mechanisms in which ontogeny recapitulates phylogeny; sartorial modernity is, in general, defined by the extreme reactions against its core aesthetic agenda, and thus ontogenetic and phylogenetic properties are largely incommensurate.[18] The links between sartorial events and sartorial tendencies often simply reflect a relationship of sequence rather than one of causality and perhaps an understandable desire for an aesthetic dimension to the creation of aesthetic theory; finding patterns in the randomness of sartorial happenings—the beauty of those patterns being more often prescribed than inherent.

The fact that certain previously unavailable materials became available is a concrete and measurable change, as definite a change as the introduction of oil pigments was in the history of painting; and the immediate and dramatic challenge to attitudes to the body, how and when it should be covered, and whether or not clothing should echo or deny its form, are foundational to the history of Japanese sartorial modernity and thus are examined here before other formal causalities. In all discussions of causality, free will in sartorial choice is still assumed, and the phenomenon this book attempts to explain is the correlation of parallel choices made by Japanese dressers endowed with free will that add up to fashions, not superorganic structures that dictate the aesthetic patterns to the wearers of clothing, nor evolutionary models, nor purely economic models.[19]

Identity and its opposite—syncretic randomness—form the central, but not exclusive, narrative of sartorial causality in modern Japan. The defining factor of modernity was not any form taken by that identity, or form defined as its opposite, but the degree to which that identity became liquid and thus also malleable. This is not to say that one couldn't be sartorially self-actualizing in Edo times, but rather that the scope and magnitude for it increased exponentially within the conditions of modernity, such that it can be perceived as an explicating element.[20] The way in which events were used to influence tendencies is part of the larger nation-building narrative of how modern Japan became ethnically and culturally homogeneous, or more properly, how the idea of ethnic and cultural homogeneity came to be a defining feature of Japanese national identity even in the face of manifest heterogeneity. The way in which clothing is used as a vessel for identity and its myriad variances is, in essence, a Kantian process of liberation, of movement from arbitrary to self-actualizing custom. Sartorial modernity, like modernity itself, is often defined by its extreme divergence from modernity's aesthetic agenda, as many of its dominant forms were reactionary with regard to this agenda.[21] The events of Japanese vestimentary modernization were thus often antithetical to the long-term tendencies which finally elucidated it, and while sartorial modernity ultimately prevailed, it was, for much of the period of modernization in Japan, a partial, minority or elitist affair.

Nakedness and Covering It

One of the first indices of a change towards a modern aesthetic in Japan was the attitude to nakedness and the body—issues with which European aesthetics had been earnestly engaging since the Renaissance. Clearly the challenge of Western clothing, as it arrived in 1853, was also a challenge in terms of the way to regard the body the fundamental reasons for clothing it in the first place.[22] In Darwinist schemas of the time, hierarchies of civilization were equated with hierarchies of clothing; with European clothing at the top, being most civilized, and nakedness cast as a primitive and uncivilized state. Darwin himself had concluded, upon seeing the Patagonian Indians greet HMS *Beagle* completely naked, that they must be at the very lowest stage of cultural and biological evolution.[23] It was these conceptual structures, which were introduced and reinforced by the expositions of the nineteenth century, and which expanded upon borrowed Chinese conceptions of the outward signs of civilization, that established the Meiji Japanese view of the body and when and how it can be seen, not just the motivation to display Western manners in order to convince Western powers to give up the unequal treaties, to which so many writers reduce it.[24] Japan accepted the tenets of the Western science which arrived with the reopening and included the belief that there was a hierarchy of race and civilization—and intended to demonstrate that they belonged to the upper strata of this hierarchy.

As part of the deliberate programme of transforming the peasantry into able and conscious citizens of the nation-state, a new conception of rule resulted in many new policies aimed at creating a highly disciplined national community and a unified and totalizing culture. Internalizing attitudes to the display of the body was one of the first stages. In Tokyo, the authorities launched aggressive campaigns against mixed bathing, public nudity, and urinating in public (*tachi shōben*). In 1876, the Tokyo police arrested 2,091 people for nudity and 4,495 others for urinating in public.[25] This attention to details of the culture of everyday life and attitudes towards the body reflected a great faith in the educability of common people—a conviction that if properly and vigorously instructed and regulated, the former unimportant commoner could become an informed and responsible member of the national community.[26] Japan's Meiji period political leaders conceived the entire cultural apparatus of the modern state as a mechanism for enlightening the masses and turning a peasantry into a citizenry.[27] Civilization was a clothing of base behaviour with customs, practices and beliefs, and rather than explaining the philosophical and political reasons for this, the regime understood that it could infiltrate everyday life more simply by regulating customs. Modernity would be enacted from the inside out; like a process of dressing, from underwear to top hat.

Decency

Tokyo, in 1872, was being vigorously instructed in imported notions of decorum, both to impress the foreign powers and to institute the modern system of internalized regulation that the modern-nation state required of its citizens.[28] Runners were required to wear more than the conventional loincloth. Edward Morse describes how a runner stopped at the city limits of Tokyo to cover himself properly,[29] as though he was, right there, entering civilization. Social regulation through sartorial formality was not new to Japan, but its extension to all areas of life and to all classes was a modern phenomenon. A central, if not *the* central, feature of the French Revolution was its faith in the ability of politics to refashion the everyday life and mentalities of a people.[30] The application of this comparison is limited; however, the Meiji Restoration was every bit as revolutionary as the French Revolution, for, like its French counterpart, the Japanese revolution set off a double movement of the 'political'. While it expanded, once and for all, the shape and the polity so that government became, preeminently, that of the nation-state, at the same time the Meiji Revolution, propelled by a faith in human plasticity and a new civilizing mission for the State, extended the State's reach into the very souls of the people. It did this by first targeting their bodies, and not immediately their clothing and the customs which governed the wearing of it. Changing various rites, symbols, customs, beliefs and practices was perhaps even more important to ruling than the formally written down ideas supporting the regime, because these innovations could more easily infiltrate everyday life, because they could, in many instances, be unconsciously inscribed in daily practices on the body in the form of clothing, hairstyles and modes of physical deportment and, most importantly, because their recent invention could more easily be forgotten.[31]

In *The Wealth of Nations*, Adam Smith wryly points out that in modern, materialistic societies, countless things that were no doubt unnecessary from the point of view of physical survival had nonetheless, in practical terms, come to be seen as 'necessaries' simply because no one could be thought respectable and so lead a psychologically comfortable life without owning them:

> By necessaries I understand not only the commodities which are indispensably necessary for the support of life, but whatever the custom of the country renders it indecent for creditable people, even of the lowest order, to be without. A linen shirt, for example, is strictly speaking, not a necessary of life. The Greeks and Romans lived, I suppose very comfortably though they had no linen. But in the present times, through the greater part of Europe, a creditable day-labourer would be ashamed to appear in public without a linen shirt, the want of which would be supposed to denote that disgraceful degree of

poverty which, it is presumed, nobody can well fall into without extreme bad conduct . . . Under necessaries, therefore, I comprehend not only those things which nature, but those things the established rules of decency, have rendered necessary to the lowest rank of people.[32]

It was this internalized value system that the Meiji government was attempting to implant in the Japanese psyche. Clothing, or more accurately the absence of the lack of it, was used to ingrain concepts of what was 'decent', and by extension, of how to behave. Through such simple contrivances, Japan's former peasantry could begin the transformation from feudal to modern consciousness. In our effort to understand this process of imposing a standard of decency, which is a more modern and sophisticated method of social control than the monopoly on violence held by the samurai elites, it is interesting to see what is created by the taboo, the breaking of rules that occurs once the rules have been imposed.

In the Japanese experience and more generally, nakedness contributes to defining how fashion is experienced: looking at and wearing clothes is a process defined against what it's not—the absence of clothes. The social imperative to wear clothing of certain types at certain times is an extension of the social imperative to wear clothing in the first place. While some fashion theorists have written of the original motivations behind the prohibition of nakedness in terms of religious constraint, such as original sin, the moment when God shows Adam and Eve that they are naked and they become ashamed, the religious inheritance is only part of the explanation, religious constraints being a subset of social constraints. Adam Smith is closer when he talks about the value placed on wealth and argues that not having adequate clothing signifies your poverty and poverty signifies 'extreme bad conduct'.[33] Morality, including its instructions regarding clothing and nakedness, is essentially a tool for maintaining social hierarchy and order. It codifies behaviour and internalizes the process by which that behaviour is monitored. People feel ashamed if they are not properly clothed, as the current public morality defines it.

Emile Durkheim's notions of social constraint are useful here. Durkheim's definition of traditional societies, in which self-sufficient subsistence farming was closely knitted together by 'mechanical' solidarity—common heritage and common occupation—was set in contrast to his definition of modern societies, in which a highly complex division of labour resulted in 'organic' solidarity—specialization creating interdependence—often finding itself in conflict with collective consciousness.[34] Mechanical solidarity relies on repressive law and punishment and in this way acts to preserve the unity of consciousness, while organic solidarity relies on restitutive law, to reinstate normal activity in a complex society. Fashionable behaviour cannot exist in traditional social structures, where collective consciousness entirely subsumes individual consciousness. Only in social structures where individual and collective consciousness are in conflict can fashion systems operate. The regulation of nakedness in the early Meiji period was an accelerated example of a shift from mechanical to organic social solidarity—a solidarity in which notions of social constraint of individuals replace a subsuming collective consciousness.

Roland Barthes attempted to crystallize the contradictions created by attitudes to nudity and nakedness and the way clothes are sexualized. In endeavouring to explain the process between dress and undress he used the metaphor of the striptease.[35] Barthes said that the striptease—at least Parisian striptease, the low burlesque—is based on a contradiction: woman is desexualized at the very moment when she is stripped naked. Barthes asserts that the ritual is a spectacle based on the pretence of fear, as if eroticism here goes no further than a sort of delicious terror, whose ritual signs have only to be announced to evoke at once the idea of sex and its conjuration. In modern Japan, the models for the exotic were often Western, and in both, the borrowed *mise en scène* aims at establishing the woman right from the start as an object in disguise. The equating of exotic femininity with the potency of foreign forms is a recurring theme in the relation of power and sex, and it spills over from the revues of Asakusa into the general urban consciousness of foreign clothing and its sexual appeal.[36] The elements of the dress go, in Barthes's revue, towards establishing this particular erotic as comfortable—towards conceiving of eroticism as a household property and by extension domesticating what was originally potently foreign.[37] Formulating eroticism makes it familiar and no longer dangerous. The revues give sex a narrative, which is often satirical, and thereby a means of interpretation.

Barthes' conception of the ritualized removal of clothing adds interpretative depth to the analysis of dress and its associated taboos.[38] The introduction to the Japanese polity of dress norms as a measure of civilization also created a sophisticated caricature of the arbitrariness of forms of attire, and of the ways in which the manipulation of these norms can create a whole vocabulary of provocation. Barthes conceives of dressing, both at the level of cloth and at the level of high abstraction—nation, culture, sexuality, civilization—as a disguise, a framing. The important part of the message is in the context, not in the actual object. This level of semiotic connotation could establish and lampoon the conventions which say that certain things or combinations of things are sexy, conservative, formal, and so on. But the challenging of certain conventions can also reestablish original forms with their original power. Hence the importance of challenging rituals, conventions, assumptions. Some of these conventions are used as a means of domesticating female sexual power. The end of the striptease is a disappointment. It is the dress which is important, which creates the prohibition, not the undress.

Barthes's understanding of the nature of the erotic and its wider application can be applied to the Japanese experience, especially by the 1920s. A version of the striptease, though it was far more tease than strip, appeared in the Taishō period and was one of the things often used to define the times: the *ero guro nansensu* (erotic grotesque nonsense). The Asakusa revues included the decadent parts of modernity: eroticism, nonsense and speed, as well as humour, jazz and legs, and most importantly, foreignness. In 1929, the Casino Folies was opened in Asakusa, based on the Folies Bergère in Paris.[39] By the 1930s, the revues had become very substantial productions and of increasing cultural influence, with huge troupes and budgets.[40] The undoubted attraction was the evocation, against a general prohibition, of issues of sex and seduction in a social structure where they constituted a threat. The clothing and unclothing of the body were of such interest that even the unsubstantiated rumour that the girls in the chorus line dropped their drawers on Friday evenings was seductive enough to draw crowds.[41] Even in the abstract, the possibility of flouting the social conventions of dress was immensely provocative; and its association with presumed sexual liberation in an exotic elsewhere made Western clothing immensely appealing, even if the presumed sexiness and liberation were more imagined that actual.

The revues were highly regulated; police forbade ad-libbing and required scripts to be presented ten days in advance. The potency of the burlesque as a means of political subversion was well-recognized. There were also masses of regulations regarding the garb and demeanour of the girls; drawers must cover at least the top ten centimetres of the thigh, flesh-coloured drawers were not permitted, there must be no suggestive lighting about the hips or pelvis, no kicking in the direction of the audience, no wriggling of the hips and so on. One day, the casino girls were herded off to the Asakusa police station to have their drawers measured.[42] This type of regulation is reminiscent of the measuring of women's bathing suits in America. The regulations create an unnecessary prohibition. But obviously in Japan the threat to order from female eroticism was taken seriously.

Foundational Choices: *Yōga* and *Nihonga*

Artists were among the first groups to engage with the unfamiliar approaches to the human form—representing and clothing it. Responsible for visualizing values, they were intensely invested in the debate over the future of Japanese culture and the place of the body within it. With the enormous wave of cultural influence that accompanied the reopening of Japan, designers of all kinds faced a choice between adapting old forms and motifs now reified as tradition, or using the new Western techniques and patterns identified with progress. Making art necessitated choosing a style, and since styles were affiliated with either Japanese or Western modes, to make art was to make a statement about culture. This same choice was experienced every day for all Japanese citizens with resources, at the moment of dressing and every time they shopped for clothing. It was not the choice faced in Western Europe between tradition and reform or within the parameters of popular fashions; it was a much more important choice at a more fundamental stage of self-identification. Isozaki Arata, the architect of the planned city, Tsukuba, in Ibaraki, said that once you make a foundational choice about what style something will be, all subsequent choices become easier as they are directed by that first choice.[43] In choosing a sartorial style, Meiji Japan faced a similar dilemma, as did its visual artists.

The art form with the highest profile was painting, and painters were, in this period of unprecedented cultural instability, faced with a stark hermeneutic choice between two modes, based primarily on their choice of materials but also upon style and cultural affiliation. These two modes were *yōga*, or Western painting, and *nihonga*, or Japanese painting. *Yōga* artists worked in oil and watercolours, were oriented toward Europe and essentially accepted modernity as the new guiding force of artistic expression. *Nihonga* artists worked in traditional pigments and formats, taking their primary inspiration from the Japanese past and denying the value of foreign forms and the capacity for hybrids. A handful of artists worked in both modes, but generally they were exclusive categories. Within *yōga* and *nihonga* are a welter of different affiliations and styles, ranging from the progressive to the conservative. Yet, on the whole, *yōga* was by its very nature associated with stylistic evolution and perhaps derivation, as a steady stream of young artists sought to keep pace with the avant-garde modes emerging from Paris.[44] *Nihonga*, by contrast, was inherently charged with finding, defining and refining values different from, and often existing prior to, those imported from the West. Indeed, the issue of dramatic evolution was a bone of contention in *nihonga* theorizing.

Another variable in painting choice was the subject. Standard *nihonga* subject categories include landscape, bird and flower, and the figure, which includes historical subjects, literary themes, genre and portraiture. Historical subjects, like portraits of famous persons, tend to favour males, especially political leaders and military heroes. Literary and genre scenes are balanced between both sexes. But female alone comprise the long-sanctioned East Asian painting category of *bijinga* or 'pictures of beautiful women'. European art had, from the Renaissance, a reengagement with humanism and the body, yet Japanese notions of the body, how it could be depicted and covered, were within *nihonga*—as perhaps with the kimono—extremely stylized.

Several artists of the *nihonga* painting elite specialized in *bijinga*, devoting their careers to representing women in stylized ways. Implicitly these artists entered the national dispute on the rise of the 'new woman' (*atarashii onna*) and of feminine styles, or social roles, as indices of cultural identity where clothing was a principal battleground. Some formulated elaborate taxonomies of historical evolution and regional distinctions in canons of feminine beauty; others sought subtle variations in feminine emotions and values.[45] *Bijinga* specialists, many of whom started as illustrators, often had their work published in newspapers and magazines and reinforced conservative corporeal values in the mass media.[46] Those with literary skills also frequently contributed essays to popular publications, debating the subject of women, largely without the influence of women themselves. And *bijinga* painters of sufficient repute even served on public committees charged with suggesting social policy concerning women. *Bijinga* artists did not merely reflect prevailing opinions about women; they helped to craft those opinions.[47]

In a multiplicity of ways, women and their situation and appropriate representation were at the very core of social and cultural tension and anxiety in late Meiji and

Taishō Japan. It was a common historical sentiment of the era that 'women could not enter public space without arousing anxiety about their presence.'[48] It was irrefutable that men had a self-evident stake in modernity with an equivalent sartorial expression, as a consequence of having to work in the new economy and wear the clothes appropriate to the milieu of modern employment in the factory or office. Women's participation in the project of modernization, however, was a far thornier matter. In a favourite Meiji formulation, the nation's goal was the adaptation of Western technology to preserve the Japanese spirit and the manifestation of this as clearly gendered. For the average urban male, modernization was mandatory. But for females— emblems of that native essence—Westernization was inherently problematic. In the dispute over the fate of Japanese culture in the modern age, women's bodies and lives thus constituted 'contested spaces'.

This contest was often played out between two antithetical images of women. On one hand, the modern girl (*modan gaaru* or *moga*)—sporting pumps, a short dress and bobbed hair and conspicuous in such modern spaces as cafés and urban streets—represented, at the least, an enchantment with the material surface of Western modernity. She also held the promise or threat of cultural and sexual liberation and the possibility of militant social action.[49] On the other hand, the traditional woman— championed in official ideology as 'good wife, wise mother' (*ryō sai kenbo*) and belonging to the space of the home—stood guard over conventional values sanctioned by Confucian and Victorian morality alike. These poles in the debate represent politico-cultural ideologies, aesthetic choices and even marketing strategies, all played out predominantly on the bodies of women and their clothing.

Between these compelling opposites of radical modernity and reactionary tradition was a rich and passionate middle ground, where the styles and values of the *moga* and the good wife/wise mother mingled. This culturally composite woman was largely the product of a sophisticated capitalistic society, where ideology was not simply expressed through visual style but could be wholly transformed into style as fashion, all the better to market it to followers who were also consumers. For instance, the June 1926 issue of *Shiseidō geppō*, published by cosmetics firm Shiseidō, included an article on the modern girl, emphasizing the coiffure, clothing and cosmetics required to achieve the *moga* look.[50]

It is a feature common to both capitalism and fashion that they assimilate rather than repudiate challenges to them. Anti-fashion is constantly being taken up by mainstream fashion; the rebellion commodified and neutralized. Japanese fashion does this as well: Shiseidō turning the *moga* from a dangerous challenge to female values and social position into merely a look, to be copied and then forgotten as with all fashions. There is also an element in Japanese magazines, even today, that tends to make them instructional (anyone can achieve any look) rather than expressing restrictions or exclusivity of fashions based in class envy. With a more highly developed tradition of aristocratic differentiation through clothing, the West developed magazines within Veblen's[51] framework of conspicuous consumption; for the aristocracy to remain visually differentiated from the rising middle classes, it had to change fashions fast enough to keep ahead of the aspirants. Japan, proudly egalitarian now—at least nominally—never had as much of a system of visual differentiation as European aristocracies. Non-samurai were simply not permitted to wear samurai clothing before the Meiji Restoration, and with the abolition of these laws in the 1870s, a new visual system was established around issues of tradition and modernity rather than simply of class. Like the merchant classes of Europe, Japanese merchants had developed a system through which they could subtly demonstrate their wealth through items like silk linings, but they were not permitted to actually imitate their samurai superiors. Certainly, after the Restoration and the abolition of the sumptuary laws, it was only those with means who could afford the new clothing, but merchant and ruling classes wore the same thing. When Japan had a fashion trend, it was embraced universally, like Louis Vuitton handbags today: everyone has one, so it no longer distinguishes social class; it simply signifies luxury, but universally accessible luxury.[52] Fashion was a modern desire for visual newness in Japan, not a means of class differentiation, because Japanese national identity was, and is, configured differently from identity in the West, where class was, and perhaps still is, more central.

The Japanese also have a tendency to reduce threats to established order to play—a strategy of fashion and of capitalism. Sadism and masochism is called *S/M play*, the *play* part being hardly what the Marquis de Sade would advocate.[53] In this way, foreign concepts which could present a challenge to Japanese culture and norms are put linguistically into an experimental, and nonserious category, where their threat is reduced. The playfulness of the terms *mobo* and *moga* hide the seriousness of their potential challenge to established order and social behaviour.

Although the binary of modernity and tradition, foreign and indigenous, comprised the basic formulation for cultural criticism in Taishō Japan, there was as much of an attempt to bridge these categories as an attempt to fix or fortify them. Theoretically, the modern girl was defined in part by the difference she presented from pre- or antimodern female styles and behaviours. Yet, because of the bridging, there was no absolute fracture between old and new, and thus the categories were not mutually exclusive but rather contingent. The concepts of modernity and tradition were hybrids, or at least heterogeneous constructs subject to modification. Not surprisingly, there were both formal efforts to deflect the potentially subversive qualities of the *moga*, by making her more like a traditional woman, and spontaneous attempts to find formal commonalities. Likewise, even as the Japanese-style woman (*wasō bijin*) was being crafted as an antidote or counterbalance to the *moga*, there were also attempts to infuse her with the vitality of the modern girl.

'Westernization' and Japanese Fashion

Japanese clothing before the 1860s was almost entirely confined to indigenous fashions, a restriction strictly policed by the State with only a few exceptions among rich, travelled eccentrics. Essentially, the indigenous fashions consisted of many varieties of the kimono, the loosely fitted robe worn with a broad belt, made of silk, mixed silk and cotton, just cotton or linen. The kimono itself was an outgrowth of a kind of undergarment called *kosode* and worn by the upper class between the eighth and twelfth centuries. This gradually became an outer garment—in a process reminiscent of the European process described by Koda and Martin of underwear becoming outerwear as social formalities evolved—and the basic style and form was fairly well set by the fourteenth century.[54] Warmth was achieved in Japan by adding layers of clothes and also by padding the garments with raw cotton or silk. Until the end of the fifteenth century, linen from flax had been the most popular fibre, but from that point on, the growing cotton industry increasingly reduced the use of linen. The silk industry developed from the end of the sixteenth century, yet silk always remained a luxury of the rich, and the sumptuary regulations—which were abolished after the Meiji Restoration—restricted its use to the samurai and noble classes, which accounted for well under 10 per cent of the population. (Other classes, notably the merchants and rich farmers, frequently violated these regulations, using silk as a lining and other means of subtly demonstrating growing wealth and refinement.)[55] There is no reliable quantitative information for this period, but it is generally agreed that just before the Meiji Restoration, the average Japanese would have worn some form of cotton or linen kimono, while a rich person might have been clad in silk.[56] At this time, woollens were very rarely manufactured in Japan—indeed, they were almost unknown.[57] Some woollen and worsted fabrics (such as Raxa and Grofgren) had been introduced at the end of the sixteenth century by Spanish, Portuguese and Dutch merchants, but the closing of the country by Tokugawa Iemitsu, in 1639, to anything but very limited Dutch and Chinese commerce prevented this importation from developing. Until the Restoration, wool remained a luxury commodity, used only by the richest nobles for accessories—in much the way that furs might have been used in Europe.[58]

Among the first Japanese to adopt Western clothing, albeit only in the form of military uniforms, were the officers and men of some units of the shogunal army and navy.[59] Some time in the 1850s, these men adopted woollen uniforms in the style of those worn by English marines stationed at Yokohama. Producing these uniforms could not have been an easy matter. All of the cloth had to be imported,[60] and tailors had to be trained in the comparatively difficult art of fitting Western-style suits. Uniforms are dealt with in more detail in Chapter 3.

The indigenous kimono, being a loose garment, presented no particular problems of cutting and fitting, and until recently, most Japanese women were capable of putting these garments together entirely by hand. Kimonos are made from one long, rectangular length of cloth cut into eight pieces; the pattern is the same for everyone, male or female, child or adult. Every inch of cloth is used, with no waste. No matter how efficiently an article of Western clothing is cut, when fitted clothing is produced there will be pieces from which nothing can be made. No buttons or hooks or other gadgets are needed to hold the kimono on: the obi—the band or sash tied around the waist—is sufficient. This means that when the garment is put on it can be adjusted for the wearer's girth and height. As already stated, the kimono creates a certain understanding of the body, as something to be wrapped. Western garments require a much closer individual fit, and the Japanese needed special training in order to become Western-style tailors—tailoring here meaning the English tradition of bespoke design: having the clothes customized to the particular body became the prime European male sartorial criterion. In the late 1850s and the 1860s, a few foreign tailors catered to the small foreign settlements in Yokohama and Kobe.[61] Some of these establishments took Japanese apprentices, and they in turn became the first native entrepreneurs in this trade. By 1886, the Association of Merchants and Manufacturers of Western Suits, founded in Tokyo, already had 123 members.[62] In 1890, the first style-book (*fukusō zasshi*) was issued, designed to introduce the newest fashions of Europe to tailors and the public.[63] Some sewing machines had been in use since the 1860s, and in 1887, a special sewing machine school was founded in Tokyo, mainly for the benefit of apprentice tailors. The Singer Co. established a school, also in Tokyo, in 1907, and here the students were largely housewives and young girls.[64] Perhaps the most significant aspect of this early adoption of Western styles was its public origin. For quite a while the public sector remained the major champion of the new garb, reflecting the aesthetic dimension of the political agenda of modernization.

The Meiji Restoration of 1868 established in Japan a strong central government, committed to abolishing feudalism and eager to use Westernization as a model for political, economic and cultural development—the idea of development itself being the operative aspiration of modernity. These policies were reflected in the clothes in which the members of the new government chose to be seen. When the Duke of Edinburgh visited Japan in 1869, the Imperial Court decided to receive him in formal Western dress.[65] In 1870, navy cadets were ordered to wear British-style uniforms, while army cadets followed the French model.[66] The turn of policemen and mailmen came in 1871, and that of workers on the sole national railway line, running between Tokyo and Yokohama, in 1872.[67]

During 1871, debate commenced as to whether the principles of sartorial reform should be extended to ministers of the central government and members of the court.[68] The issue was whether, to what extent and at what occasions, senior officials of the central and local government should wear Japanese or Western dress. The agenda of wider Westernization prevailed, and an imperial rescript of that year reflected the official view: the court was ordered to abandon its Sinicized costumes—they were considered effeminate and un-Japanese—and courtiers and bureaucrats were urged to adopt Western clothing; it was thought that this was much more practical and would demonstrate their new alignment with Western rather than Chinese civilization.[69] The government had the Emperor speak as follows: 'The national polity [*kokutai*] is indomitable, but manners and customs should be adaptable. We greatly regret that the uniform of our court has been established following the Chinese custom,

and it has become exceedingly effeminate in style and character . . . The Emperor
Jimmu [660–585 BCE] who founded Japan, and the Empress Jingu [201–269 CE] who
conquered Korea, were not attired in the present style. We should no longer appear
before the people in these effeminate styles, and we have therefore decided to reform
dress regulations entirely.'[70] The emphasis was on the new adaptability that the State
would require of the people in order for Japan to modernize and remain independent,
and it was recognized that the reform of simple sartorial customs—the fundamental
marker and means of enacting individual and collective identity—would be a crucial
instrument in effecting this required malleability. The evocation of Emperor Jimmu,
whose reaction to the cutaway can only be imagined, illustrates the State's willingness
to enlist and manipulate history and custom and reinvent it in the service of fostering
nationalism and expedient, if untrue, collective memory.

When, in 1877, the new conscript armies of the central government faced the
last internal challenge to the new regime during the Satsuma Rebellion, they were
dressed in woollen uniforms while the insurgents wore the traditional cottons and
silks of the samurai. The symbolic aspects of the battle were probably clear to both
victor and vanquished.[71]

Thus, by the 1880s, European clothing fashions had conquered some small
but symbolically important corners of the market, and their influence was spread-
ing slowly—mainly from the top down.[72] The higher echelons of society in Tokyo
started to frequent European-style entertainments—social dances, garden parties,
musicales—and they would often appear in a tuxedo or other forms of European evening dress. At the time foreigners had extraterritorial rights in Japan, and the government believed, perhaps naively, that the rapid spread of Western manners and dress
would enable it to get rid of the unequal treaties by simply demonstrating Japan's
level of civilization and ability to adapt to European customs. In line with this policy,
the government sponsored, beginning in 1883, a variety of nightly social affairs at
the Rokumeikan, a Western-style building in Tokyo. These affairs were attended by
foreigners and high-class Japanese, all in Western dress.[73] Some department stores
also opened Western-dress sections at this time.[74] The Empress and ladies of the
court began to be seen in dresses. During this decade, the Ministry of Education
ordered that Western-style student uniforms be worn in public colleges and universities; private universities followed only at a much later date.[75] Businessmen, teachers,
doctors, bankers and other leaders of the new society made use of Western suits by
the end of the nineteenth century, mainly at work or at large social functions, and
in 1898, the total consumption of woollen fabrics reached about 3,000,000 yards,
almost all imported from England and Germany.[76]

By the early years of the twentieth century—about thirty years after the
Restoration—Western dress had become a symbol of social dignity and progres-
siveness, an accepted symbol of civic progress. In addition, it was usually a reasonably good indication of public employment. The victory in the Russo-Japanese
War (1904–1905), and the economic boom associated with it, turned the eyes of Japan

even more towards Europe, as the Japanese had proved to themselves and the world that they were able to defeat a European power, and somewhat broadened the narrow circle of people using wool and Western suits. It is necessary to underline how limited the use of this type of dress still was at that time. The vast majority of Japanese stuck to their own styles, within which fashion systems had begun to operate in the modern sense, and even those few who, voluntarily or involuntarily, changed to 'modern' dress replaced it, when they returned home, with the more (physically and mentally) comfortable kimono, Japanese interiors were impractical for Western clothing until the later trend towards European furniture. Western dress in public and Japanese dress at home remained the general rule for a very long time.[77]

At the beginning of the twentieth century, a development of much greater long-range consequence was taking place within indigenous Japanese styles. Western clothing was confined to a small elite, but the nature of indigenous clothing was also affected by the new times. From the turn of the century, woollens and worsteds showed their real gains, not in the narrow demand for Western suits but in the adoption of these materials for the kimono. Thus the experience of sartorial modernism was, for many, not one of form, body and movement change but one of textural change. In line with the general samuraization of tastes, many adopted what the ruling class had already known about for some time.

Almost up to the time of the First World War, from the point of view of the majority of Japanese, there was no general Westernization of clothes but rather a gradual adoption of a new fibre, wool, together with a continued use of silk and cotton. The people had become acquainted with wool, but there were still two enormous obstacles to the more widespread use of Western fashions: the Japanese continued to prefer their own styles, and wool remained comparatively expensive. There were always cheaper substitutes among traditional clothes. Among other things, the kimono has the advantage of lasting much longer than Western clothes. Styles—usually designs of the cloth, not designs of the clothes—change less frequently, and since the garment is loose it can fit successive generations of wearers.[78] Since the mid-Tokugawa period, there had been many used clothing shops in Edo, and business was so brisk that people began stealing clothing to sell it, precipitating an unsuccessful attempt to close down the market in 1724. By the eighteenth century, wholesalers of used clothing emerged; and the volume of trade was huge.[79] The standardization of the kimono made this trade much more vibrant than the trade in used clothing in Europe and America; when you can fit into anything on display, the opportunities for consumption greatly increase. This fact reduced accessibility to Western clothing through the traditional channel of traders in second-hand clothes.

The Japanese economy underwent extremely rapid development during the First World War, and this was a great stimulus to the Westernization of national life. Among what might be called the 'smart set', the slogan *bunka seikatsu*—literally, cultured or civilized life, actually meaning a Western style of life—began to be heard. These people craved *bunka jūtaku* (cultured houses), *bunka shoku* (cultured food) and *bunka fuku* (cultured clothes), and all this meant the same thing—that European and American customs were considered superior.[80] While this may have been the general opinion, reinforced by the arrival of Hollywood cinema and the like, the actual result was the creation of an abundance of stylistic hybrids in these areas which better suited the Japanese experience of modernity than either the indigenous or the foreign models. These tendencies continued in the 1920s, and spread considerably due to the Great Kantō Earthquake of 1923.[81] The disaster almost completely destroyed Tokyo and Yokohama, the largest metropolitan complex in the country, and this tragic event caused something of a turning point in Japanese fashion history. Over 700,000 dwellings were levelled, and millions lost all their possessions—including their clothes.[82] Many victims replaced their clothing with a larger proportion of Western items, in part because the pattern of demand had slowly shifted to a greater emphasis on this type of fashion, and also because it was said that the kimono had proved dangerous during the quake since its long sleeves and train prevented rapid movement. Even though the latter allegation was not very plausible—after all, the Japanese had long experience with both earthquakes and kimonos—it may well have affected popular tastes. Also in the 1920s, primary and secondary school students contributed to increased Westernization as, after the Great Kantō Earthquake, many of the schools adopted plain, blue serge, Western-style uniforms, and the popularity of social dancing and gymnastics intensified the tendencies to Westernization.

Until the 1930s, however, the majority of Japanese still continued to wear the kimono, and Western clothes were still pretty much restricted to public, nondomestic use by certain classes. Since most Japanese women were still largely confined to the home, a large potential market was eliminated. Even when Japanese women began to appear more frequently as members of the labour force, either in industry or in service occupations, they usually remained in the kimono. It is true that the conductresses on Tokyo's municipal buses changed to Western wool uniforms in 1924, but that was an exception.[83] Wherever Japanese women worked—in department stores, offices, bars, as telephone operators or factory workers—they usually performed their tasks in kimonos, if necessary covered with aprons and dusters. It was another disaster that provoked a big conversion in women's dress.

The Shirokiya, an eight-storey department store constructed after the earthquake, was the chief retail rival of the Mitsukoshi through the years of diversifying and expanding. On the morning of 16 December 1932, a fire broke out in the toy department on the fourth floor. The end of the year in Japan had traditionally been a time of giving gifts, and Christmas gifts had in the 1920s been added to those based on older customs, just as pagan ritual had been co-opted by Christianity. Christmas Eve was becoming what New Year's Eve is in the West. The Shirokiya was bright with festive decorations and a technician was repairing Christmas lights when a tree caught fire. Fortunately this happened a few minutes after nine, before the store had filled with customers. The utility poles and wires along the main streets and the narrowness of the side streets made it difficult to use ladders, though some rescues were effected.

Ropes and improvised lines using kimono fabrics in the store were used to help people escape. It may be that no one except a single victim of asphyxiation need have died. The other thirteen deaths were caused by jumping and falling. The bears and monkeys on the roof came through uninjured, demonstrating that the garden zoo on the roof was safe throughout. The jumping was of course from panic. The falling had more subtle causes, having to do with dress. All shop girls in those days wore Japanese dress and underwear; wrap-around skirts were worn in various numbers depending on the season. Traditional dress for women included nothing by way of shaped, tight-fitting undergarments. The older women at the Shirokiya, being bolder, made it safely down the ropes.[84] Some of the younger girls, however, used a hand for the rope and a hand to keep their skirts from flying into disarray, and so they fell. In 1933, newly rebuilt, the Shirokiya started paying its girls subsidies for wearing foreign dress, and required that they wear underpants.[85]

This expression of fatal modesty is reminiscent of the passage on the training and position of women in Inazo Nitobe's *Bushido*; 'It was a disgrace to her not to know the proper way in which she had to perpetrate self-destruction. For example, little as she was taught in anatomy, she must know how to tie her lower limbs together with a belt so that, whatever the agonies of death might be, her corpse be found in utmost modesty with the limbs properly composed.'[86] This purportedly samurai morality was deliberately spread throughout the public during the Meiji period, and the Shirokiya fire demonstrates how ingrained it had become amongst ordinary girls. Going from society in which mixed bathing and public nudity had been common to one in which young girls risked death to protect themselves against a brief lapse in modesty reflects an extraordinary change in attitude towards the body and how it can be seen.

From about the time of the earthquake, advertising men had been pushing Western underwear for women, which they made a symbol of sexual equality. But a disaster like the Shirokiya fire was needed to effect decisive change. It demonstrated that women were still lamentably backward, and the newspapers loved it.[87] Underpants became one of their favourite causes and one in which they enjoyed quick success, though the reform would actually seem to have begun earlier. In the early 1930s, Kawabata Yasunari noted that all the little girls sliding down the slides in Hama Park were wearing underpants.[88]

The general trend towards Western dress in the 1930s is explainable in more rational terms. By this time most of the people had worn Western-style school or army uniforms and presumably had acquired a kind of taste or habit for fitted and divided clothes. From 1873, all able-bodied Japanese men had to serve three years in the army and four years in the reserves, wearing Western-style uniforms and living in Western-style barracks. In addition, the stature of young Japanese men and women had also changed—their very bodies had become more modern through diet and lifestyle. They had grown taller, their legs were longer and the women's busts were a little larger, and this made new styles more flattering. For example in 1900, the average twenty-year-old male was 160 cm tall and the average female 147.9 cm tall.

By 1940, they were 164.5 and 152.7 cm tall, respectively.[89] Furthermore, Western fashions themselves—especially women's fashions—had changed. The skirts were shorter and the sleeves narrower, increasing the comparative advantage of dresses vis-à-vis the kimono if one wanted to lead a more active life. Western fashions for women changed, from the reaction away from modernity in the Victorian era, towards more modern forms. Meanwhile, the woollen and worsted industries had experienced considerable growth—they were now more productive and the real price of woollen textiles had declined.[90] As a result of all these factors, by the outbreak of the Second World War most working women in Japan and quite a few housewives wore Western dress. The same was true of the men working in offices or factories. Already, in the 1920s, the Western suit had reached the upper classes in the provincial cities, and in the 1930s, it was ubiquitous in general business circles. Male work clothes also reflected the Westernizing influences. Cotton, woollen or worsted work clothes, following Western patterns, were used in most factories and the use of bicycles for delivery and message purposes contributed in no small measure to the wearing of pants.[91] The group least affected by all of these changes must have been the farmers, who still made up over 40 per cent of the gainfully occupied population in the late 1930s.[92] More important, however, at home, in the cities and the country, most Japanese continued to relax, eat and sleep in their indigenous clothes.[93]

The adoption of aspects of Western material culture was for the most part superficial and took the form of short-lived fads well into the twentieth century. The changes that occurred during the early Meiji period—carrying Western umbrellas or wearing Western shawls with traditional kimonos—were primarily changes of style and didn't really constitute a radical cultural shift. It is interesting that Japan, superficially one of the most faddish nations when it comes to fashion, is also extremely slow to abandon traditions—as with 'S/M play', fashions are viewed as play and are engaged with on a superficial level only, with any contexts or deeper meanings or social challenges being ignored. This argument has often been made at a linguistic level.[94] The distance at which Japan keeps foreign influence, is also clear in the katakana alphabet used exclusively for foreign words, which are not allowed to be absorbed into the Japanese language; thus, foreign and indigenous are immediately distinguished, just as gender is immediately distinguished in European. While the argument is not without flaws and exceptions, it still has merit for demonstrating, if only partly, this phenomenon of keeping foreign influence in a separate category, to distinguish it from what is considered essentially Japanese.

Because of the early preference for the larger income of the middle and lower classes in the Meiji period to be spent on a samuraization, consumption patterns tended to favour many local products.[95] Increases in the standard of living resulted, by and large, in a greater demand for traditional goods, and this went towards stabilizing the economy, as it meant that the producers of traditional goods did not suddenly find themselves out of work or technologically obsolete—the textile industry is a good example. The new large-scale textile factories produced cloth that was too wide for the kimono, so that while they contributed to an increase in the consumption of cotton cloth for other purposes, they also enabled the survival of the traditional industry that produced the material for the kimono. Furthermore, consumer preference for traditional goods meant that the country did not spend its valuable foreign currency on consumer goods during the early stages of industrialization.[96] This was particularly important for Japan, which not only set out on its industrialization with a somewhat lower per capita income than that of Western nations but was also nearly a century behind England when it began to industrialize.

The impetus for the eventual diffusion of new lifestyles and of a preference for new goods can be attributed to a large degree to the military. Just as the Sengoku wars transformed life in the sixteenth century, the Sino-Japanese and Russo-Japanese wars at the turn of the twentieth century transformed life in the Meiji period. The adoption of cotton for military use by the Sengoku daimyo led to its diffusion among the population as the favoured material for clothing. So, too, the soldiers' contact with Western uniforms, mainly woollen, and foods helped create a demand for such goods when the troops returned home after the wars with China and Russia.[97] This will be examined in further detail in Chapter 3.

Consumption

Advertising is one of the essential modern institutions. The canny merchant of Edo had been aware of its merits, and there are well-known stories of kabuki actors who promoted lines of dress.[98] Edo was a closed world, however, in which vogues, led by the theatre and the pleasure quarters, spread like contagions. People knew their stores, and stores knew their people. Even the largest and richest were highly specialized, and faster transportation led to the development of a wide clientele, gradually becoming something like a national clientele. At the same time came the idea of offering everything to everyone.

Through most of the Meiji period, the old ways prevailed. The big shops specialized in dry goods. The customer removed his footwear before stepping up to the matted floor of the main sales room. There was no window-shopping; only seeing of clothes on other people, as in the case of kabuki promotions, could provide suggestive marketing. If customers in the stores did not know precisely what they wanted, the clerk had to guess, and bring likely items from a warehouse. Wealthy ladies did not go the shops themselves but had the dry goods shops come to them. The Mitsui dry-goods store, which would become Mitsukoshi, had a fixed schedule of prices from an early period in its history.[99] The last decades of the Meiji period saw the advent of the department store; in many of its details, it represented the emergence of a Western institution and the retreat of the traditional to the lesser realm of the speciality store. Certainly there was direct imitation; the big Taishō-era Mitsukoshi store, which was destroyed in the earthquake, was an imitation of Wanamaker's in the United States.[100]

If the department store symbolized the new city, however, it remained in many ways a Japanese sort of symbol. Department stores sold their wares by drawing crowds with culture and entertainment as well as merchandise. Modernity was a spectacle to be experienced, not just owned. Shopping was an essential part of that experience— the act itself, not just the results. Department stores were the heirs to the shrine and temple markets. Mitsukoshi and Shirokiya, at opposite approaches to the Nihonbashi Bridge, led the way into the great mercantile transformation.[101]

Mitsukoshi was better at advertising and image-making than Shirokiya. Though purveying almost everything to almost everyone, it has preserved an air of doing so with elegance. In the late Meiji period, standing face to face across the bridge to which all roads led, the two stores sought to outdo each other with bold innovations. Shortly after the Russo-Japanese War of 1904–1905, Mitsukoshi added a second floor, with showcases. These were innovations so startling that they were for a time resisted. Edo had done its shopping on platforms perhaps two or three feet from the ground, with no wares on display. The addition of a visual dimension to shopping cannot be underestimated in its part in creating a visual modernity.

Shirokiya was ahead in other respects, and in 1886, it became the first of the old silk stores to sell Western clothing, perhaps one of the most significant decisions in widening the availability of sartorial modernism in Japan. Before then, only through tailors, or by making it from the patterns oneself, could one get into Western cloth- ing, and this greatly limited access, socially and economically. Shirokiya had one of the first telephones in Tokyo, and it provided the country with its first shop-girls. All the clerks in the old dry-goods stores had been men. In 1904, Mitsukoshi began selling hats, leather goods and sundries. In 1911, Shirokiya had a new building, with four storeys and a tower; it had game rooms and the first of the exhibition halls that give the modern Japanese department store something of the look of museums and amusement parks. By 1914, Mitsukoshi had central heating, a roof garden and even elevators.[102]

Mitsukoshi was better at the big sell—selling the context—and at the turn of the century, a life-size picture of a pretty girl stood in Shimbashi Station inviting every- one to Mitsukoshi.[103] Early in the Taishō period, the store joined the Imperial Theatre in a famous advertising campaign: 'Today the Imperial, tomorrow Mitsukoshi.'[104] The Nihonbashi stores were clearly aimed, earlier on, at a very high-collar market. 'High-collar' (*haikara*) was originally the word used to describe, somewhat criti- cally, those men who experimented with Western clothing, but it later came to mean simply stylish but with a definite Western (of the real or imagined West) sense of style. The department stores worked the beginnings of a huge cultural shift in the way they initiated the desire for new clothing and new fashions and in the way people consumed clothing.

The problem of what to do with footwear was not solved until after the earth- quake, and the delay was, in some measure, responsible for the long time it took the big stores to attract a mass clientele. Footwear was checked at the door in traditional fashion, sometimes tens of thousands of items per day, and replaced by specially furnished slippers. On the day of the dedication of the new Nihonbashi Bridge, Mitsukoshi misplaced five hundred pairs of footwear.[105]

Department stores as a means of embourgeoisement were essential; they democratized consumption. They were also an example of the awe-inspiring stasis that capitalism can achieve—for it is insensitivity to the immediate pressure of the market that separates big-ticket capitalism from the rug bazaar and the vegetable store. Department stores slow down the market and place it within a shell. In the marketplace, everyone barters and everyone expects to be cheated, but in the department store everything works to take people's minds off the price. It is no longer a place where women simply buy things, but a place to which they simply and necessarily go, just as people wander into and out of a shrine or temple. Shopping becomes an act not solely for procurement but also for entertainment.

All life in a mercantile society, it sometimes seems, is dedicated to disguising wants. This is an acutely middle-class, modern phenomenon. The sin of capitalism, perhaps, is to make wants feel like needs, to give to simple, silly stuff, like clothing, the urgency of near-physical necessity. The grace of capitalism is to make wants feel like hopes, so that material objects and things can acquire the aura of the heroic and civic. Department stores made consumption aspirational in the sense that it served as a self-construction of one's subjectivity. The urge of the great department stores, in Japan, as everywhere else, was to disguise acquisition as sociability, to disguise acquisitiveness as membership, like entering a library or a club, striding in with pleasure.

The department store provides a stage for a modern act, like the cafés of Ginza. The consumption of clothing is the point at which people make their first choice about what they will wear, about what will become part of them. And being able to look and choose these items marks a huge step on the path to a modern consciousness: people's ability to create their own identity, choose their own look. The department store also became a sign of the greater embourgeoisement of Japanese society: now anyone could buy anything, as long as they had the money.

In 1929, a survey was made in the afternoon at all the *sakariba* places in Tokyo.[106] A *Sakariba* means a bustling place where revelry and shopping occur with the greatest intensity. At the time the places considered to be *sakariba* were Ginza, Shinjuku, Ueno, Asakusa, Shibuya, Ningyōchō and Kagurazaka. In none of the places did women outnumber men. Shinjuku in mid-afternoon had the highest proportion of women, 43 per cent, and of these only a third were recognizable as housewives. In Ginza at 4.00 p.m., young men accounted for almost half, young women only a little over one-tenth; and so those who went strolling seem to have done it mostly by themselves or with male companions. *Mobo* were most commonly without *moga*. Thus *gimbura*—the first syllable coming from Ginza, the other two from *burabura*, a mimetic word which indicates an aimless wandering or an idling away of time: thus the word means fooling around in Ginza—was done primarily by men.

Another survey conducted in 1929, of department store visitors, reveals that there were as many men as women.[107] Almost two-thirds of the men were in Western dress, but only one-sixth of the women, and only 2 or 3 per cent of 'adult women', a category that was not clearly defined. The tendency of women to stay longer than men in traditional dress seems to be universal, and it was clear in Japan from the beginning of the Meiji period. In the survey, cosmetics seem to have provided a way of distinguishing the urban lady from the provincial. A heavy application of cosmetics was the mark of the provincial, still unaware of the shift from the indigenous, stylized face to naturalism in cosmetics.

Cotton, silk, wool, skilled labour, industrial textile processes and new means of consumption were the tools that allowed the new forms of visual expression and to a small degree—in so far as the acts of making clothing, choosing it and wearing it count as art—new artistic practices to come into being. As art objects of the everyday, they provided the vocabulary and the detail for the expression of modernity in 'higher' art forms—literature, painting and so forth. The majority of people at the majority of times did not wear Western clothing, although the spread of new material, especially wool, and the availability of new colours for kimonos, did give the broader Japan a partial experience of modern change. Modernity, however, remained for much of the Meiji and Taishō periods the domain of the few; the urban, elite and predominantly male part of the population. But even though, for material as well as cultural reasons, modernism belonged only to a few, its apparent and discursive forms began the transformation to visual modernity. Clothing had to be culturally practical and match people's lifestyles, and it wasn't until Western homes or *bunka jūtaku*—the cultural dwelling—a euphemism for the kind of dwelling of the salaryman or office worker—department stores and cafés appeared that real changes began. Western clothing, especially Victorian women's fashions, was unsuitable for traditional Japanese homes, workplaces, shopping practices and pleasure quarters. But costume alone wasn't enough: Japan needed the stages and sets of modern life as well. Throughout much of the Meiji period, the samuraization of culture, and of tastes, was the dominant cultural force, with Western fads in clothing being mainly superficial. It was the military, however, that created a desire for a new relationship with the body, mediated by new clothing, and once economic development allowed it, and consumption in department store style facilitated it, the growing middle classes were able to indulge in these new tastes.

The separation of events from tendencies is a formulation borrowed in part from Winston Churchill, who defined modernity in war by saying: 'In ancient times, the episodes were more important than tendencies; in modern times, the tendencies are more important than episodes.'[108] It is a feature of modernity in fashion that the tendencies within the populace become more important than the events within the palace or the government, and that something once governable and regulated becomes so complex and laden with elaborate meanings that it takes on a life of its own. The tendency towards modernity in clothing—tailoring, divided garments, shifting erogenous display, simplification of etiquette, streamlining and reductionism—is eventually more important than any episode of reactionary or conservative dress. The equating of fashion with modernity—meaning that change for change's sake is in fact a progressive development—is at the heart of Churchill's formulation. Tendencies require events to lubricate them, and it is not particularly important what those events are: only stasis is antagonistic. Yet tendencies are still only the sum of their profuse parts, not super-organic processes beyond mortal influence, and so perhaps the most appropriate conclusion is that the tendencies of modernity tended toward those forms most universally appropriate to the condition of modern consciousness, despite many interludes to the contrary. In this way, as in the other arts, the ultimate project of sartorial modernism was a Kantian veracity of form, and political, social and material concerns were only ancillary to the significance of this aesthetic tendency.

−3−

Japanese Menswear: Masculinity and Sartorial Statecraft

The separation of vestimentary objects by gender is an obvious division within early modern Japan, as indeed the role of the modern, while abstractly gender-equalizing, was initially in practice one of extreme gender differentiation. Masculinity and the ways it could be performed and expressed in dress were among the first things challenged by the wave of American and European aesthetics which arrived with the Meiji Restoration. Japanese notions of sartorial femininity, while toyed with by the elite in the 1870s, remained essentially untouched until the 1920s, and, while not directly in the province of this book, political and social freedoms were also partitioned in this way, with masculine modernity beginning much earlier and for different reasons than feminine modernity, which, while hopeful beginnings cannot totally be discounted, stagnated for much of the Meiji period. This chapter seeks to approach the Japanese solutions to problems posed by modernity for menswear by first examining the political motivation for uniforms and their impact and then the development of the suit in the European and American contexts, before examining the comparability of the Japanese experience.

Meiji modernity had a deliberate and methodically discharged political agenda which first attended to the male occupations of the military, the state bureaucracy and commerce.[1] The clothing forms for these occupations were naturally the first areas to experience reform, though it should be stressed that the men involved dressed in modern styles only while performing these occupations, their leisure and domestic wardrobes remaining indigenous. This is the inverse of the central narrative of sartorial modernization in Europe, where men's leisure wear drove clothing reform in the modern directions of abstraction, streamlining, simplification and deliberate dourness, while the state bureaucracy and the military forces of most European powers remained conservative and reactionary in their dress agendas.[2] While many monarchies and militaries of Europe entered the First World War without really having engaged with modern dress imperatives, the role of the Japanese monarchy and military was, by then, that of being the models of a new modern agenda rather than hankering after an older aristocratic order and its accompanying sartorial aesthetic.[3] Thus it was a unique avant-garde that drove early Japanese sartorial modernity and indeed Meiji modernity in general; it was not an artist or intellectual class but an ambitious political class, though this changed by the time of the later waves of modernity in the 1920s. The central narrative of these later waves of modernity belongs to consumption, leisure and women, but the earliest chapters of the story of Japanese dress modernity belong most definitely to the crisis of Japanese masculinity and abundant the solutions to this crisis.

The penetration and reach of early clothing modernity was, as stated earlier, greatly limited. There was a definite period of eclectic combination of kimonos and foreign elements—hairstyles, shoes, hats, gloves, glasses, umbrellas and so on— which can be seen in early Meiji photography and prints, but it is logical that this would be reflective mainly of the urban areas and the wealthy social classes that had access to photography and print-making. Access to more extensive experimentation was also limited by availability, and by the lack of compatibility of Western suits with lifestyle until changes in furniture, relaxation in the removal of shoes and so forth, allowed them to be worn more often without too much discomfort.[4]

The essential aesthetic change in Japanese masculine sartorial priorities was in contrast to the feminine, and indeed it reconstructed that very gender demarcation. As in Europe before it, the first concern of modernity in Japanese masculinity was to rid itself of the feminine, and the essential movement was one that disavowed sanctioned male vanity, flamboyance and insouciance—repudiating both aristocracy and femininity.[5] The inclination of modernity towards seriousness and abstraction, against frivolousness and ornamentation, was naturally first applied by the sex that considered itself, rightly or wrongly, to be serious and non-ornamental, while it was half a century before women's clothing began an equivalent programme of reform. Thus the primary tendencies in clothing modernity in Japan were masculine and bound up with the affairs and priorities of the emerging state, its principal actors and the identity it wished to fashion for itself.

Uniforms and the State

'The official ideologies of the emerging Meiji State were meticulously displayed in the multiple scenes of the performances painstakingly inscribed directly onto the bodies of the emperor and members of his entourage and brilliantly represented in the *mise-en-scène* upon which the symbolic action took place and in the costumes worn by the actors.'[6] Details of the newly restored Japanese monarchy, which could be as seemingly arbitrary as a moustache, a hairstyle, a particular clothing fashion, an intimation of gender, a choice of transport, were all intentionally fabricated and meaningful signs, together forming systems of signs designed to convey particular messages to the Japanese people and to the world.[7] Modernity was that message, and those who could not understand its philosophical details were provided with a visual rendering in the body of the newly restyled Emperor.

The Emperor himself was portrayed as leading his fellow Japanese along the path towards civilization, as it was then understood, and visually comprehensible by way of aesthetic modernism. He commenced the journey in 1872 by cutting his topknot (in 1872 only 10 per cent of Japanese men had cut their hair), donning Western cloth-ing for official appearances (though he continued to wear his more familiar Japanese garments at home) and eating meat, this last despite the fact that it's said he really did not care for foreign food and never became a large consumer of flesh. Like many as-pects of his life, his eating of meat served as a model which facilitated rapid reform, in this case reversing a counterproductive nutritional prohibition. He did, however, take to foreign wines, especially Château la Rose, and one of his physicians later testified that it was his alcoholic indulgences, among other things, that shortened his life.[8] Needless to say, not all foreign influence was productive.

In an albumen print thought to date from 1872 and attributed[9] to Tokyo portrait photographer Uchida Kuichi (1844–1875), the twenty-year-old emperor is striking in full-dress French-style uniform, heavy with gold braid.[10] His left hand rests on the golden hilt of his dress sword and a splendid hat ornamented with luxurious ostrich plumes is set on the table at his side. Though still uncomfortable in his new clothes and unnatural pose (he appears to slouch a bit, his right foot is bent at a peculiar angle and his epaulettes look to be a size too large), this rather glamorous image of author-ity, reminiscent of Napoleon III, was consciously exploited by government officials as a symbol of national continuity as well as unity, making the transition from sho-gunal rule an easier task. Visually demonstrating the return of military authority to the monarchy and the sophistication of that authority in its grasp of modern military methods was an early priority.[11]

The choice of a French-style uniform at this stage is significant. James Laver noted that the fashion in uniforms and the main inspiration for uniform reform come from the successes of certain uniforms in battle.[12] In 1868, the French army was still the most powerful in Europe. Napoleon III's challenge to Russia's claims to influ-ence in the Ottoman Empire led to France's successful participation in the Crimean War (1854–1856). Napoleon III approved the launching of a naval expedition in 1858 to punish the Vietnamese and force their court to accept a French presence in the country. In May–July 1859, French intervention secured the defeat of Austria in Italy. But intervention in Mexico (1862–1867) ended in defeat and the execution of the French-backed Emperor Maximilian, and France saw her influence further eroded by Prussia's crushing victory over Austria in June–August 1866. Due to his Carbonari past, Napoleon III was unable to ally himself with Austria, despite the ob-vious threat that a victorious Prussia would present to France. He would pay the price for this blunder in 1870 when, forced by the diplomacy of the German chancellor, Otto von Bismarck, he began the Franco-Prussian War. This war proved disastrous and was instrumental in giving birth to the German Empire. The French Emperor was captured at the Battle of Sedan (2 September) and was deposed by the forces of the Third Republic in Paris two days later. He died in exile in England on 9 January 1873, and with this shift in the balance of power in Europe, Japan also changed, from the more showy French uniforms to the more somber Prussian ones.

Before this, Takashima Shuhan, perhaps Japan's first modern military scientist, who had been imprisoned by the Tokugawa shogunate because of his advocacy of military modernization, created an original uniform for the Meiji military from traditional Japanese working suits.[13] The Tokugawa shogunate issued several orders prohibiting people from wearing 'strange clothes', later permitting a restricted use of Westernized dress for military training only.[14] Another famous proto-modern military scientist named Egawa Tarozaemon, who was a petty local governor in Izu, volunteered to organize a platoon of musketeers from peasant soldiers recruited within his jurisdiction. To train them, Egawa invented shirts, trousers and hats which resembled traditional Japanese wear. Utilizing local materials and even waste paper from his office, Egawa consciously created Japanese uniforms, changing them step by step for reasons of utility. For instance, he created a new hat by cutting the brim of the traditional broad-brimmed hat to facilitate the handling and carrying of a gun. He made the hat in the shape of Mount Fuji. These are examples of conscious rejection of outright imitation and pursuit of indigenous rationality, but they are very much a subplot to the main narrative of importation of foreign forms in the service of Japanese modernizing needs.

The central interest was in military imitation, not in the reinvention of Japanese military styles under a modern imperative. In 1858, a translation of a Dutch book on the uniforms of the Dutch Royal Army, with colour illustrations, was published by the Fukui clan. It demonstrated the strong interest shown by the Tokugawa Japanese in Western military uniforms; however, they seemed most interested in how to differentiate ranks by uniforms, colours and ornaments than in direct imitation or combat efficiency. Military uniforms became more and more varied in order to differentiate ranks, platoons, arms, clans and so forth.[15] When the Tokugawa government sought France's military assistance in its final days, Napoleon III was responsive enough to send a whole set of French military uniforms, along with a group of military teachers.[16]

The victory of the reforming forces of the Restoration also brought military uniform imitation along French lines but on a much larger scale. Reform was central to their programme, not a desperate afterthought. And this acceptance of change as an essential value in itself continued. In 1887, around the time when nationalism was on the rise, the army uniforms were changed to the Prussian style, that of the latest victorious power. As a military with a very reformist culture, the Japanese army was most sensitive to changes in the geopolitical balance of power and to reproducing the details of the most recent, most successful military performance. In 1905, the year of Japan's victory in the Russo-Japanese war, the Japanese army adopted the notorious khaki uniform, which acted as an integrating force for the Japanese people, while being repugnant to all other peoples in Asia and in the world.[17] This uniform recognized, once again very perceptively, the shift in global power after Britain's successful use of khaki in Africa and the growing importance of camouflage in an age of improvement in firearms.[18] The catalyst was, once again, the success of a military force in war and the desire to imitate it, even in details such as uniform. The transformation from French cavalry uniforms to the sober uniforms of the Prussians was also a step towards a purer interpretation of modernity's transference of all elements of ornamentation to the female and its adoption of a high seriousness in male dress. It was taken further with the switch to khaki uniforms, which again emphasized utility and usefulness.

The Japanese schoolboy started wearing a Westernized uniform, essentially a Prussian military uniform, around 1884, shortly before the upsurge in nationalism.[19] The basic form has always been the same throughout the country, with variations only in such small symbols as the badge, the style of buttons and the number of white lines on the cap differentiating schools. It is singular in that it was introduced in public schools and then spread to private schools.[20] The Japanese schoolgirl was far behind the boy in wearing a Westernized uniform. The first national women's teaching college adopted a proto-Westernized uniform even before the Rokumeikan period, but this was soon abandoned and a more traditional style readopted.[21] Women's education had its own influence on clothing styles, but it was through claiming gendered male indigenous clothing, not foreign clothes. It was well into the Taishō period before some private girls' high schools introduced Westernized uniforms.[22]

Most countries in the West were attempting to restructure their militaries at the time when the Japanese were building theirs in the 1880s. In Japan, the military's newness was one of its strongest features; European militaries, and the aristocracies which dominated them, were sometimes charged with being backward or conservative, and this was witnessed in the tragic miscalculations and inflexible thinking of cavalry officer generals in the First World War. But 'Japan's new army considered itself to be the embodiment of the spirit of a new age.'[23] At the time when the Meiji leaders became established in their authority, every country in the West with the possible exception of the United States, which had just demobilized after the Civil War of 1861–1865, was rebuilding and rethinking its military system on the basis of the lessons of the wars of Italian (ca. 1859) and German (ca. 1871) unification, the American Civil War and especially the Franco-Prussian War. Industrial development and population growth made for new possibilities in the movement, equipment and direction of mass armies of citizen-soldiers. The Meiji leaders, themselves so recently samurai, did not fail to absorb these lessons on their missions to the West and apply them to their own country.[24] This more responsive agenda for reform allowed for the principles of sartorial modernism to be effected in Japanese uniforms, because there was none of the conservative resistance of aristocratic or military tradition to insist on the retention of impractical or outdated uniforms.

In the immediate post-Restoration days, the Meiji leaders also continued to look to French officers and tactics for guidance. Despite the French defeat at the hands of Prussia, the Meiji government initially still regarded French military theory and military structure as preeminent. Moreover, substantial moves in the direction of French guidance had been begun in the late Tokugawa period, and it was logical for the regime to order, as it did in 1870, all domains to follow the French model for their land forces and the English model for their navies. Land forces turned to German models by the 1880s under the leadership of Yamagata Arimoto's principal disciple and future *genrō* (elder statesman) Katsura Tarō (1847–1913), who had spent a total of almost eight years in Germany.[25] He brought back not only the structural theory of the Prussian general staff but also their uniform principles, symbolizing the winning practicality and efficiency of the Prussian war machine under Bismarck.

As well as its role on the battlefield, the military naturally also has a social and cultural role, in particular in its visual styling, massed and individual, which provided the Meiji state with a malleable and extremely useful tool in its agenda of rapid modernization. The great imperial pageants of the Meiji era were central to the construction of a kind of ocular domination in modern Japan. It was an ocular domination that had comparable results and yet was different in the tools used from the visual domination that, according to Michel Foucault, emerged in France around the time of the Enlightenment.[26] As is well known, Foucault argued that Jeremy Bentham's model for the penitentiary—with its prisoners made completely visible to an anonymous gaze located in the structure's central tower—was a diagram of modern power. Because the Panopticon's arrangement made the prisoners in their cells visible from one central point while rendering the prison's overseer invisible, prisoners could never know whether they were being observed. As a consequence, they would always have to behave as if they were being watched—they would have to internalize their own surveillance. Yet Foucault's argument was less concerned with the Panopticon as an instrument of the penal system than with the Panopticon as a model of modern power that was replicated in practice throughout the social formation. Following this model, T. Fujitani argues that far from being feudal, the monarchy in Meiji Japan was central to the production of Japan's modernity.[27] Through instruments such as costume and spectacle, the monarchy and the military were avant-garde in their enthusiasm for, and understanding of, modernization, leading the rest of the society, rather than the monarchy and military having to keep pace with a changing society. Unlike France, where the monarchy's demise ushered in a new mode of consciousness, a modern one, in Japan the monarchy's rise from the position of a largely irrelevant ritual icon to the centre of Japanese political and cultural life was crucial to Japanese modernity in creating a culture of a self-administered regulatory regime of ocular domination.

The mass distribution of images was at the centre of this process of elite provision of examples—the primary vocabulary of these images being sartorial. The photographic portrait of the Emperor, based on a drawing by the Italian Edoardo Chiossone, which in 1888 became the official portrait, which was distributed throughout Japan in the second half of the Meiji period, did even more than previous portraits to construct the Emperor as a dignified man. Like so much of modernity, while the art form is photography, the vocabulary is dress, which announces its modernity and drains the Emperor of femininity and frivolousness and establishes seriousness, strength and dignity.[28] Interestingly, this portrait was not a photograph of the Emperor himself, but rather a copy of a copy of a representation of the Emperor. Chiossone, who was employed by Japan's mint, first sketched the Emperor. He then drew a seated portrait of the Emperor based on his sketches. The Japanese photographer Maruki Toshiaki then photographed Chiossone's drawing. Yet, for most people in Japan in the late nineteenth and early twentieth century, this simulacrum three steps removed was the Emperor's real presence. This *real* Emperor of the portrait was a considerably more dignified, militarized and masculinized man than even the Emperor of Uchida's 1873 photograph, some way along in modernity's early project of polarizing gender signs. The Emperor of the 1873 portrait is slouching in his chair, whereas the Emperor of the 1888 portrait sits forward stiffly with his back straightened. The later, more disciplined and more militarized posture gives the Emperor a far more majestic bearing and suggests his greater capacity as a political actor—the association of this serious mode of masculinity with action being a new connotation of early modernity. Elements of the photograph were manipulated for effect: the earlier portrait, even though it portrays the full length of the emperor's body, contains a considerable amount of empty space, so that the imperial body relative to the entire frame seems much smaller and has a less imposing presence than the body in the later photograph. The later Emperor places his right arm away from the front of his body to reveal a large and heavily decorated chest, while the earlier Emperor has his arms crossed weakly in front of his body in order to grasp his sabre.[29] Here we not only have an emperor in physical motion, an image enhanced by the militarized body, but we also see him marked with what had been emerging as a sign of masculinity: facial hair. Most importantly—unlike the earlier photograph—he now belongs in his clothes; they have become a legitimate part of him, and he is in control of them, master of the identity he projects.

The Meiji Emperor became masculinized only to the extent that he was refashioned according to the modern norms of masculinity that were being produced at precisely the moment when the ruling elites created him. A corresponding claim could be made for the women of the Imperial Family.[30] At the same time, the men and women of the Imperial Family acted out what it meant to be men and women—the former were dynamic and actively involved in political affairs—and were marked as such as they participated in the construction of dominant expectations of manhood and womanhood. This provided a deliberate guide to the population on how to construct gender relationships both socially and visually and, by extension, it provided a model of social order. Fujitani says:

> An emperor was constructed who could be imagined to have not one but at least two bodies. Homologous to the relationship of the two capital cities on the nation's symbolic and ritual landscape, the one imperial body was a human and masculinized body that represented the mundane and changing prosperity of the national community in history, while the other body, often invisible or described as wrapped in ancient courtly robes, represented the emperor's godliness or transcendence and the immutability of the nation.[31]

Clothing was the visual language of this process. It is a feature of modernity every-where that it first changes masculinity, primarily at the expense of femininity, and that femininity's equivalent reformations occur only much later. No matter how universally applicable modernity's Kantian processes may be, this gender differ-entiation demonstrates that their application has always had elements of arbitrary cultural throwback within it.

The era of mass image reproduction and its use as a tool of social control sometimes utilized religious associations that were profoundly antimodernist. In the August 1872 issue of *Kyōchū shimbun* of Yamanashi Prefecture, the editor praised the patriotism and national feeling of a local man who brought back from Tokyo several dozen photographs of the Emperor so that he and others in this remote corner of the country might worship the image and place it on their house-hold shrine (*kamidana*). In this way he was blending the new means of imperial propaganda with old religious devotional ones. Interestingly, the photograph was designed, and the Emperor dressed, to further modern means of hierarchical re-enforcement, not to be used in premodern devotion, yet it was the opinion of the newspaper editor that this man should be singled out and rewarded for this form of propagation of the imperial image.[32]

The educational reforms throughout Japan at this time emphasized the absolute obligations of loyalty to the Emperor on the part of all Japanese, and bowing be-fore the emperor's portrait soon became customary—blending modern mass image reproduction and religious displays of reverence. The use of the imperial figure, in the form of a portrait, to publicize the new regime was a radical departure from tra-ditional uses of the imperial image. In the past, the Emperor had never made public appearances and was approached only by high court officials. Furthermore, imperial portraits were commissioned only as private religious dedicational purposes: Japa-nese portraiture had developed in a Buddhist context, and such works were often intended as devotional objects to be enshrined in a particular temple with which the subject was closely associated. This was true, for example, in the case of the seven portraits of himself that Emperor Hanazono commissioned in the fourteenth century. They show him as he looked after abdicating the throne, with aristocratic and slightly idealized features but attired in the sombre vestments of a tonsured Buddhist monk, for he had taken religious vows, as was the custom upon retirement. On the whole, however, the use of imperial images, and thus the sartorial messages contained in them, was extremely limited if compared to the use of portraiture (oil painting) by European monarchies and their fastidious attention to sartorial detail.

In contrast to earlier emperors, Emperor Meiji was a very public figure, and his public image and the attention paid to his clothing were, accordingly, heightened. By 1872, the importance of his visibility had been realized: he was being displayed around Tokyo in his open Western-style carriage, free to be gazed upon by one and all, and his subjects were no longer expected to prostrate themselves in his pres-ence.[33] His first public state ceremony took place on New Year's Day, 1872, when he visited the Imperial Dockyard and Arsenal at Yokosuka, near Yokohama. The Emperor was dressed in traditional white robes with a tall black lacquered hat, but he was accompanied by two young pages wearing European-style clothing in a shade of violet and neckties in the most extravagant colours.[34] Throughout the 1870s, he was shown in more distant parts of the country as well, and although at first he disliked these public appearances (some Western observers found him overly detached and even sullen), his advisors persistently sent him off on exhaustive rounds of inspection as far north as remote and backward Aomori Prefecture.[35] He opened large numbers of Western-style buildings and technical sites along the way, helping to sanction the spread of civilization and enlightenment (*bummei kaika*). The sentiment of the people who turned out in their thousands at every rural stopover was one of religious veneration as well as increasing affection. At one site, villagers actually rushed to scoop up and preserve the earth on which he had walked, believing he had sanctified it by his very footsteps.[36]

It is the very exploitation of this veneration that according to Fujitani allowed the rapid construction of a new, modern nation-state with the Emperor as the central tool in the transformation from feudal to modern consciousness. His last public appearance in ancient court costume was, perhaps symbolically, the grand ceremonial opening of the railway line in October 1872, but he was seen several times earlier that year in fancy foreign clothing.

This was an early experiment in which not everything was yet quite right; the details—so important as the vocabulary of sartorial propaganda—had not yet been perfectly mastered. However, there seems to have been no shortage of exacting foreigners to point out the shortcomings, from which the monarch and his tailors chose to learn rather than take offence.

Mastery did not take long, but mass image-making took a little longer to be fully established. The elite that had seen the value of the Emperor as a tool of modernization saw usefulness in the extension of this means of social influence via the Emperor cult for even greater social control, especially in the service of empire-building. The portrait by Uchida was one of only a few authorized photographs of the Emperor, who apparently hated to have his picture taken. Some prints and paintings produced a full decade later were simply copies of this photograph. Until 1877, when rising nationalism and an increasingly strong central government began to foster the emperor cult, no attempt was made to show the Emperor's countenance in coloured woodcuts—his presence was merely suggested by indirect means.[37] Later in the Meiji period, as printing and image-making became more sophisticated and publishers felt free to capitalize on the now familiar face, artists presented an ever more idealized and handsome visage. Despite the image construction, though, the original object, the Emperor, was on balance a youthful and virile ruler whose manliness and looks helped the Meiji oligarchy rally the people to their cause. Emperors Taishō and Shōwa, neither of whom can be described as particularly charismatic personalities, were beneficiaries of the way the imperial institution learned to manage its image through Emperor Meiji.

Sartorial modernity in general reduces the importance of more codified totemic, even tribal, elements of dress in favour of more subtle and flexible signs. Early on in the Meiji period, however, there was a particular interest in foreign means of sartorial differentiation of rank, especially in uniforms. The amount of gold decoration on the emperor's jacket, especially the chrysanthemum, the royal emblem, is remarkable in Uchida's photograph and was often commented upon. When the Emperor rode into Kyoto in July 1872 wearing the uniform of a French cavalry general and accompanied by his gentlemen-in-waiting in black dress suits, the crowds later went home to 'wonder which was the Mikado, as very few Japanese recognized him amongst the many gorgeously dressed persons they saw on horseback, and who ... all resembled each other in the amount of gold lace about their dresses'.[38] It was simply not possible for the Emperor and his high officials to appear dressed like commoners; court costumes had always signalled rank and status in Japan. The peerage was now expected to wear the elaborate uniform of a frock coat with gold lace, while civil officials wore a tuxedo with gold lace. This is an influence coming more from the European military aristocracy than from European modernity. Writing in 1874, Japanese intellectual Tsuda Mamichi confessed that he could not accept the extravagance of the full court dress (*taireifuku*) of his country's civil officials; he pointed out that in Europe and America all persons from king to commoners wore the same formal dress in their capacity as civil officials—a dress that was the equivalent of the Japanese semiformal dress.

With the coming of a new generation, by the middle of the Meiji period, the showier aristocratic French uniforms were being replaced both in the military and in its areas of more immediate influence—education, nursing, livery and so on.—with the simpler, streamlined, more subtle and serious Prussian uniforms. In Hashimoto Chikanobu's 1887 print, *Mirror of Japanese Nobility*, the principal subject is the young Crown Prince Haru (1879–1925), who is given the place of honour at the centre of the composition. He was officially named crown prince at age ten. The prince was the Emperor's only living son, the child of one of five imperial concubines; seven of the emperor's ten children died in infancy. The Empress had no children of her own. Chikanobu has portrayed the Prince as he would look on his first day of school in his new double-breasted school uniform, with an impressive stack of textbooks near at hand.

This is an example of a uniform influence that had a truly lasting impact; the student's black uniform has persisted almost without change to the present day. Another lasting influence was the white nurse's uniform introduced by the Red Cross. This followed the revolution in nursing led by Florence Nightingale (1820–1910) during the Crimean War, from 1854 to 1856. The standardization and modernization of nursing techniques included equivalent sartorial reform with the adoption of the white uniform, which was functional, easily revealing when it became dirty, allowing ease of movement and being easily recognizable, and it yet retained a mothering quality. Japan realized the importance of nursing reform as part of military effectiveness and adopted the sartorial reforms in nursing uniforms. While this might seem a minor point, it influenced a major theme in female sartorial modernization, where items of particular importance were the livery of bus conductors and other female uniforms, which were closely based on the feminized practicality and aesthetic modernism of nursing uniforms.

The Crimean War—the first major European conflict since Waterloo—had the effect of making the leaders of armed forces realize that the uniforms of their soldiers were utterly unfit for combat. There was a general loosening up; the tunic finally replaced the tail coat, indicating, incidentally, a growing divergence between military and civil dress, although there was an obvious connection between the undress frock coat of officers and the civilian mode of the day. Everything took on a slightly French look, for the French were very successful in the 1850s and their military fashions became supremely attractive to the world, as those of successful nations tend to do. The American Civil War (1861–1865) was fought, both by North and South, in what were in effect, French uniforms, even to the peculiar form of the kepi.

Then, in 1870, with the French disaster of Sedan, the military world, including Japan, switched to essentially German uniforms. It is not a particular stretch to argue that the German uniform was more aesthetically modern than the French; it was simpler, more sober, more practical and its form was more closely aligned with its principal function. The *Pickelhaube* had beaten the kepi, and some variety of the spiked helmet made its appearance in most of the armies of the world, though interestingly, not in usually German-admiring Japan, where the kepi was retained during the Sino-Japanese (1894–95) and Russo-Japanese wars (1905). In many armies of Europe, infantry regiments adopted the spiked helmet, which remained in use, at first in battle and later for ceremonial occasions, until the First World War. The black coats of the German army were also widely adopted, and the Meiji Emperor is often seen in this style of uniform, as are many schoolboys to this day. The Boer War of 1899–1902 was Britain's first khaki war, as the technology of warfare, particularly the rifle, changed and the need for camouflage became imperative. Khaki was also adopted by the Imperial Japanese Army by the time of the Russo-Japanese war, and at the Triumphal Army Review of 1905, the Meiji Emperor can be seen in khaki in his carriage.

The newness of the Japanese army and the relative lack of inflexible class structure within it reflects James Laver's pattern of global military fashion almost perfectly and, in contrast to Europe, makes the military avant-garde in its attachment to the principles of sartorial modernity. Laver tries to establish some further fundamental principles governing the evolution of military costumes:[30]

1. The seduction principle
2. The hierarchical principle
3. The utility principle

The first principle attempts to make the wearer of uniforms as attractive as possible to the opposite sex. According to Laver, it is, in general, the governing principle of female costume, but it was not without influence on men's, and particularly soldiers', dress at a time when male civilian dress was becoming more serious and abstract. It widens the military man's shoulders, narrows his hips, puffs out his chest, lengthens his leg and increases his apparent height. It played, therefore, before the days of conscription, an important part in recruiting. It adds appeal to soldiering, symbolizing a monopoly on violence and thus on physical power. The heightening of masculine characteristics might also be considered of value, at least in its early days, in intimidating the enemy, a particular concern for the very height-conscious Japanese—though internal control, making camaraderie and rank look visually natural, of modern armed forces was of greater importance than any intimidatory feature, the enemy rarely being seen.

The second principle establishes and naturalizes social position. It is the general principle governing male dress. In military costume, it shrinks into rigid ritualism of rank—wealth, education and so on, being of little or no relevance in that context.

The utility principle has comparatively little influence on civilian costume in Europe, besides certain types of livery. In general, suits replaced the type of dress which had indicated profession and homogenized the sartorial symbols identifying a member of the professional class. In modern male civilian dress, the utility principle produced a succession of sports outfits which gradually formalized themselves until they were too uncomfortable to be worn for any active pursuit and had to be replaced by something easier to wear. The same is true of military costume; something practical was formalized successively until it became impractical—hence the existence of 'dress' uniforms.

In considering military uniforms, therefore, having taken due note of the succession of stars and stripes on sleeve and shoulder, Laver ignores the hierarchical principle. The hierarchy is real and imposed more immediately than in civilian life where it has to be signalled and expressed visually. For Laver, military uniform is a tug of war between the seduction principle, in the sense of the heightening of masculinity and martial bearing, and the utility principle, that is the adoption of an outfit that is efficient in war. Given a long peace, the seduction principle triumphs and soldiers become more and more gorgeous, but a war, especially a long war, brings the utility principle once more into operation. Laver's analysis can be readily applied to the experience of the Japanese military in the modern era—uniforms becoming more elaborate in periods of peace and suddenly becoming more simple and practical during the conflicts of 1895 and 1905.

What Laver neglects is the possibility of any larger aesthetic currents manifesting themselves in the development and fashion of military uniforms. From our later vantage point, there is a clear movement in uniforms away from the aristocratic, from ornamentation, from sanctioned male vanity and the arbitrary, towards the serious, abstract, streamlined and manifestly functional. Uniforms were, in Japan, one of the first crucial visual expressions of modernity; the armed forces being the paramount place for modernization in the minds of the Meiji political elites, fearing Western domination. With astonishing speed, Japan not only created a modern force clothed in Western uniforms but also came to understand the importance of the fashion system which operated in the world's militaries, imitating the most recent victorious power so as to appear as advanced as that power. We see this in the major shifts from French uniforms to Prussian ones and then to English khakis. In terms of gendering, military uniforms constructed the visual division that is still in place today. Further, in Japan national service introduced and popularized many new sartorial innovations, from divided garments to wool and tailoring. Uniforms also established one of the two essential principles of Western fashion systems, uniformity. The idea of looking the same, carried over into livery and in group identification, is at the heart of all fashionable desire, to be uniform with those we identify with. In modern societies, the need to identify visually becomes much more important than in feudal societies. As the social becomes more liquid, the visual lexicons that operate become, by necessity, more sophisticated—to meet the dual psychological needs of fitting in and standing out, they become an essential means of creating individual and collective identity. Uniforms were, in this way, a major expressive form of modernity and, to the extent that the State had agency in developing a modern consciousness in Japan, a tool of modernization as well.

Suits: Modern and Classic Masculinity

Authenticity, appropriation and legitimacy were recurring themes and anxieties for the Japanese in the adoption of wholly foreign sartorial schemas. Mori Arinori's debate with the Chinese leader Li Hongzhang in 1876 articulated the central dilemma of practicality and national identity with regard to formal clothing. Li, looking disdainfully at Mori's Western suit, had asked if Mori's Japanese ancestors had dressed that way. No, Mori replied, they had adopted Chinese dress, but it was no longer practical; Japan had always taken the best of other civilizations for itself, and it was doing so once more. He then went on to remind Li that Li's ancestors had not worn the official robes prescribed by China's Manchu conqueror either; Japan, by inference, had at least made its own choice.[40] The first and longest lasting of all the sartorial choices of modern Japan had been to adopt a garment—or a system of garments—that had almost evolved into the suit, which is still universally worn for the same reasons 130 years after Mori and Li's encounter.

Anne Hollander's definitive characterization of the suit as a 'fluid, multipartite envelope for the body, complementing its shape and movement and establishing a constant visible harmony between the body's structure and that of the clothes without heavily emphasizing either one'[41] is a profoundly modern definition. It touches on many of the defining elements of sartorial modernism: movement, practicality, systematic elements and a new relationship with the body, and implies important others: the banishment of frivolity and unnecessary ornament, form following function, abstraction and formal seriousness. It corresponds to J. C. Flügel's modern psychological motivational definition of clothing as compromise formations between exhibitionism and modesty—clothing hides and shows the body in equal measure.[42]

While the suit became a modern garment rather than one with a particular national association, it originated in tailoring for the English rural gentry, Western European revolutionary movements and American theology.[43] Central to this Western popularity of the suit was the rise of the bourgeoisie, though this term has been put to so many uses since the popularity of Marxism and sociology that its meaning is unspecific and rather blurry. One of the clichés in explanations of the creation of modern Europe, and indeed its clothing history, is 'the rising bourgeoisie'. Most often this class is represented as emerging in nineteenth-century England as a class made up of manufacturers. The phrase has also served to explain various reform movements in England and revolutions elsewhere. In clothing it is called to account for the rise of the suit and its evolution into the garment that has been adopted universally by government and commerce in the developed world. When it was enthusiastically taken on in modernizing Meiji Japan, many of the same explanations were applied, not necessarily appropriately.

It was argued earlier that the economic and cultural embourgeoisement of most of the first world was a twentieth-century phenomenon; however, the roots of the embourgeoisement of clothing tastes are much further back. While much of what influenced this shift in Europe was irrelevant to the Japanese adoption of suits, there were parallels in the dress practices of Edo merchants and urbanites, whose increasing civic concentration and enrichment—financial and cultural—well predates direct European influence. The bourgeoisie first began to rise not in the nineteenth century but in the twelfth century, when towns in Europe began to revive, roads were improved and trade flourished again beyond town walls. In Japan the rise of the bourgeoisie can be traced to the second half of the sixteenth century, when Toyotomi Hideyoshi unified and integrated the various regional samurai warlords into a singular feudal system for the first time, providing the necessary stability and structure for the growth of trade. Upon Hideyoshi's death, power was assumed by Tokugawa Ieyasu, who founded the Tokugawa dynasty which was to last 250 years, imposing the formal closure of Japan to aid the dynasty's longevity. Hideyoshi's feudal reforms included the division of the population into four closed orders: samurai, peasants, artisans and merchants. The merchant class was forbidden to purchase land, and the samurai were excluded from commerce.

Within this agrarian feudal economy, as in feudal Europe, there developed important urban centres, engaged in mercantile operations and manufacturing.[44] Though these gave rise to merchant councils and artisan guilds, they had less political power in Japan than rural village leaders.[45] As well as the general pacification of the nation, Hideyoshi also established the *sankin kōtai* system whereby regional lords had to maintain a residence in Edo and leave family members there when not in residence themselves—a centralization system not unlike that of France at Versailles. In Edo, this stimulated unprecedented commercial demand in the urban economy because of the resultant aristocratic consumption of luxury goods in the city and the necessary expenditure on the maintenance of the official city residence or *yashiki* and on the frequent movement of aristocratic households between Edo and their rural domains. These costs required the conversion of rice tributes into cash and thus gave rise to specialized merchants managing this, advancing credit against future taxes and speculating in commodity futures. The enforced monetization of feudal revenues paved the way for a rapid expansion of mercantile capital in the cities.[46] Banned from legally acquiring agricultural property, Japanese merchants, enriched by the enforced centralization of wealth, could not divert their capital into rural property, and thus the very rigidity of Hideyoshi's class system incongruously encouraged the growth of large, purely urban fortunes.[47]

By the eighteenth century, Edo had population of over a million people, and Osaka and Kyoto each had over four hundred thousand. At least one-tenth of the population lived in towns with more than ten thousand residents, demonstrating the demographic concentration of urban, bourgeois economic (and approaching cultural) dominance.[48] Despite what might be assumed to be a demographic and economic inevitability, Tokugawa isolationism meant that merchant capital was constantly constrained and artificially redistributed towards parasitic dependence on the feudal nobility. The fundamental economic precondition of rudimentary capital accumulation in early modern Europe, which was lacking in Japan, was the dramatic internationalization of commodity exchange that removes the need for aristocratic domestic markets.[49]

By the beginning of the modern era, European trade was global. The sartorial needs, however, of the class responsible for trade were similar in Europe of the Age of Discoveries to those in Edo Japan. Merchants were becoming much wealthier, but feudal systems—with wealth and status based on land—forbade ostentatious displays of wealth, or even nonpecuniary sartorial expression and aesthetic self-actualization, in their dress. Thus a code of subtle finery became the vocabulary of trading-class clothing. In Edo Japan, the merchant classes used the legal dull colours for their kimonos but used fine silk linings and other means of muted conspicuous display.[50] These were the mechanisms that were also at work in the European merchant princes' gravitation towards the subtle forms of display and class markings that gave birth to the system of clothing which became the male suit.

Modernity and its cultural products were, in Japan as elsewhere, primarily urban both in inspiration and developmental character. Amongst the European merchant classes, a particular type of subtlety was required in order to allow the wearer to be seen and not seen—to display wealth and finery that would not be construed as a threat to the ruling class. The particular sartorial lexicon that developed was a reflection of this. Edo Japan experienced similar circumstances, in which the trading classes, and the multitude of industries and professions that their concentration of wealth facilitated, were urban, while traditional ruling-class samurai were attached to the land.

The European bourgeoisie should not be regarded, and nor should any class, as a uniformly constituted group moving up or down the centuries in concert. If the early bourgeoisie was made up of town dwellers, it is clear that at any given time some of its members were wealthy patricians ruling the town, others were ordinary trades-men, others lawyers, builders, artists and writers, still others shopkeepers. In the State's recruitment from such a mixed group, the literate and well-brought-up man's qualification for service was obvious. In this development, the theme of meritocratic emancipation can be detected, and clothing comes to reflect this.

In Tokugawa Japan there were many indicators that a middle class had been rising for some time. Abortion and infanticide were widely practised, controlling middle-class population growth, not for reasons of abject poverty but in an effort to maintain and improve standards of living.[51] Mid-nineteenth-century Japanese were able to buy books, furniture, sweets, fresh fish, hair ornaments and all sorts of small luxuries, even in remote villages.[52] A dramatic increase in consumer goods among the general populace was also found in seventeenth-century England, just prior to industrialization.[53] Prior to the Meiji Restoration there was high agricultural pro-ductivity, commerce on a nationwide basis and institutions and practices essential for industrialization, such as a monetized economy and bank-like money exchang-ers. The trade in clothing and textiles was also highly developed, as mentioned ear-lier; by the eighteenth century, cotton was the second most important commercial commodity, after rice, and second in value to rice in goods shipped into Osaka.[54] All these commercial activities were performed by a merchant class whose power and financial strength were rapidly growing. To be true to Marx's definition, they did not yet own the means of production. Samurai lords were still the landowners and privileged in law and social custom, but the source of wealth was shifting towards industry and cities. Thus a significant indigenous middle class was already in existence when the suit arrived, and they took to wearing it. This was not the case in places where merchant classes were not as firmly established.

Though it came late to the process of embourgeoisement, it is hardly likely that Japan had a very low standard of living, particularly in light of the evidence that life expectancy in Japan in the mid-nineteenth century was higher than that of industrial-ized countries at the beginning of their industrialization and was similar to Western life expectancy in the mid-nineteenth century.[55] In economic terms, a low standard of living signifies a low savings rate, since the poor consume a very large proportion of their income. Savings are important because they provide the investment neces-sary for industrialization, and since the Japanese industrialized rapidly and without borrowing significant amounts of foreign capital, it would seem logical that they had had the necessary standard of living, indicating a growing middle class in Edo times. However, income, or the amount of goods and services one can purchase, is not a sufficient measure of how healthy or productive people are—it does not tell us how well-educated or alert they are, or the extent of their physical and mental stamina. For our purposes, the important measures are the size of the potential middle class, and how willingly it would define itself as such through clothing. The rise of the new social class was facilitated by education, production, urbanism and freedom, and all these principles were reflected in the clothing they chose.

The concept of the 'modern' is multidimensional: it involves not only a set of ideas that affected the intellectual environment but also the way in which a new industrial, metropolitan social environment affected the people who inhabited it. Modernity is both the ideas that made new forms and also what those new forms made of the ideas. What made such a formal and conceptual revolution possible was not only new ideas but, more importantly, the tools to turn such ideas into reality: reason, industrialization and the urbanization of culture.

The male three-piece suit was both a remarkable affirmation of a belief in a classical aesthetic and the first manifestation of what a new 'modern' world would be capable of achieving through social and political rearrangement of education, class and nationality, and as a result, of how people's consciousness changed from self-definition primarily by class and occupation to self-definition primarily as educated citizens. This process was actively encouraged by the Meiji rulers, as Fujitani argued, with a view to turning the passive, ruled, feudal subjects of Tokugawa Japan into active participants in the State and in their own history; in short, they were to become modern citizens rather than feudal subjects.

The bourgeoisie's replacement of the aristocracy as the economically and culturally dominant class in modernizing society meant that a much larger group took control of the mechanics of state and nationhood. With this change also came the shift of power from the land to the city as the source of wealth creation, through an industrial revolution and the expansion of trade, money markets and population that preceded it and was accelerated by it. The economic power that had rested with the few now rested with the many, and the interests of this larger group had to be accommodated politically. A uniform representing the democratic bourgeois spirit had to distinguish itself as not aristocratic, and thus audacious with wealth, but also had to reveal the bearers of this spirit as the new masters of the universe.

Japan had a much shorter time than Europe to come to terms with these ideas and to transform itself from a feudal state into a modern one, yet it also had many advantages. The level of wealth and the inherent efficiency in the Japanese lifestyle allowed for a rapid economic change. The degree to which religion affected the population was less than in Europe; Christian dogma on such simple matters as borrowing money took centuries of enlightenment to reverse in Europe. Literacy and education were also a great boon in the rapid creation of a bourgeois society and meritocratic government in Japan. These factors would have allowed the adoption of the suit—a garment already evolved for modern life—to seem more appropriate.

The Suit in Europe and America

The suit was an expression of modern political and social structure. Baudelaire expresses this in *Selected Writings on Art and Artists*: '. . . observe that the black frock-coat and the tail-coat may boast not only their political beauty, which is an expression of universal equality, but also their poetic beauty, which is the expression of the public soul.'[56] One of the political reasons for the French Revolution had been the huge financial support in France for the American Revolution. This had hastened Louis XVI's fall and allowed the republican aesthetic to be born in America. The chief project of American culture before, during and in the years after the Revolution of 1776 was to graft pagan antiquity onto puritan newness.[57] In this regard the suit can be seen as both classical—for reasons of symmetry, simplicity and adherence to the body—and puritan—for reasons of austerity, sobriety and uniform equality.

The state style that came out of the American Revolution was neoclassical, a sartorial correlate to Greek democracy and Roman republicanism. The newness lay, as it did for the French revolutionaries a decade later, in its power to abolish whatever was frivolous, luxurious, trivial or rococo, an early parallel to the way in which modernity strives to remove ornament and romantic expression from clothing. American republicans did not think in terms of copying antiquity, but rather of understanding its principles, grasping its essence, which was in Johann Winckelmann's phrase a 'noble simplicity and calm grandeur'.[58]

Clothing for the young Americans, as with art, design, architecture and literature, was to be didactic, to be stoic and to clearly manifest the values of restraint, self-sacrifice and patriotism. In this mindset, God or Providence governs wisely and does not interfere with its own laws; nor does it reward or punish in this world. Most early American revolutionaries were deists, believing that God could be discovered through reason. Stoicism teaches that to make the best of life, moral conduct is imperative; it causes the least trouble and leaves the fewest regrets. In the face of life the goal is composure, a 'calm grandeur'.

When thought of in these terms—didactic, stoic, restrained, serious—how much like the classical toga the modern suit becomes as an outer manifestation of inner values. They both reflect an aesthetic of male clothing which endures beyond mere transient and arbitrary fashion, because it represents a political philosophy and a particular way of performing gender. Both take an architectural form, to follow Hollander, rather than one of fashion, because their symmetry and formal coherence are more stable and appropriate for their political and social condition—symmetry, stability, balance and restraint are all both the message and the means of expressing it.[59] As the columns of Athens are replayed in Washington to represent the same democratic and rational values, the suit, like the toga, represents reason without artifice—politically and aesthetically in concert.

There are other religious influences on the suit, in particular the inheritance from Puritanism and Protestantism. This is particularly important in the clothing chosen by the young American nation, a nation founded, somewhat problematically, on the principle of equality and also on religious freedom. The bourgeois American revolutionary values had a direct aesthetic correlative in sartorial simplicity and utility. This was a link between the intellectualism of the Sons of Liberty and the merchant-class people of Boston; artisans and small shopkeepers indicated in their dress that the American Revolution was not only about political independence but also reflective of the rise of a new set of middle-class values—still interchangeable at this stage with its religious Protestantism.

Bourgeois thinkers like Benjamin Franklin, Diderot and Rousseau had recategorized work not only as a means to earn money but also as a way of 'becoming oneself'. It was a reconciliation of necessity and happiness typical of the bourgeois and Protestant attitude, exactly mirroring the bourgeois reevaluation of marriage. Just as marriage was re-described as an institution that could deliver both practical benefits and sexual and emotional fulfilment (a convenient conjunction once thought impossible by the aristocracy, both European and Japanese, who saw a need for a wife and a mistress in separate roles), so too work was alleged to be capable of delivering both the money necessary for survival and the stimulation and self-expression that had once been seen as the exclusive preserve of the leisured.[60] Bourgeois clothing, correspondingly, also reflects this conceptual duality; the suit being suitable both to work in and to be at leisure in—an expression of self and social worth.

Boston's mercantile ascendancy had chosen this form of dress because it was both embedded in a world of substance, lists and inventories, the parts of the suit adding up to a man of the world—honest, comfortable and utilitarian, and was also the symbol of puritan and democratic equality, the civilized centre of respectability without ostentation, empowerment without rank and elegance without artifice. In this way, it was completely possible to link neoclassicism with puritan tradition, because they both shared a radicalism, with one making everyone equal because of reason and the other making everyone equal because of death; puritan and rationalist both wore black suits.

As Weber noted, Protestantism's crucial and radically new assumption was predestination—leaving the believer in doubt about his salvation yet holding out the chance of grace encourages him to act as if already an elect—sober, earnest, hardworking.[61] His moral code makes him calculating at every turn, the ideal man of commerce. On earth and beyond, he faces risk with fortitude while taking all thoughtful precautions. The Catholic, by comparison is easy-going, paying his way spiritually by symbolic 'works', most of which have no practical effects on earth. Far from praising real work, the Catholic sees it as Adam's curse. And the model man is not the one who achieves material success, as for the Protestant; on the contrary, for the Catholic, poor and humble is the mark of sanctity. The Protestant work ethic was, for Weber, the ideal moral code for the entrepreneur, the economic actor in the social organization of capitalism: hence for Weber the commercial success of Dutch, English, German and American merchants. The rise of the merchant prince coincided with the decline of fashion as a theatre in which men wore romantic costumes. It coincided with the decline of culturally sanctioned male vanity, flamboyance and insouciance. The ceaseless effort to prove one's worth, a Protestant legacy, diverts ambition from more luxuriant forms of self-expression in clothing.

Though it arrived in the middle of this Western religious process, and it was mostly, therefore, irrelevant to it, Japan also experienced this phenomenon in men's clothing and in performing masculinity, where the proof of material worth—a measurable and therefore rational scientific imperative—became its governing principle. While the theological details were irrelevant to the Japanese, the forms were not, and the wider process of replacing an arbitrary religious value system with a rational economic one, where everything can be measured, is almost a universal feature of modernity everywhere.

It was the long period of enlightenment in America and Europe that Japan had to imitate, though in a much shorter time. It was able to do this because of certain favourable preexisting social and economic conditions. The political, aesthetic and sartorial victory of the classical over the baroque had particular relevance for Western history but its relevance for Japan was far more general and tied up with the need to catch up with nations that had stepped on to the path to modernity well before it, rather than being tied up with internal religious debates. However, the ends had to be the same for the achievement of a truly modern society and state. The *bummei kaika* (civilization and enlightenment) movement of the early Meiji period recognized this and saw in the suit the manifestation of modern values that had taken a century to evolve in the West.

Embourgeoisement and the Civilized Centre

Essential to the self-conceptualization of the middle class is the idea of a civilized centre.[62] Most bourgeois clothing signs are signs of negation. In the West, suit was not aristocratic, not decadent, not Catholic, not religious, not part of a hierarchy and not feminine. For Japan the meaning was slightly, but not substantially, different: the suit was not aristocratic (samurai), not primitive, not isolationist, not backward-looking and not—for the first time—feminine. The suit pulled away from the movement that sanctioned male vanity, flamboyance and insouciance: dandyism.

The dominant concepts of masculinity instruct that men should not be too aware of what they wear or take too much time considering what they wear. The suit provides the answer to this modern dictate on the seriousness of masculinity; it is a uniform that can be worn every day and allows men to look good without having to consider their outfits too much and therefore becoming feminine.

Dandyism was a reaction against this bourgeois sartorial construct which limited male clothing consciousness. Dandyism was a way of being, a particular romantic reaction against the bourgeois prohibition against male sartorial vanity, not just a clothing style; returning to male dressing its status as a form of artistic expression. Dandyism was not particularly ostentatious; it was non -aristocratic, it was restrained, and it simplified movement; though it valued perfection at a level that bourgeois tastes would have thought excessive. Dandyism was a sartorial seriousness and it was always an attribute of the individual—never a group activity. Dandyism represented the collapse of religious faith and a different masculinity, not homoerotic but more sexless. It had an ambiguous sexuality, both sexless and solitary, and it represented a form of nihilism—its value was not given by religion, nature or the social, and by extension it believed that the social favoured mediocrity and was corrupt. In this way it was a profoundly modern aesthetic movement, taking Kant's reasoning, that art should have a value only in itself, to its logical conclusion in clothing. Dandyism valued perfection in dress as an end in itself.

Kuki Shūzō questioned whether Dandyism had the same structure as the Japanese aesthetic of *iki*. He claimed that Baudelaire's *Les Fleurs du mal* expresses a passion close to *iki*, which was born in the urban, wealthy culture of Edo. It was part of the non-profit-making life of the rich man who has become accustomed to enjoying himself.[63] Dandyism, Kuki argued, was the 'dogma of elegance' and he argued that Dandyism has a structure analogous to *iki* but that its semantic content is appropriate almost entirely to the male sex. As an end in itself, and therefore an aesthetic practice, *iki* was analogous to European Dandyism, and women could practise it too. While coquetry seeks consummation and thereby self-extinction, Kuki argues that it is the continuation of the relational, the preservation of its possibility as possibility, which is the secret of the success of *kanraku* (pleasure).[64] The second feature of *iki* is chic—a brave composure (*ikiji*). This is close to the 'cool' component in dandyism.[65] Self-composed even when starving, *iki* courtesans displayed a 'haughty disdain'.[66] Through *isagiyosa*—a proud resignation to the truth of life and an indifference to its outcomes—coquetry is spiritualized through the 'brave composure' produced by idealism. The third attribute of *iki* is resignation (*akirame*), which has renounced attachment and is based on knowledge of fate. *Iki* must be urbane.[67]

There existed, then, an equivalent to European Dandyism in the Japanese context. While some reservations can be made as to its exact equivalence, it can be concluded that some of the aesthetic factors which shaped the development of the suit in Europe were at work in the Japanese experience as well. A code of sartorial practice in which the end purpose was dressing itself was perhaps the most important factor in dress modernity. The fact that this aesthetic developed under the same sort of cultural conditions, with increasing urbanization and a middle class expanding in power but as yet unrecognized by the State, is important in answering the question as to why the suit was deemed so appropriate to modernity in Japan and why it was so widely and quickly adopted.

There are other ways in which *iki* prefigured and prepared Japan for the embrace of modernity. 'In *Ukiyo-buro* (bath-houses of the floating world) there is the series of adjectives: 'slim, pretty, chic'.[68] Within this vocabulary, Kuki argues that the formal reason for the pursuit of *iki* was a-realistic ideality. In general, Kuki argues, were we to try and express a-reality and ideality objectively, they would tend to adopt a long slim form. In addition to revealing the weakening of the flesh, the long slim form speaks of the power of the soul. Kuki argues that El Greco, who tried to express the spirit itself, painted only long slim figures; Gothic sculpture also makes a feature of the long and slim. Even ghosts are usually imagined as having a long slim form. So to the extent that *iki* is spiritualized coquetry, its pose must be slender.[69] Attenuation and repudiation of the human body as the basis of form is profoundly modern, though clothing and other arts diverge here. Modern clothing tends to become more rational and therefore true to the form of the body, while in becoming more rational a painting need only look more like a painting, and a Shaker wardrobe need only look like a wardrobe.[70] *Iki* expressed this modern sophistication in the rejection of humanity as a standard for beauty. 'In geometric figures there is nothing which better expresses [the relational quality of coquetry], than parallel lines. Parallel lines which run forever without meeting are the purest visual objectification of the relational. It is certainly no accident that the stripe, as design, is regarded as *iki*.'[71] Only the cool and the disinterested have angles and straight lines.

However, the European Dandyism that was a part of the lineage of the suit was, as Kuki notes, exclusively masculine. This was part of the cleavage within sartorial modernity along gender lines. The preexistence of a dress sensibility which raised dress to an art form amongst the merchant classes was certainly a significant factor in the adoption of the modern suit, which had an equivalent antecedent. An essential element of European Dandyism's influence on the suit was, however, the draining of elements of both aristocratic opulence and feminine frivolity from male dress. While *iki* served the first purpose, as it was not interested in displays of rank or wealth, it did not serve the second.

In an exhibition at the Tokyo Photography Museum entitled Samurai Dandyism, the change in the concept of sanctioned male sartorial display was documented through some of the earliest portrait photography in Japan. The title is not quite accurate, as the early samurai were not dandies in the strictest sense of the historical definition. They were not sexless, nor were they particularly nonaristocratic, but the pictures do show a class of male dressing before the gendering function of the suit transferred the full weight of conscious attention to self-presentation onto women. The early samurai were extremely self-conscious of their clothing and there was no prohibition against this at the time.

Like the middle class itself, the sartorial philosophy that came to dominate the performance of masculinity in modernity was a balance between extremes. It became an idea of a civilized centre—a middle-class system of identification—and its principal expression in the male wardrobe was the suit. It was entirely masculine and did not sanction too much male vanity on the surface; nor did it sanction a negligence in male dress. It was also balanced in that it was a set of replaceable components: over time, pumps replaced boots, trousers replaced stockings, collar and tie replaced neck cloths and bow ties. The tie was, however, the aristocratic remnant in the middle-class suit, the flash of ostentation in the austere black. The bowler hat replaced the top hat and then disappeared entirely, and watches appeared to enable the checking of time, the new rhythm of the world. As Japan rapidly developed a middle class, a stricter semiotic gendering and a modern economy, it by necessity adopted the garment system that had already evolved in the West to accompany these changes.

The streamlining of the suit—from the frock coats and top hats that first arrived in Japan to the simpler suits of the Taishō and early Shōwa periods—followed the modernist desire for form to follow function long before anyone had thought to phrase it that way. This pattern was similar to that in women's clothing where underwear increasingly became outerwear, simplifying and redefining levels of intimacy and social behaviour. The suit too reflected the gradual progression towards garments which best fitted what would be done in them—form following function. Therefore ornament was dropped. The form of the body was shown and the garment was shown in equal measure—the brush strokes were visible. Streamlining was an essential concept of the twentieth century and can be thought of as a product of enlightenment reason.[72] The suit was designed to enable greater movement, and because it is a system of garments, rather than just a single garment, variations could be made to suit certain conditions. Being able to move was part of freedom.

The entrance into modern society can only be a voluntary contract. Rousseau argues in his *Social Contract* that 'The law of majority-voting itself rests on an agreement, and implies that there has been on at least one occasion unanimity.'[73] The suit as a manifestation of this was also entered into as a covenant. It was not a national dress which could only be legitimately taken on by ethnic members of that nation; it was involved in modern political ideas that went beyond nationalism. As with the Roman toga, it was worn by citizens, not peoples. The Meiji elite wanted very much to create a nation of citizens, whose active spiritual participation could be used in the achievement of national objects, out of the passive, uneducated, feudal masses. Like American enlightenment, Japanese enlightenment required the individual—only the male individual at that stage—to become more than just an object of rule, to become knowledgeable and self-disciplined, not only subjected to control and dependence but possessing his own identity through conscience and self-knowledge. Simply, The Meiji elite wanted to accelerate the process of creating a modern citizenry from a feudal mass, and to do this they imitated the clothing choices which had defined that process in America and Europe.

The point was intellectual agreement rather than racial identity. Postrevolutionary French citizens had defined themselves in terms of a social contract, in terms of likeminded similarity rather than genetic similarity. To be a member of the suit-wearing world, one originally had to believe in the values of modernism and, to some extent, liberal internationalism. This was opposed to the Meiji elite's other goal of creating a unifying national identity. These twin objectives were often rivals in the battleground of clothing, as demonstrated by the stark difference in the Meiji period between men's modern Western suits and women's traditional indigenous kimonos.

The suit was a repudiation of tribalism and was first taken up by the risen middle classes of America, France and England, as a demonstration of mainly Protestant, puritan values. It was also a repudiation of class and the rococo fashion of leisured, frivolous aristocracies. Modern political thought sought to end the leprosy of unreality that consumed the ruling classes of Paris and London and infected Boston's Tories. The first exhibition of this was the clothes worn by the new 'modern' man. Japan too, wanted to end the leprosy of unreality that had informed Tokugawa isolationism, but the Japanese also had the problem that this was being forced rapidly upon them and was a movement from without, not from within. It was no wonder that the first need of American enlightenment was to adopt highly symbolic new ways of dressing, appropriate to new ways of thinking, life and organizing society, as simple and egalitarian as the toga was for the Roman republic. Japan's change too, had to be highly symbolic, but it was a symbol as much for the outside world as it was for the Japanese population.

The suit was also an exhibition of education; it referred to growing literacy and universal education and for a gentleman of the early Meiji period it referred to a certain cosmopolitanism and worldliness. Those who wore a suit were educated without being part of the aristocracy—they were members of the growing meritocracy of the Japanese civil service. Voltaire had ridiculed the French elite of his day, pointing out that, apart from title and money, its members were pitifully ignorant, though, sometimes unfortunately for Voltaire, never ignorant when it came to threats to their power. Hereditary elites mostly bought knowledge and advice. The spread of literacy to larger and larger proportions of the populace meant that civilization became a much more shared experience. This is the process that the rising middle classes were experiencing first in the West and then in Japan, which always enjoyed high literacy rates, for they were taking part in civilization through education, not through title and privilege. The suit, in Japan, was a symbol of the fact that the middle classes were becoming part of civilization, that the masses were now important and that culture was now dictated from the middle, not the top. The masses could aspire to middle-class privilege through education, and this was a kind of upward mobility representative of meritocracy.

Two attempts at dress legislation in Europe had demonstrated that the suit was endemic among people who had reached a certain stage in political thinking, particularly a sense of their own participation in civilization. First there were the attempts in France after the 1824 restoration of Charles X to reintroduce court dress, which failed to alter the preference amongst the new ruling class for embryonic early versions of the suit. Although costume change is never a linear progression, it was clear that the French Revolution had greatly influenced costume through political ideas. The members of the ruling class at court in 1824 did not want to give up their status as men of the world and take up court dress, which would again indicate the frivolity of aristocracy.

The same is true of the new, developing meritocracy of Japan, which did not want to be associated with the feudalism of the recently abolished samurai, although many Meiji elite members had previously been samurai, and identity issues continued to create inevitable contradictions. In France it was clear that a blatant exhibition of rank and privilege through court dress could only be seen as in contradiction to the rights of man and the citizen; in Japan it would have been antimodern. French revolutionary political ideas were too strong and too widely accepted, amongst both upper and lower classes in France, to risk violating them with a display of romantic individuality or ostentatious wealth through court dress. It is these ideas which are at once both part of the cause of, and part of the effect of, the 'modern' entering peoples' lives. In a world accepting reason and science as new epistemological underpinnings, clothes reflected the change from ornamental to utilitarian. The principal cause of the political and aesthetic streamlining, the modernization of form, both physical and abstract, was the rebirth and domination of reason as the central method of conducting human affairs. As such, the suit was one of the first examples of modernization because it was a physical manifestation of reason. Despite the fact that many nationalist movements elsewhere were calling for a return to indigenous clothing, in Japan the suit persisted as the principal male garment for reasons similar to those in France: it was appropriate to the new political, social and aesthetic organization of the nation.[74]

The second example of attempts to regulate dress, cited by Rousseau, is the failed attempt of Peter the Great to sartorially modernize the Russian people. Peter the Great had talent as an imitator, in the spirit of the early Meiji missions to Europe and America, but he did not see the unreadiness of the Russian people to adopt the reforms of Western Europe, Rousseau argued. Whereas France and England had the industrial, metropolitan, educational and intellectual development required for the adoption of modern reforms, the Russia of Peter the Great was unready, and his attempts to modernize his people were crude and tactless. His dress reform and his imposition of compulsory shaving sought to alter appearance without particularly reflecting any larger reform of Russian society. A nation's costume had to reflect its inner intellectual state—merely adopting the dress of Western Europe did not make a Russian more civilized if he did it because it was imposed on him. It was irrelevant to his own cultural and social circumstances. Although this dress reform was away from peasant dress and not towards the three-piece suit, the logic remains the same: costume is a reflection of perceived identity and self-actualization but can not be used to effect change from the outside in. This is because it is a voluntary covenant, and all attempts to create utopias by designing the clothes first and the politics second are doomed to failure. The leaders of China now wear suits rather than Mao's Cultural Revolution uniform because these reflect internal changes in their self-identity.

It can be assumed by comparison to Russia in Rousseau's analysis that Japan was ready to embrace modernity and its reforms. Its leadership had more extensive knowledge and larger-scale ambitions in its reforms. The Western model was a lot more advanced than it had been in Peter's day, but the central assumption is that Japan was educationally and economically ready for massive reforms, and when the Japanese put on frock coats they looked, after a while, natural; whereas Peter's Russia was not ready, and just putting a man in a new coat or removing his beard could not change the character of a Russia that was not willing and able to change. Forms and means had to make sense in terms of the secondary context—there was a performative and transformative quality to the Japanese adoption of Western sartorial models, not a simple donning of modern male attire. Imitation is generally an inadequate explanation for sartorial modernity; there need to be intrinsic changes in forms of life for new clothing forms to feel appropriate.

There are psychological elements to the transformation of national identity, and the process of fundamentally altering a way of dress—essential to self- and group perception—is alienating and traumatic, and thus 'readiness' is impossible to judge. However, looking alike is an essential part of the whole system of fashion. It is scientifically recognized that 'isopraxism [is] a non-learned neuro-behaviour in which members of a species act in a like manner: Dressing like your colleagues and neighbours dress reflects a deep reptilian behaviour . . . '[75] This is also valid for the suit's paramount position in modern dress as a reflection of the human desire for group acceptance in the growing urban crowds of modernity. Flügel's suggestion that perhaps there are two motivations governing our sartorial behaviour, one encouraging exhibitionism, the other modesty, and in balancing these we dress, wanting to fit in and stand out at the same time and in equal measure. The suit allows this to happen, with elements sufficient to distinguish the individual but also a structure that does not allow too much variation from the primary form. It suits the needs of modernizing Japanese group identification.

Born out of political ideas that themselves were born out of the new science and reason, the suit presented the first glimpse of a modern Kantian aesthetic, based on principles of form which are partly classical and partly utilitarian—a formal fidelity. The modern aesthetic was the victory of the classical over the baroque, black and white over colour and formalism over frivolity. The republican values of America and France attempted to remove the artifice and ornamentation of aristocracy from their cultures and replace them with the classical architectural form of noble simplicity and calm grandeur as their governments removed the arbitrary from the body politic. Mankind's consciousness was to be defined first as that of a citizenry, and not by occupation or rank as in premodern times, hence the need for a new form of dress demonstrating this. An international rational idealism was to replace the tribalism and ethnicity of costume. The risen middle classes of the Western world were to take their place as the new ruling classes of this transatlantic modern world of trade and new money, and their puritan faith was both their driving motivation and the shaper of their new cultural values. A social contract was to replace divine right as the central weave of society's fabric. Part of this new, voluntary covenant was the display of the individual's membership of this modern, rational, educated world.

This membership was displayed by the dark, three-piece suit, which expressed worldliness—politically powerful because its wearer was republican, economically powerful as a reward from God and culturally powerful because its wearer was educated. To wear the uniform of the democratic, bourgeois spirit was to sign the social contract, declare one's independence and remember mortality, while celebrating reason at the same time. It reflected modernism with all its contradiction and nuance. It was a quintessential, classic, modern form.

An essential point in this complex dress evolution is that Japan arrived in the middle of many processes that were largely irrelevant to it. While certain universal trends towards modernity and citizenship were signalled through changes in dress, other issues of Protestantism, or baroque aesthetics, were meaningless to the Japanese in 1868. The meaning of many of the elements of male dress, in so far as they had meaning, was unimportant to the early Meiji elites. This is not to say that the suit did not have meaning, just that the meaning was mostly different. The abolishing of aristocratic rank and the transformation from a feudal social structure to a less arbitrary modern structure was shared, but the forms this transformation took in Japan were very different from those in the West. Essentially the suit was a sign of alignment with a change in policy—the new policy of looking out to the world rather than closing it off. It signalled that a foundational choice had been made by the wearer to be part of the change, to be modern, not traditional. The rise of the merchant classes took place by a process similar to that in Europe and America and did have the same implications for male dress, in that it involved a change from a feudal theatre in which men wore essential romantic costumes to one in which the culturally sanctioned male vanity, flamboyance and insouciance that allowed for more luxuriant forms of self-expression in clothing declined and were replaced with the imperative of ceaselessly proving one's wealth within a framework of conforming as equal members of a citizenry. This was a universal phenomenon which accompanied the embourgeoisement of peoples everywhere. In Japan it was a critical field in which the traditional did battle with the modern, socially and aesthetically.

The Japanese Suit

The political inequities of the 1858 Harris Treaty (extraterritoriality for treaty ports, low import levies and a most-favoured-nation clause) provided a strong stimulus to Japanese nationalism but simultaneously reinforced a traditional underlying sense of inferiority, and this contradiction was also at work in attitudes to male clothing reform.[76] One reason why the Japanese government implemented changes so quickly in the Meiji era, adopting Western laws, technology and clothes, was to demonstrate that they were in fact civilized on Western terms and deserved to be treated as equals—hence the adoption of *bummei kaika* (civilization and enlightenment) as an official government slogan for the 1870s. As Japan's government lurched into the modern world, there was a tremendous outburst of energy and euphoria for all things Western. Serious and otherwise responsible intellectuals advocated adopting English as the national language, or at least adopting the Western alphabet in place of Chinese characters. Mori Arinori, then a diplomat at the Japanese embassy in Washington, greeted incoming Japanese students by advising them to intermarry and produce children with superior Caucasian ethnic qualities.[77] The immediate switch to Western clothing was similarly self-alienating. These were extremes, of course, but on the whole it seemed that in the beginning, modernization and Westernization were virtually synonymous.

Japan's willingness to accept Western learning and culture is not without precedent. It reflects a long history of fascination with anything new, foreign and exotic— perhaps the result of geographic remoteness. In the past this had meant an absorption of continuous waves of influence from China, and to a lesser extent from Korea, and even, in the late sixteenth century, from Europe. This adaptability, combined with widespread education, a common language, large urban commercial centres with a skilled labour force, a strong secular tradition and a rising agricultural surplus, helped to ease the transition from a feudal world.

In the early Meiji period, Western civilization was very effectively publicized and popularized by the educator and writer Fukuzawa Yūkichi (1835–1901). Fukuzawa had begun as a student of Dutch learning in Osaka in the 1850s, and he founded Keiō Gijuku (later Keiō University) as a private school for the study of Dutch in Edo in 1858.[78] After a visit to Yokohama, he astutely turned his attention to English, gained a reputation as a translator and was sent overseas in 1860 as an attendant to the head of the first embassy to the United States.[79] In 1862 he was recruited as a member of an official shogunal mission to Europe, and in 1867 he was ordered to accompany a delegation to America. Armed with first-hand information, he quickly published several books that established him as a serious authority on Western matters. Sales of the first volume of his *Seiyō jijō* (Conditions in the West) in 1866 reached the huge figure of 150,000. He was thus the first knowledge source on foreign clothing for many Japanese.[80]

Fukuzawa's *Seiyō ishokujū* (Western clothing, food and homes) was published in 1867 on the eve of the Meiji Restoration as a detailed and neatly illustrated wood-block-printed guide to Western customs and manners. Written in simple, readable style, Fukuzawa's advice had the meritocratic aim of educating able young samurai of low rank who, like himself, were eager to rise in the hierarchy of the emerging new Japan and 'obtain power commensurate with their talents'.[81] The book provided fundamental kinds of information for which there was obviously a desperate need. Fukuzawa illustrated, to his obviously curious and probably bewildered readers, how to eat, dress and even urinate in proper Western style. Each illustration used kanji as well as phonetic katakana for an approximation of English pronunciation and was thus intended to begin a process not just of informing and entertaining but of deliberately incorporating these manners and words in Japanese cultural consciousness.

The detailed and intentionally useful information on clothing in Fukuzawa's manual soon percolated down to schoolchildren throughout the country in the form of illustrated woodblock-printed English primers such as the *Eiji kummō zukai* (Illustrated Manual of English Instruction) of 1871. It has been argued that a fundamental difference in tone existed and still exists between the fashion press of Europe and America and that of Japan; with the former being about envy and class re-enforcement—a voyeuristic glimpse of a world of clothing that is unavailable, socially more than economically, to the reader, and the latter simply more instructional—any foreign look is achievable by anyone. Fukuzawa's publications on clothing perhaps demonstrate the origin of this difference: to the Japanese all foreign clothing is alien, and thus to adopt and incorporate any is equal in its strangeness, while for those of European cultural inheritance the alienation is in wearing clothing from a social class that is not their own.

Hybridity in early Japanese clothing and some original combinations of East and West (the newest style of felt hat from Paris combined with a kimono) and of imports worn improperly according to European criteria (ankles protruding from trousers, collar unfastened and cravat askew) were a source of both amusement and irritation for Westerners, who were often of the opinion that the Japanese figure was 'too dumpy and the legs too short to appear to advantage in this foreign dress'.[82] Even if the skills of early Japanese tailors and wearers were poor, what really seemed to be at work was a challenge to the rules of group sartorial identification which, though it was thought absurd, was only so according to Westerners' preconceptions of race and racial characteristics. An English traveller and writer, Isabella Bird, who arrived in 1878, showed little mercy for the early, somewhat eccentric attempts at sartorial modernization: 'The Japanese look most diminutive in European dress,' she wrote. 'Each garment is misfit, and exaggerates the miserable physique and the national defects of concave chest and bow legs.'[83] Again, the preconceptions attached to Bird's racial constructs—defectiveness and inferiority—made the suit of a Japanese seem alien and inappropriate: the very notion that in their sartorial reforms the Meiji leaders wanted to refute.

The Rokumeikan

The notion of inferiority was not limited to foreign visitors, and measured against what they perceived as a successful and vigorous West, the editors of the *Hōchi shimbun* in 1885 found Japan to be a young, weak, indolent and uncivilized nation:

> If a Japanese be compared with an Englishman or an American it is not necessary to go very deep into the subject to discover which is the more industrious, better educated, more courageous, and more intelligent. What a difference there is between Japan and either England or the United States in strength, wealth, and civilization! It will be impossible for us ever to stand on the same level in civilization with England and

America unless we increase the rate of speed towards that goal to which we have been lately moving. It is true our recent progress has surprised the world, but our work so far has been simply casting off the garments of inaction, and taking a sudden dive into the waters of progress and improvement. But our movement towards civilization would attract notice in a country of the cultured West, where progress is constant and perpetual. It is certain that if we aim at approaching England and America we must step out or we shall never reach the goal.[84]

'The Japanese . . . do not know that time is money,' scolded the editors, taking a somewhat Protestant tone. 'Some will lay aside their work for idle talk.'[85] In the interest of developing a rich nation, citizens were exhorted to follow the example of their government and of prominent members of society by increasing contact with foreigners and learning their customs—an activity that would develop Japanese mental power, business capacity, spirit and sagacity. The importation of foreigners would theoretically rouse the lethargic population. Standing in the way of this progress, however, were the unequal treaties, and the government and press reasoned that only their revision would ensure the opening of the country for mixed residence along the lines of the United States, which was becoming powerful by encouraging migration from all the countries of Europe.

Inoue Kaoru, the Foreign Minister from 1879 to 1887, devoted himself to treaty revision to engender these reforms, designing the first legal modernization, as required by the foreign powers, but also devising original and highly visible social programmes of Westernization and modernization—then understood as the same thing.[86] Inoue, one of the most influential architects of early modern Japan, was born into a samurai clan in the fief of Chōshū (in almost Prussian style, he bore enormous scars and old sword wounds on his body and face). He had studied Dutch learning, the English language and Western-style gunnery, and he was secretly sent to London for a period of study together with Itō Hirobumi. Active in the new Meiji government as Minister of Finance, member of the Genrōin (Senate) and vice-envoy extraordinary to Korea, he travelled in Europe for two years, from 1876 to 1878, studying fiscal and economic matters. Like his friend Itō, whose parents had been poor farmers, he was named to the new peerage of government officials with meritorious service to the nation who were given titles in July 1884 in anticipation of the projected House of Peers. 'He is a little man with a very bright and intelligent expression,' wrote Erwin Baelz in 1881, 'and he has adapted himself to western civilization and habits more perfectly than any of his compatriots. He is having his daughter, now seventeen, educated in the European way.'[87] His knowledge of, and enthusiasm for, European clothing was probably amongst the greatest in the early days of the reopening of the country, since he had been amongst the very few Japanese to have travelled widely and thus he understood the meaning and significance of sartorial modernity. In a document Inoue prepared for the Cabinet he stated his opinion that

. . . what we must do is to transform our Empire and our people, make the Empire like the countries of Europe and our people like the people of Europe. To put it differently, we have to establish a new European-style Empire on the Eastern Sea . . . The Japanese must achieve a system of self-government and a vigour of conduct sufficient to assure the creation of a strong people and a powerful and effective government . . . How can we impress upon the minds of our thirty-eight million people this daring spirit and attitude of independence and self-government? In my opinion, the only course is to have them clash with Europeans, so that they will personally feel inconvenienced, realize their disadvantage, and absorb an awareness of Western vigorousness . . . I consider that the way to do this is to provide for truly free intercourse between Japanese and foreigners . . . Only thus can our Empire achieve a position equal to that of the Western countries with respect to treaties. Only thus can our Empire be independent, prosperous, and powerful.[88]

Inoue, understanding the importance, both for domestic and international perceptions, of symbolism, conceived the Rokumeikan (Deer Cry Pavilion), which was such an important element of early Japanese sartorial modernity and of government policy on cultural direction that it gave its name to the span of years from 1884 to about 1889. Designed by British architect Josiah Conder and opened on 28 November 1883 under the jurisdiction of the Foreign Ministry after nearly three years of construction financed by the government, it was, after the Emperor, the most important major tool of sartorial statecraft. The agenda, naturally, was more complex than that, reflecting Inoue's belief both that the Japanese needed to be Westernized and that the West should be witness to that change with the result that they would accept Japan as a cultural, and thus political, equal.

The Rokumeikan functioned as a space where the new Japanese urban elite could mingle with, influence and be influenced by foreign dignitaries and the many imported experts in a setting emulating the elegant clubs of Paris or London, which were acknowledged as the informal power structures in European society. It demonstrated Japan's willingness to imitate the civilized—on foreign terms—and was a concrete visualization, in a complex piece of state theatre, of Inoue's ideal European-style empire on the Eastern Sea. The actual site was a government property in the Hibiya district of central Tokyo, close to the Imperial Palace, and across from what was later to become Hibiya Park. Conder, the architect, had come to Japan early in 1877 in the employ of the Ministry of Technology and was thus one of the foreign experts, the ambassadors of the civilization that the building was built to impress. As has been argued before, the embrace of Western aesthetics did not mean any distaste on the part of the Rokumeikan's Japanese guests for indigenous culture, and all would have changed into traditional clothing when they returned home—the Rokumeikan was very much a tool.

The food was supervised by a French chef, another imported foreign expert, whose banquet menus included many exotic foreign delicacies.[89] English cigarettes, German beer and American cocktails were served at the bars to demonstrate, overtly, the cosmopolitanism and internationalism that was so desperately sought. As an exercise in the deliberate creation of cosmopolitan tastes, the Rokumeikan prefigured the plethora of influences in contemporary Japan, and it was at pains to show that the trappings of 'enlightened' leisure time came from a variety of European and American sources rather than just one.

The agenda of aesthetic and cultural change was real, and to almost any sensibility, violent. And it was not an evolution. There was nothing random about these changes—the approach to clothing at this stage was very much designed and directed for cultural and ultimately political change, by the elite of the Meiji State. While it could be considered a failure according to the terms of its creation—to reverse global perceptions of inequality and to reverse the unequal treaty arrangements—the Rokumeikan became a cultural phenomenon that gave its name to the brief years of its operation and was a symbol of the Meiji government's belief that changes in culture, custom and costume were essential for political change and national development. And it should be noted that while women in general did not adopt the clothing of the Rokumeikan example, men gradually did, and the tail coats worn in 1885 are still the official portrait dress of male politicians and the Imperial House today, some hundred and twenty years later. The elites' provision of an example is the defining and unique element in early male costume in Japan, and the Rokumeikan was its principal instrument. The fact that ruling elites provided an example they expected to be copied also provided for great sartorial equality. The Rokumeikan period effected a profound and lasting change in the Japanese conception of the male body and how it should be covered—and it also established the governing principle that cultural forms should adapt and imitate rather than resist foreign challenges and that no matter how ridiculous the Japanese felt at first, modernity and its sartorial aesthetics should be embraced and incorporated as rapidly as possible.

Four stages mark the progression of suit-based clothing in becoming the dominant forms of male dress, as white-collar work clothing and formal wear.

1. Use by eccentrics (in the late Tokugawa and early Meiji periods)
2. Involvement of political elites (from the 1872 rescript)
3. Partial experimentation (in the mid-Meiji period)
4. Assimilation (in the late Meiji period) with generational change

These stages followed the general cultural developments in Japan. While the nation was closed, before 1868, only those rich enough to be smuggled secretly out of the country developed an understanding of and taste for Western clothing, and it wasn't until housing and lifestyle changed in the Taishō period that Western suits and their adaptations—casual and formal—really took hold in all areas of Japanese male life. The period of partial experimentation was often the object of both native and foreign satire, but in many instances this seems more like an indicator that Japanese dressers were getting it right than an indicator that they were getting it wrong—the satire reflecting the fact that both Japanese and visiting Europeans felt threatened by the displacement of the perceived sartorial norms of race. The changes in aesthetic tastes that underpinned the suit's impact were partially universal and partially unique. The change in gendering in the Meiji period, which accompanied the rise of the merchant classes, restricted male vanity and placed an emphasis on demonstrating wealth but without aristocratic ostentation, was a process that echoed European embourgeoise-ment. In male clothing, romantic expression was considered in Japan, as in the West, to be an attribute of a feudal ruling class and was thus shunned. Unique to Japan was the question of foreignness, the foundational choices which had to be made by every suit wearer as to whether they should adopt modernity so fully as to change their bodily appearance in a totally fundamental way. The new relationship to the body, not nearly as hidden in a suit as in a kimono, was also part of one of modernity's primary projects: physically redefining humanity.

The intentionally fabricated and meaningful sartorial signs of the Meiji State, in the form of the Emperor, the civil service, the Rokumeikan, the army and public schooling, were an essential part of its programme of cultural and political modern-ization and the desired accompanying aesthetic shift to modernity. The reconstruc-tion of gender demarcation in the aesthetics of personal adornment was as important a dichotomy in modernity as others such as *civilized* and *uncivilized*. It was as a Kantian truth in form adopted into masculinity with male clothing becoming serious, useful and abstract. Femininity was accordingly reconstructed as ever more frivolous and ornamental. Both positions were, of course, abstractions and arbitrary, yet in the universal conditions of modernity, coupled with the particular gendering norms that predated it, in both Europe and in Japan, masculinity was the aesthetic that mod-ernized first. The central sartorial form that the new aesthetic took was the various versions of the suit, which repudiated both aristocracy and femininity and was true to the body at the same time as to the garment itself—as with modern art, the brush strokes were visible.

−4−

Japanese Womenswear:
Femininity and Modernity

The second part of the sartorial aesthetic shift towards modernity in Japan was the reform of notions of femininity; how it could be visually performed, what constituted feminine beauty and how femininity and feminine beauty could integrate an awareness of modernity within their forms. As argued in Chapter 3, at the beginning of the Meiji period, femininity was defined by the rapid reshaping of masculinity, which increasingly defined itself against the feminine. By the end of the Meiji period, however, the aesthetic principles of modernity were being assimilated into women's clothing styles—seeking their own Kantian truth in form rather than merely expressing an aspect of masculine sartorial repudiation.

The clothing styles of women in Europe and America fluctuated rapidly in the nineteenth century, reacting dramatically to conceptual history, whimsy and the mood of the period. Only twenty years elapsed between the sheer, simple gowns of the neoclassical Napoleonic period and the heavy, dowdy styles of the early Victorian age. This pattern of fashion followed the shifting erogenous zone theory, where the desired female silhouette swelled or diminished in differing directions with every decade and the term 'ideal figure' was relevant only to the specific style of the day.[1]

In Japan, women were slower than men to converge with and join the modern fashion world. There was significant experimentation in the Rokumeikan period. However, soon after this, it was for the most part renounced until the age of the 'modern girl' (*moga*) a generation later. As in Europe, finding a feminine aesthetic, equivalent to the masculine sartorial aesthetic of the suit, that was appropriate for modernity, as lived, and that reflected social, political and aesthetic aspirations was extremely complex without the disavowal of gender, nation or status. These issues of sartorial reflection on and expression of identity were naturally more pronounced for Japanese women because of their lower social and economic status in the Meiji period and their own need for emancipation, in which sartorial aesthetics was only one element.

The history of sartorial modernity in women's costume in nineteenth-century Japan could be argued as being equivalent to modernity in Euro-American styles, in that foreign trends instigated a desire for constant renewal and therefore rapid changes in sartorial form. The very valuing of this may be defined as the sum and substance of modernity in dress, and is divisible into four distinct successive phases: a period of observation in the 1860s and 1870s; a period of experimentation in the 1880s; a period of stagnation in the 1890s; and a period of assimilation in the closing years of the Meiji era and at the beginning of the Taishō era.[2] It is the relaxation after the first substantial modernization drive, the relative peace and prosperity and the generational change of the Taishō period that provided the soil for the first real expressions of a truly modern feminine form in clothing, the manifestation of which was the modern girls (*moga*) and also the repercussions on Japanese aesthetics of their provocation to traditional notions of femininity, beauty and deportment.

It would seem that the attraction of a modern sartorial aesthetic and the attraction of foreign and exotic dress were indistinguishable in the very early Meiji period and exhibited itself in intense curiosity about the clothing of the foreign experts and their families living in Yokohama in the early 1860s. This curiosity was predominantly evinced by the publication of a multitude of prints that recorded, often in great detail, the frilled and flounced crinoline skirts, lacy mantillas, and beribboned bonnets of the fashions of the foreign community. When the Japanese government decided to adopt European clothing during the early stages of the Meiji era, it was primarily for political rather than aesthetic reasons, and the elite members who modelled the new fashions were not selective—they were in no position to modify the borrowed costumes according to Japanese taste. The taste was simply for foreign clothing, without knowledge of its intricacies. It was a wholesale adoption, without any creative reflexivity. As a result, those who adopted it often looked uncomfortable, even a bit ridiculous, and this was recorded rather harshly by the satirists of the time. This was especially true of Japanese women's clothing, as the brief period when foreign dresses were copied most assiduously, from 1887 until about 1889, corresponded in America and Europe with the height of the bustle style, which represented an extreme deviation from the natural shape of the body and was a matchless example of the sartorial gender differentiations of early modernity, where the burden of the feminine was apportioned almost entirely to women as ornamental and impractical, as a radical reaction against the aesthetic agenda of modernity.

For the few Japanese women who attempted it, the bustle style proved to be convoluted and completely alien to any indigenous style; women strung and fastened themselves into disfiguring, waist-shrinking corsets and bustles, a painful self-sacrifice that deformed the body in an extraordinary way. The bodice, with its high, tight neckline and elongated pointed waistline, was closely moulded to the waist and bust, while the enormous posterior-exaggerating rear protrusion known as the *queue de Paris* (Parisian tail) 'was nearly equal to another half woman from the waist down and so perpendicular at the back that it could easily support a saucer with a cup of tea without spilling it'.[3] The rear-extending bustle arched away from the body before plunging to the ground. The support for this tail was a short crinoline cut in half, made of steel or whalebone, never reaching beyond the side-seams at the hips, and mounted on a lining. Cushions, sometimes made of rattan, could also be attached to the back of the corset and petticoat. The impracticality of all this in a modernizing world of crowds and motorized transport is acute, and maybe it is best seen as the death rattle of the passing baroque age, and, for this reason, it had even less relevance to early Meiji women and their aesthetic needs. While the tastes of the Edo period, the aesthetic antecedent of the Meiji period, were elaborate, they could never be characterized as baroque, and thus there could be no nostalgia or reactionary refuge from a rapidly changing world in baroque forms.

The bustle style was favoured by the nouveaux riches wives of European and American industrialists, whose French couturiers designed clothing that was suitably opulent, even garish, made with yards of heavy satins, velvets, and brocades overloaded with ornaments that were completely heterogenous in colour and material. This fashion was the one particularly seen in Japan, as it was members of the entrepreneurial classes that ventured there, and corresponded to a larger shift from aristocratic tastes, which were losing their supremacy to the tastes of the newly wealthy bourgeois, eager to show off their new material power. The weight of these costumes did little to enhance mobility, so greatly needed in industrializing cities. According to costume historian Stella Blum, many of the fabrics were upholstery-like in quality, made even heavier by the profuse use of beading, fringes, braids and furs.[4] Some dresses alone weighed over five kilograms, and to carry this excess of material a woman adopted a stance in which the bust was thrown forward and the head held back. Petite Japanese ladies who were less busty, for which the kimono style allows, must at times have had the perception of physical inferiority harshly reinforced, as tall, fleshy women with big bosoms and heavy hips were held up as examples of perfection. That Western female clothing was introduced to Japan with these styles is perhaps one reason, along with the growing nationalism, for the backlash against and rejection of European and American clothing for women that occurred in the mid-Meiji period, with many women returning to indigenous styles. Unlike the suit, bustle dresses were not appropriate to the conditions of modernity, nor did they adhere to its aesthetic tenets.

Thus, while Japanese women did have a limited knowledge of foreign feminine dress, their own clothing did not change significantly during the second half of the nineteenth century, notwithstanding the great popularity of Western goods in the large cities. The styles worn by European and American women were antithetical to the demands of modernity, both practical and aesthetic, and even if such styles of clothing had been readily available, the full skirts fashionable in the West during the early Meiji period would have been most impractical in Japanese housing and impossible for women to manage in Japanese toilets, which had to be used in a squatting position.[5] The incompatibility with housing and social spaces was a major restriction on the uptake of Western clothing during the early period, and it was not until the Taishō period, when many Western-style public spaces and physical environments came into existence—cafés, department stores and furniture for seating—that modern clothing really became feasible for the average Japanese woman.

The conservatism with regard to the status of women that accompanied the early modernization of Japan, and was articulated in the *ryōsai kenbo* (good wife, wise mother) doctrine of 1898, already had an indigenous sartorial archetype and there was no need to appropriate the bustle styles, which were themselves a reactionary formation against the currents of modernity. The adoption of foreign clothing by Japanese women was generally a progressive gesture, but the redefining of sartorial masculinity in the early Meiji period demanded a conservative antithesis in women's dress and precluded broad feminine reshaping until the end of the Meiji period.

At the beginning of the Meiji period, there were relatively few occasions for observing Western costume directly, so many Japanese artists relied upon fashion illustrations, which were, by the time of the Restoration, surprisingly common in Europe and America and were brought with the foreign community to Yokohama. Fashion prints were, at the time, the means of instruction for both men and especially women of economic means in the selection of their attire. Improvements in printing techniques in the second half of the nineteenth century, and a reliable income for skilled artists, resulted in the provision of magnificent lithographs for fashion magazines of the period. Fashion plates were published, beginning in the 1780s, in prototypes of today's modern fashion magazines, and by 1870, there were fifty fashion magazines in five languages in Europe, with one, *Die Modenwelt*, published in thirteen languages.[6] Plates were hand-coloured until the 1880s, when the chromolithograph process began to dominate fashion printing.

Despite the general disinclination to foreign women's clothing during the early Meiji period, there was a very limited use of it amongst the elite, and especially in the royal household, where the influence of Western fashion prints—French via America—can be discerned almost immediately in their Japanese equivalents. While the clothing had been adopted wholesale without any regional interpretations yet, the artistic representations of that clothing were subject to much interpretation, and influenced by the lingering conventions and norms of native costume and the traditional body image.[7]

The Empress was a paramount symbol in the political agenda of demonstrating a sophistication on a par with America and Western Europe, and in prints it was thought essential to show that at the highest level, Japanese feminine fashion was up to date with the world—the Empress's white gloves, folded fan and pointed shoes were all absolutely the latest style in France in 1887, and feathers were perhaps the most popular form of hat decoration during the spring and summer of 1887, indicating that by this time, and at this exalted level at least, Japanese fashion was impeccably synchronized with global fashions.

Many early French fashion magazines from the 1880s—informing sartorial and bodily praxis as well as form—contain similarities in costumes and in poses to those illustrated in Meiji prints by Chikanobu and others. But the Japanese representations never seem to have appropriated entire compositions or looks, and all that was borrowed was, even in this early phase, transfigured into something distinctively

Japanese. Some costumes were composites—they contained many Western elements, but in combination they became Japanese. Some prints employed original textile designs and combined fabrics in accordance with the interpretive judgements of the traditional standards of Japanese woodblock prints. Japanese fashions of Edo had been purely textile, not structural: hence the lingering emphasis on combinations of patterns.

As with all purportedly realistic art, there is a fine line between realism, the artistically convenient, the nationalistic idealization and the purely imaginary in any Japanese woodblock print—perhaps the primary source for early Meiji period dress history. Because in Edo and more modern times their primary subject matter is taken from everyday life, Japanese woodblock prints are often deceptively realistic, even though their fanciful composition makes it unlikely that many were actually sketched from life. It is always difficult to figure out what has resulted from diligent and faithful observation and what is the product of expediency or imagination, especially with Meiji prints. So many of these profess to record noteworthy public events, duly witnessed and recorded by the artist for a patriotic public hungry for souvenirs that they could venerate. However it is often apparent from prints by different artists devoted to the same theme, or rare early photographs, that numerous discrepancies exist in the factual details, especially in the pliant visual vocabulary of dress.

The salient details of clothing and fashions are especially difficult to appraise in this regard. It is often impossible to ascertain whether the prints depict an accurate rendering of a Japanese adaptation of a European costume or an artistic intervention, altered to produce a more compelling composition or to make the costume appeal more to traditional taste or nationalistic pride. However, repeated aspects of pictorial manipulation seem to indicate certain elements at least of deliberate refining of some sartorial elements of prints, in line with an aesthetic more familiar to the tastes of the Japanese Meiji-era public. In the very early Meiji period, the Yokohama printmaker Utagawa Yoshikazu rendered the bodice of a woman's dress in such a way that it resembled a tight-sleeved kimono—no collar or lapels, and a simple, overlapping closure. More subtly, in the 1880s, printmaker Chikanobu accentuated the bustle to make it resemble the obi; and the trailing yardage of the train recalls the hem of an *uchikake* (bridal kimono).

Certainly, traditional print conventions, expectations of anatomical representation and mores of judgement and taste with regard to sartorial depiction were less subject to change than the actual new European and French clothes that were worn. As Julia Meech-Pekarik has shown, another Yokohama printmaker, Utagawa Sadahide, and Chikanobu both reduced foreign costumes pictorially to their component parts and arranged the resulting geometric shapes in abstract patterns of line and colour. This tendency to emphasize the decorative surface pattern over the structural qualities is an aspect of premodern Japanese aesthetics. Both artists seem to have deliberately exaggerated parts of the costume to render them more effective in the overall composition, reflecting the overriding concern for unified composition that was characteristic of many earlier *ukiyo-e* masters and the traditional aesthetic. These artists were clearly innovators, however, in that they recognized and exploited the new vocabulary of decorative patterns, shapes, curves and frills represented by foreign dress and its underpinning modern aesthetic. Sadahide was the first to carefully detail the lace trimmings, feathers, ruffles and novel textile patterns of the foreigners' costumes, piling pattern upon pattern to make fascinating, semi-abstract designs, though he still understood clothing from a premodern Japanese aesthetic that had yet to adopt the human body as the primary source of form.[8]

The real challenge of Western clothing was that it forced the artist and the viewer to consider the human figure underneath the garment. The classicism and emphasis on form over motif of the figure was a radical departure from both Japanese sartorial practice and its artistic depiction. In Europe, the classical academic traditions of drawing the naked body, sometimes even the skeleton, and building up form and clothing over it began in the Renaissance and even have their descendants in today's computer animation—starting with skeleton form and building up muscles and so forth to create the most realistic form.

Considering form over texture was a key break from Japanese artistic practices and a movement towards the artistic practices of the West. Unlike the kimono, which wraps the body in smooth, straight lines, effectively eliminating the figure underneath, the close-fitting bodice and bustle reduced the figure to a series of angles and curves. The challenge of body, which goes back in Western art to the practice of commencing with a naked form before applying the clothing, was a profound one to Japanese artists and to every Japanese person confronted with a new system of dress that did not hide or wrap the body but made it the very basis of design. Chikanobu was perhaps the first chronicler of this dramatic sartorial restructuring, and he not only depicted the new curves and form of clothing, but he celebrated and delighted in them. Consequently, his women are uniformly coy, flirtatious, even seductive— quite the opposite of the sedate matrons presented by many of his contemporaries who were still steeped in premodern notions of vestimentary practice. Chikanobu discerned and proclaimed the modern feminine sartorial aesthetic that came with European clothing and, rather than moderating its formal qualities to align them with traditional hermeneutic structures, he foresaw new opportunities for elegance and grace afforded by different ways of performing femininity.

Throughout the Victorian era in Europe and America, and correspondingly throughout the Meiji period in Japan, every costume was a unique creation. Fashionable behaviour involved selecting a desired design from a fashion magazine, determining a fabric and then having it made up by a seamstress. The design was then varied with ornamentation—the addition of a bit of lace, a frill or flounce or a new arrangement of drapery. This fluid and idiosyncratic conception of fashion, so alien to the industrialized and standardized marketplace of today, was fully appreciated by Chikanobu, who was very particular in varying the details and accessories of each costume he limned. When the imperial couple made a tour of inspection of a local area, the Empress was known to bestow pieces of cloth on the wives of local officials of high rank beforehand, so that they could wear European clothes to greet her, but they had to have the dresses made-up themselves.[9] The separation of dress form from fabric pattern was the unique and novel element for Japanese women, who previously would have only been able to select the cloth, for it would have been assumed that the form would be that of the standard kimono.

Early feminine experiments and the wider public knowledge of them meant that later experiments, especially by modern girls of the 1920s and 1930s, were perceived not so much as foreign in form but as modern, there having been an entire generation with experience, although sometimes only in print, of clothing based on non-Japanese aesthetics. While it has been argued that the Meiji Japanese never really fully adopted European costume at all—since it was worn only outside the house as a business or military uniform, a 'protection by mimicry', as nineteenth-century Japanologist Basil Hall Chamberlain claimed—it is tenable that almost all Japanese women were influenced by the visual possibilities of modern femininity in this early period.[10] This was the case even though the women's dress of Europe and America in the Meiji period was far from modern; the prominence of the body as the basis of clothing design and the valuing of change as a value in itself was instilled, rather than the genuine application of modern aesthetics in feminine dress. Japanese clothing still remained central in private life, especially for women, whose participation in employment and public life remained limited throughout the Meiji period; but their education in the dress possibilities of modernity was greatly enhanced by the (albeit limited) provision of examples by the elite, by the cataloguing of those examples by artists and by inculcation through the press and public education. The Meiji-era public world of brick buildings in Ginza and corsets and bustles had been established with contemporary Europe as the model, but private life was an extension of the Edo period, in sartorial practice and in taste, with the real changes in women's dress culture yet to come.

Taishō Decadence and the *Moga*

Change from Meiji to Taishō times exhibited many political, social and aesthetic similarities to the change from Victorian to Edwardian times. After lengthy, earnest, industrious and diligent reigns by serious and steadfast monarchs, Victoria and Meiji, there were comparable feelings of release from worlds of nationalism and self-sacrifice and entry into new ages in which novel freedoms and decadence followed as the rewards of the prolonged modernization, under Edward VII and Taishō. As with the rise of the postwar English flapper, this new, freer age in Japan also had a female personification in the form of the modern girl, the *moga*. If a specific date can be given for the emergence of the *moga*, or at least her nomination as a symbol of the anxieties and optimisms of the accelerated stage of modernity, then it was 1924.[11] In that year, Kitazawa Shūichi coined the term *moga* for an article in the women's magazine *Josei*;[12] Tanizaki Jun'ichirō's novel *Chijin no ai* (A Fool's Love) appeared,[13] featuring the scandalous *moga* Naomi (whose name became the title of the English translation of the novel); and Yamamura Kōka designed the famous woodblock print *New Carleton Dancers, Shanghai*. If the *moga* was defined, and defined the times, by her fashionable Western clothes, cropped hair, manifest freedom, taste for nightlife and unfettered physicality, then Kōka captured her appearance and her essence in this work. Aesthetically, this was the more genuine inception of a modern sartorial performance of femininity in Japan, an equivalent to the modern sartorial masculinity that had commenced decades earlier.

The ways in which femininity could be performed, from the late Meiji period, had been reinforced by the initially very conservative growth in women's magazines. Publications such as *Fujin sekai* (Woman's World, 1906), *Fujokai* (Woman's Sphere, 1910), *Fujin Kōron* (Woman's Review, 1916), *Shufu no tomo* (Housewife's Companion, 1917) and *Fujin Kurabu* (Woman's Club, 1920) at the outset advocated the *ryōsai kenbo* (good wife, wise mother) philosophy that was the official morality of Japanese women from 1898. The room within the political needs or social confines of the developing Meiji State for urban women to find agency was limited, in forms such as attitudes towards work, love and sexuality, marriage and family life, communication, changing fashions, personal fulfilment and aesthetic self-actualization. In 1920s Japan, new images of the feminine emerged in the wake of the First World War, in the embrace of consumerism. Barbara Satō argues that this constituted a form of agency sufficient to question existing social mores.[14] Moreover, Satō argues that because affordable commodities for mass consumption remained limited and full industrialization was still some way off, this early consumerism reflected mainly the fantasies identified with consumerism, and any new feminine sartorial aesthetic or agency was performed mainly in print, but that this, nevertheless, was the birth of modern feminine identity in Japan.

The *moga* became the visible product of the consumer dream and was, for Satō, a creation of the media, reflecting both the potential agency and freedom of professional working women and a sexual and social decadence that could be simultaneously repudiated and coveted. Thus, the media could redefine behavioural codes amongst urban women and habituate the population to progressive and unfamiliar roles and forms of femininity. Magazines used several narrative forms, the family article (*katei kiji*), the fashionable article (*ryūkō kiji*) and the confessional article (*kokuhaku kiji*), to articulate the modern in lifestyle, attitude and dress. *Shufu no tomo* published articles on birth control methods in January 1922, and on Western clothes and the proper way to wear them in June 1923, demonstrating the express agenda of the promotion of feminine agency and the means of visually enacting it in the early 1920s. Women's magazines also reduced the gap between rural and urban understanding and assimilation of visual modernity; taking knowledge of, and instruction in, more modern forms of feminine behaviour and dress to rural hamlets.[15]

As the evolving focus of the fashion spectacle, magazines allowed women a space to debate and explore alternative forms of femininity and a chance to effect self-cultivation and even a degree of social fluidity. Yamakawa Kikue argues that engagement with feminine modernity through magazines amounted to the domestication of modernism because of the print media's inherent conservatism. It was, as such, counter-revolutionary, redirecting the transformative energy of modernism into benign bourgeois consumption rather than into socialist, emancipating activism.[16]

Yet the resulting modern girls, whose look and behaviour was the recurring theme of many magazines, and their corollaries in art, literature and dress, were certainly revolutionary socially and aesthetically, if not politically. Women's magazines were not the only influence on modernity in femininity, naturally, and the reasons for aspiring to be a modern girl would also have included compulsory education from 1880, which, by the early twentieth century, meant that women's high school graduates increasingly sought and entered employment. Young women were not driven to become professional, working women solely for economic reasons, as the newly employed were mainly middle class; also served as a vehicle for self-actualization, a desire for which was engendered by education and had a direct sartorial correlative.

The economic boom that accompanied the First World War for Japan, and the extensive precedent of European female employment during it, also provided a stimulus for feminine sartorial amelioration, but another crucial catalyst for aesthetic reorganization was the massive destruction of the Great Kantō Earthquake of 1 September 1923. In 1924, Tokyo was still rebuilding after the great earthquake, but the enthusiasm of artists like Yamamura Kōka to represent the emerging new feminine aesthetic led them to Shanghai, the Asian capital of Western-influenced cosmopolitan nightlife while Tokyo could not provide it.

Artists and young women themselves recognized and revelled in the new incarnation of feminine beauty and its closer alignment to the aesthetic dictates of modernity. That alignment was represented both in a woman's couture and coiffure and in her deportment—a pursuit of pleasure, self-confidence and autonomy. Confidence and physicality were commensurate. The *moga* represented not just a new style of clothing but a new way of being in those clothes. The activities in which women of means were engaging drove the need for new sartorial codes. The essential and intimidating part of these new feminine activities was the element of looking. Promenading, shopping and engaging in leisure activities at the seaside all involved the element of being seen that started to permeate Japanese youth culture in the early Taishō period as part of an expanding and deliquescing fashion spectacle.

The self-confidence of these women stemmed not only from their abundant beauty and leisure but from their mastery of fashion. Modernity was present not only in the emancipatory assurance of self-actualized elegance but also in the naturalism of skin and body and the declaration of shape of *moga* clothing—both sexy and in a Kantian sense truer to both body and cloth. The worth of change in form, as a value in and for itself, was extolled in the perfect adherence to the latest refinements of fashion and in the modern aesthetic virtue of feminine attenuation. Attenuation in modern aesthetics inherently means that long slender things are chic, as with every fashion model, and they approach intangibility—being aloof, superior and irreproachable.

The modernization of women's costume became necessary in the early part of the twentieth century in Japan for three main reasons:

1. Political agenda: emancipation
2. Aesthetic demand: modernity
3. Functional need: appropriate to new urban movement and new activities women were engaged in, such as sport

These demands were somewhat contradictory. Female traditional dress had to be modernized because of the new status of women as consumers within the expanding Japanese economy and the new political agenda born of compulsory female education and the Enlightenment rationale of equality. Reform dress among English and American suffragettes had tried to duplicate male sartorial principles and thereby visually promote female emancipation. This endeavour was not merely a delayed modernization of feminine sartorial aesthetics; it was a deliberate and calculated attempt to modernize feminine sartorial principles and to institute a truly feminine version of male costume. In Japan, this process was first distinguishable with the adoption by women of the formally exclusively male *hakama*, especially at women's colleges, as a symbol of emancipation through education. As it had been in Europe, in Japan, the salient area of formal contention in the formation of an equivalent modern feminine outfit was below the waist. Male dress modernization, predominantly in the form of the suit, was not equivalent to female dress modernization, largely because female subjectivity oscillated dramatically in the modern period. In Europe and America in the 1850s, the formal means of performing gender were the most divergent perhaps in the whole history of dress, arguably as a reaction to modernity and its unfamiliar aesthetic agenda. To achieve equivalence to modern male costume, what was required was either to tame female dress to aesthetic inclinations of modernity, or to imitate male dress while maintaining the marks of difference. In Japan, costume was moderately homogenous in the Edo period—gender differentiation being primarily signalled with colour and pattern—so the inception of European clothing after the Meiji Restoration marked an altogether new system of sartorial gendering.

In the period of modernity, male costume renounced vanity and insouciance, thereby obliging the full weight of the feminine to be assumed by female dress. The male suit contained almost no element of the feminine, in accordance with the modern masculine aesthetic of seriousness, abstraction and utility. An equivalent feminine dress reform had to embrace the same Kantian adherence to a formal autonomy. As the suit had done to men's bodies, to achieve a modern feminine sartorial aesthetic a woman's body casing would need to be extensively restructured, following the principle of revealing and concealing the body in equal measure—emphasizing neither a woman's body nor her clothes disproportionately.

American dress reform in the mid-nineteenth century was informed by the aspirations to political emancipation, which was generally limited to the middle classes and did not properly include a reform in work dress. The ambition was to embody political reforms—the female equivalent of the republican principles of the suit in a female costume. The attendant objective was to lessen the degree to which a feminine aesthetic equated with male sexual desire. So American Dress Reform, as a political dress movement, contained a contradiction: women were ostensibly meant to be uninterested in the frivolity and superficiality of clothing and to avoid this, their clothing should be serious, nonornamental and self-determining. But Dress Reform itself was merely a clothing movement. As logically untenable as followers of other fashion movements claiming vehement indifference to what they wear—like contemporary counterculture anti-fashion—Dress Reform adherents nevertheless defined themselves by what they wore in a negative formulation. Consequently, Dress Reform never became a viable possibility for a modern feminine sartorial aesthetic, eliminating the route of adapting modern male dress using feminine signifiers and leaving the course of the reform of feminine clothing in line with modern aesthetic imperatives.

By the 1920s in Europe and America, female clothing of the affluent classes had attained a certain compliance with the aesthetic dictates of modernity and was regarded as definitively modern. Elites were aware of modernity, and feminine costume became a crucial sign of its enactment—primarily involving a shortening of the skirt, exposing the body, especially the legs, and creating a divided garment, a radical simplification or abstraction of ornament and a general streamlining. Aesthetic adherence to modernity was a means of establishing class distinction and affirming cosmopolitanism, but also, beyond this, it could also be a feminine instrument of self-actualization, pliable enough to reflect unique identity and aesthetic agency. From 1909, Coco Chanel brought to fulfilment the strand of feminine sartorial aesthetics in modernity in clothing systems exemplified by a new, feminine version of male dress and divided clothes. Though it was limited to the elites, Japanese women by the 1920s had an understanding of, and participated in, this modernization, as images and accounts of *moga* demonstrate.

Sport, both as an actual activity and as a metaphor in clothing design for movement more generally became a prime functional reason for the advocating of fundamental changes in feminine sartorial form in Taishō Japan and *moga* culture. In the nineteenth century, the spectrum of sports in Japan increased greatly as it had in Europe and America, corresponding with industrialization and the transformation of leisure. Middle-class leisure became a more important self-defining feature of the middle-class lifestyle— and modern leisure evolved. Accompanying this came new ways of moving and living in the female body—new ways of performing femininity in movement and new ensuing sartorial casings for that motion. In particular, the sports involved were cycling, swimming—seaside leisure in general—and tennis, all of which sanctioned a new eroticism, a new female body and a new sexual exchange. The visual consequence of the flourishing popularity of physical recreation in Japan was the novel exhibition which the female body articulated: the moving body in an envelope, which necessitated unprecedented sartorial forms.

The issue of the appropriateness of imported sartorial forms for their new, energetic applications is complicated in Japanese modernity by the question of whether equally efficient forms adapted from indigenous clothing could have been devised. Tanizaki Jun'ichirō makes this argument with regard to other products of modernity— that the choice to adopt foreign forms was arbitrary and that a modernization of Japanese forms would have looked quite different but would have been as efficient.[17] The example of Taishō sports clothing would seem to support the position of modernity as a universal aesthetic reaction to the particular conditions of developmental consciousness, rather than the possibility of modernity as culturally distinct that Tanizaki asserts. Initially Japanese leisure remained totally indifferent to Western leisure, there being a clear division between home and work throughout the Meiji period. However, by the Taishō era modern leisure activities became normalized, such that they were no longer just fads or experimentations, and the sartorial forms they took were almost identical to their European or American equivalents. Particularly important were the café society of Ginza and elsewhere, the transformation of acquisition into an act of entertainment and the enthusiasm for outdoor, seaside leisure. Many of these new leisure activities became popular at the same time as they did in America and Europe, most being internationally a strictly twentieth-century phenomenon.

The new woman principally engaging in these new sports in Europe and America, comparable to the *moga* in Japan, was the flapper. F. Scott Fitzgerald wrote about her in 1925 in the jazz age classic, *The Great Gatsby*—'She wore her evening dresses, all her dresses, like sports clothes—there was a jauntiness about her movements as if she had first learned to walk upon golf courses on clean crisp mornings.'[18] Fitzgerald captures the vitality and dynamism of the new way of performing femininity in behaviour and dress.

In the 1920s, fashion in America and Europe was defined by a totally new body awareness, which did not simply manifest itself in ideals of beauty but also went hand in hand with a more permissive society and new types of sports. Flowing fabrics enveloped the extremely stylized female figure—boyishly slim with matchstick-short hair. Jerseys and knits, wide-legged pants, fringed dance dresses, long chains or strings of pearls and opulent tassels were used to bolster the new lifestyle. This influence, far more than the unbefitting bustle dress of the Victorian age, was appropriate to modernity in Japan, aesthetically, politically and socially, and was thus adopted with far greater enthusiasm and persistence. It agreed with the feminine sartorial needs of modern developmental consciousness of Taishō Japan because these needs were identical to those of modernity elsewhere: a political need for freedom and agency, a social need to identify with modern values and conform to fashions, a functional need to move in a new physical environment, including playing sports, and an aesthetic need for fidelity to the female body and assimilation of the new visual codes of sartorial modernism.

The most interesting feature in fashion was the new preference for unevenness and asymmetry. In contrast to earlier balanced and symmetrical designs, this brought animation and tension into clothing design. The central conflict in the feminine aesthetic of clothing is one between crystal symmetry and organic symmetry.[19] Diagonal lines, cloth draped on one side only, pleated skirts, fluttering pieces of fabric as ornamentation, bows and narrow ribbons, loose trim, scarves and asymmetrically trimmed necklines allowed for considerable scope in individual designs. The love of asymmetry, which seems to be regarded as so sophisticated in modernity, involves a conscious violation of a crucial aesthetic taboo, since symmetry is at the centre of human beauty. Clothing designed to mimic the human body, as in classical architecture and other objects, is unconsciously flattering. To a degree that we hardly credit, nearly everything in our built and crafted environment traditionally echoes human shape—pediments for heads and claw and ball feet, watch faces and objects that proceed from trunk-like bases to fragile tops. One dictate of Kantian aesthetics is that clothing need only look like clothing and that it should follow a nonhuman law of design. The contradiction in sartorial modernism, unlike other crafted objects, is that clothing can never be entirely divorced from the body and there is hence an antagonism between fidelity to two forms: body and clothes. Humanist classicism is an Enlightenment-spawned vestimentary principle which, reasoning that form should follow function, abstracts only slightly from the body, while modernism, which rejects humanity as a necessary primary source of form, requires no fidelity to the body at all, only the vestimentary object itself. Asymmetry is in opposition to the body but innate in the object, and thus there is continual contention in the clothing of modernity.

While the suit, quite early in masculine clothing development, had reconciled these opposed modern aesthetic tendencies by emphasizing neither the body nor the clothes excessively, the first attempts at such a congruency in feminine clothing required major social upheavals and reordering after significant devastation that required utterly new values—like the French Revolution or the arrival of Commodore Perry's black ships with regard to masculine dress. After the First World War in France, writers and social observers produced a new image of female identity—*la femme moderne*—whose independence required a radically appropriate sartorial equivalent. The image of the modern woman—scandalous in her dress and manner, giddy with freedom—dances through most historical accounts of women in the 1920s in both Europe and Japan. Social and political independence could be directly performed in behaviour and through the visual medium of dress. The modern woman in Europe was above all a creation of the war, as that egregious event had allowed her to work and live independently for the first time. This provided a sartorial model and precedent for Japanese women, who were also seeking to express independence and agency—it provided the dress vocabulary for feminine self-determination. As a popular image, the new woman can be traced to prewar avant-garde circles, though it took the war to spread the sartorial parlance of feminine independence more widely. The new woman had embodied a modernist ideal of womanhood, pioneered by cultural radicals and representing economic and sexual freedom. But she had also been considered strictly a bohemian, avant-garde phenomenon, confined to the eccentric fringes of society where her style of life served as a critique of Victorian bourgeois culture. By contrast the *femme moderne* could be the bourgeois girl next door.

Even the clothes that *la femme moderne* wore reproduced the inability of defining her within the boundaries of traditional concepts of womanhood. Her lack of a distinctly female form symbolized the unrestrained social and cultural space she seemed to inhabit—a space that was, above all, the creation of war. While Japan had no analogous society-changing conflict like the First World War, and its wars in China and Russia inspired a nationalist revival of traditional roles and clothing for women, idealized for the soldiers, it did have a major destructive event in the Great Kantō earthquake. Many writers mention the earthquake, which razed most of Tokyo, as a moment of enormous destruction, including the destruction of women's clothing, and as a pivotal point of change, and they noted that the rebuilding of the city and the replacement of clothes that were burnt or buried tended to be more in the modern than the traditional style. The psychological renewal also permitted new ideas and forms to spread. It was just after the earthquake that Tanizaki Jun'ichirō had his vision of a splendid flapper-age rebuilding, a vision with which he eventually became disillusioned. 'But what effect has all this surface change had on the customs, the manners, the words, the acts of the city and its people? . . . Westernization has not been as I foresaw. To be sure, there have recently appeared such persons as the stick girls of Ginza, and the prosperity of bars and cafés quite overshadows that of the Geisha quarters . . . How many women and girls wear Western dress that really passes as Western dress? In summer the number increases somewhat but in winter you see not one in ten among shoppers and pedestrians. Even among office girls, one in two would be a generous estimate.'[20] (Stick girls were female gigolos who like walking sticks attached themselves to men, in this case young men strolling in Ginza.) While the earthquake did not have the totally reforming effect desired by Tanizaki, Nagai Kafū portrays the changes in the cafés as more fully modern in his *During the Rains* (*Tsuyo no Atosaki*).[21] He sees the cafés of Ginza as being outposts of the demimonde and views their sensitivity to new fashions and tastes as thoroughly modern. Tanizaki does not see changes in customs and manners as Kafū does, distinguishing between surface appearances and deeper change. For Tanizaki it is not enough that women wear modern styles; to satisfy him, they must fully assimilate them, to satisfy him, as in his novel, *Naomi*, where the *moga* title character even appears to change her face and body to look more European, an obsession which the narrator hates in himself. Writing during the 1930s at the same time as Tanizaki and Kafū, although quite a bit younger than they were, Kawabata Yasunari was more interested in physical change than his older contemporaries. He discerned a kind of revivalism directed not at Edo and the Japanese tradition but at early Westernization. He found that Western tendencies, in other words, had become thoroughly Japanized.

It is almost as if in all the debates—conducted by men—over Japanese and Western beauty, these writers actually missed the point of assimilation. Too busy with abstract notions of the feminine, the actual feminine changed, and they didn't know when. The *moga* arrived and they couldn't decide if there were suddenly too many, or too few. Modern girls seem to have been very limited in number, but enough to challenge the entire system and to capture the popular imagination in celebration or condemnation, or just plain confusion. Like the flappers, their challenge was so radical that in the reaction the pendulum swung far back the other way, with a return to traditional dress in the nationalism of the war and the period immediately preceding it. But in the larger scheme of things, the emancipation of Japanese women, both conceptually and sartorially, was irreversible, and in that revolution, the *moga* and their clothes were the pioneers. They made modernity visual, performable, and most importantly, desirable. The visual needs of the change to a modern consciousness, as dreamed of by Tanizaki, were, despite his reservations, manifested in the clothing of the *moga* women, for it was that very act of wearing that was the substance of modernism.

Sportswear, Swimwear and Movement

A predominant characteristic of the *moga* was her healthy physique and athleticism—as it was with the European and American flapper. In Japan, as well as the introduction of volleyball, archery, tennis, and golf into girl's secondary education, the 1920s also witnessed the influence of Japan's first international female sports star of the track and field, Hitomi Kinue (1907–1931), who set ten world records in seven different events at international competitions between 1926 and 1929.[22] Female athletes began to be marketed domestically, to inspire national pride, but the interest also derived in part from the contrast between conventional ideas of femininity and these strong, dynamic and vigorously independent women. The reconstructed aesthetic values of modernity meant that athletics and femininity were not necessarily incompatible. The booklet *Bijingaku* (Study of Beautiful Women), published in 1927 to teach women 'how to be a *bijin*', explains, in a chapter on sports and *bijin*, how physical exercise is conducive to beauty.[23] Again there is a Japanese emphasis on instruction in such publications—as opposed to the envy and class differentiation in their European equivalents. The change in the perception of beauty was not limited to Japan but was taking place globally at the same time, and the new emphasis on a healthy physicality greatly altered sartorial aesthetics and perceptions of appropriate manifestations of the feminine.

As with interwar flappers in Europe and America, a new philosophy was emerging in which physical activity became a space of fashion-spectacle and its product of a healthy body was considered prepossessing and feminine. The new body consciousness of the *moga* was manifested in the popularity of ocean bathing and the swimsuit, though the first bathing resort opened well before the arrival of the *moga*, in 1886 at Ōiso in Kanagawa Prefecture, primarily to service the foreign community in Yokohama. By the mid-Taishō period, however, bathing was increasingly common for young middle-class Tokyoites. In *Naomi*, Tanizaki sets several scenes on a beach in Kamakura where the *moga* Naomi swims and sports with her male companions. The narrator describes her resemblance to the 'bathing beauties' in Mack Sennett's Hollywood films.[24] The summer issues of magazines of the early 1930s often include pictures of women in the latest swimsuit fashions. The influence of Hollywood on Japanese *moga* fashions is undeniable and helped spawn the new sexuality based on a healthy physicality, but the change was essentially a product of the processes of modernism. The discourses of liberation and utility played out their logical conclusions on the bodies and in the clothing of young women with the financial ability to participate in the new fashion spectacle.

The Shōwa government saw in the characteristics of the *moga* the future of the nation, albeit a somewhat violent, futurist vision. In January 1941, the Kokumin seikatsu shidōbu (national life guidance department) of the Taisei yokusankai (imperial rule assistance association) declared that Miss Nippon should not be the old *bijin* from *ukiyo-e*, but rather a 'modern, athletic' woman with a 'suntanned face, upright carriage, rather broad stature, sprightly walk, inclination for work and keen appetite . . .' The declaration also stipulated, however, that this ideal woman should have 'gentle speech, and sound sleeping habits' as well as a 'natural, unpainted complexion, and bright, unsophisticated mind'.[25] While the physical vigour of the modern girl was applauded, there was no desire to encourage similarly active minds or social habits as the government consolidated its wartime integration. But by this time, the liberty and hope of Taishō had been replaced and disfigured, as it had been in Weimar Germany. The freedom of culture and social acceptance reflected in the *moga* and her clothing was soon to be swept away in the tide of nationalism and war.

In Japan the *moga*, with her new clothes and her invasion of the world of men, was seen as a threat by conservative elements. Within the past hundred and fifty years, Japan has witnessed the emergence of a sport culture and the concurrent acceptance of athletic men and women as cultural ideals. Yet the leisure revolution diverged immediately into separate men's and women's paths. Gender served a transcendent role in shaping the Japanese sporting experience, and the development of sports clothing was an integral part of this gendering process. To an extraordinary degree, the same definition has been used for the virile male and the athlete. Only war has rivalled sports as the proving ground for masculine behaviour. The female athlete, however, has long been considered a contradiction in terms. Conditioned by a long tradition of sex role stereotyping, Japanese women sought reassurance that womanly instincts superseded athletic aspirations, and sportswomen's appearance was scrutinized for tangible signs of femininity—rendered primarily though clothing, even when this was physically impractical.

The evolution of sports clothing reflected the development of gradual, then increasing, participation in sporting activities. The influence of sports clothing on daywear is much clearer in women's dress, where the practical need to move and the obvious metaphorical significance of freedom were in play. It was the fashions from America and Europe that already incorporated a freer, sportier, style—the clothes of the *moga*—that lasted the longest, unlike the earlier Victorian fashions, which were soon abandoned, replaced by a return to traditional kimonos. Clothing had to be appropriate for the needs of the Japanese woman in modernity, physically and aesthetically. Victorian corsets and bustles were not, but the sporty flapper-influenced clothes of the 1920s were, and thus they remained in the Japanese woman's sartorial vocabulary. Sport and more active leisure, such as seaside bathing, were part of the general acceleration of the pace of society, and clothing had to accommodate these new physical and psychological conditions.

Sport is taken on by modernizing populations, if not as military training then certainly as a metaphor for a population's efficiency and dynamism. Like fashion itself, sport was a release valve for the growing amount of spare human energy freed by industrial practice. Sports clothes and leisurewear were needed for the new activities available to the modern girl and boy for the new spaces of modernity which they now inhabited. The new activity of visiting the café required a new code of social interaction and new clothes to go with it. The aisles in department stores were considered to be like streets, meaning women could leave their shoes on when they shopped, a small sign that there were places for them, places where they were not required to be totally subservient to the family. The liberation of customs to accompany these new places went hand in hand with the adoption of Western dress: clothing that not only allows freedom of movement but represents modernity's movement as well. Clothing enacts meaning, rather than just signifying it.

Modernity has forms—it does not necessarily need a fully articulated idea. For the *moga*, the sporty clothing that she adopted as her form of modernity was as much about desexualizing her body as it was about sexualizing it. The modern girl entered into a new discourse of desire with its model being American movie culture, dynamic, fluid and vital, and her clothes reflected this. Some parts of the body, which for so long had been wrapped and hidden by the kimono, were shown by modern dress—ankles, wrists, necks, waists, hips, busts. The physical form of the female body was reflected in clothes rather than repudiated by them. This form of display is congruent with Kishida Ryūsei's concept of Western beauty as a beauty that instantly attracts, instantly shows itself.[26] Such clothing has no sense of 'stillness' because it is made to move in, to go forward towards modernity's promised ideal at full speed. That is part of the desexualization—it abolishes the secret. A woman needs to be able to be part of this modern acceleration, her clothes need to be efficient and their form needs to follow the new functions they will have. This is a dual process, both sexualizing female dress, because the female form is displayed as a functional object, and at the same time desexualizing it, because displaying this form removes its element of seduction, its mystery. These processes can become blurred—there are elements in each which echo the other. A woman's clothes no longer emphasize the body by hiding it away as something to be discovered and possessed. It is on display, it is of the order of production, because it brings itself into view, rather than being of the order of seduction which removes from view.

Cosmetics and Substance

The history of facial adjustment follows a similar path in modernizing nations, often transforming from a stylized, unisex, hierarchical system with huge adjustments for formality to a naturalistic—hiding imperfection but not remaking the face—highly gendered, nonhierarchical system, with small adjustments for formality. Underlying these changes are the principles found throughout the modernization of clothing, reflecting political empowerment, sexual emancipation and aesthetic modernity, in addition to the changes in lifestyle, economic capacity and levels of education and technology. White powder, a surviving vestige of the Edo period, remained the paramount element of make-up in Japan in the early Meiji period. The arbitrary preference for whiteness as a measure of beauty in Japanese facial adjustment remains to this day, with only minor deference to tanning by *moga* in the Taishō period. Initially lip rouge and face powder were worn only for religious ceremonies, marriages and other festive occasions; however, either because people desired to carry the gala spirit of festivals over into routine days, as that distinction broke down, or because elaborately made-up women in religious service often came to be employed as dancers and singers at secular affairs, make-up became fashionable and commonplace amongst ordinary women. The ceremonial distinction in make-up use was retained in the early Meiji period in some rural areas; however, at the same time, many traditional cosmetic practices, like tooth-blackening, eyebrow-shaving and eyebrow-painting, were discontinued and died out.

Tooth-blackening was in origin associated with puberty rites for girls, but gradually it became established as proper for all married women. The stain was made by heating iron scraps and plunging them in strong tea, often sweetened with rice wine. A powder of gall nuts was added to make the mixture adhere, and the whole substance was applied with a brush. The extinction of this practice clearly came about because these customs appeared strange, even revolting, to the eyes of foreigners who came to Japan, and an ordinance issued by the Grand Council of State in 1870 prohibited them. In 1873, Empress Shōken took the initiative in ceasing these practices, and ordinary women followed her example. In 1875, Fukuzawa Yūkichi published a satire called *The Deformed Maiden*, in which he chided women for these manmade deformities, compounding the social pressure to move away from these practices.

In the Meiji era, just as in the antecedent Edo period, the essential cosmetic base in white powder make-up was white lead particles, because they spread smoothly and adhered well to the skin. After 1887, however, recognition that the habitually use of lead powder was extremely harmful gradually came to prevail.

Indicating its foreign provenance, soap was known in the Tokugawa period under the name of *shabon*, from the French *savon*, and in 1874 manufacture of it was begun in Tokyo.[27] European-style perfume debuted on the Japanese market in 1872, when a Tokyo shop named the Arame-ya put on sale a Japanese perfume under the name 'fragrant oil of enlightenment' (*kaika kōyu*). Lip rouge used in the Meiji period was made from safflower, and it was sold and used in small cups or dishes, just as it had been in the Edo period. At that time, red was the only colour available; with this, people painted small areas of their lips in the shape of a pursed-up mouth, not all over the lips as became common by the Taishō period. The Hirao Sanpei store introduced the powder-based lotion named Komachisui to the market in 1878. The Meiji period also saw the introduction of cosmetic creams to the Japanese market. In 1908, Nagase Tomirō created a cream through a production method of his own, and obtained the first patent for such an invention. Hirao Sanpei store launched the vanishing cream called Cream Lait in 1909, and Nakayama Taiyōdō Company introduced Club Cream in the following year. Cream products came out in quick succession subsequent to these early successes, and Western-style make-up employing those creams became increasingly predominant from the Taishō through Shōwa eras.

Another aid to beauty that was characteristic of the Meiji era was hygienic facial culture, presently referred to in Japanese as 'aesthetics'. (*Bigaku* being the word also used for the academic branch of philosophy.) It was introduced to Japan around 1905, and Endō Hatsuko is said to have been the first to provide such a service in 1906. Endō Hatsuko's salon offered a facial treatment of approximately forty minutes for fifty *sen* (0.5 yen).[28] The service proved immensely popular, primarily amongst the upper middle classes. Again, revealing the growing influence of newspapers, curious reporters tried the service and popularized it among their readers.

The optimism of the early Taishō period, along with the precedent of postwar Europe, saw a greater participation of women in public affairs and the rise of the Japanese feminist movement led by Hiratsuka Raichō which established *Seitō* (Bluestocking) magazine.[29] Amongst other developments, the actress Mori Ritsuko made a trip to Europe, becoming perhaps Japan's first female international celebrity; a training school for a girls' operetta company was established in Takarazuka near Kobe; and increasingly, women obtained employment as schoolteachers, nurses, telephone operators and bus attendants. As women began to take on a larger role in public life, their make-up became both more practical for everyday use and a social necessity as personal grooming and etiquette norms were established for women in the workforce.

While traditional face powder was always white, in the early Taishō period, coloured varieties were introduced into the market, signalling a shift from the stylized facial adjustment of Edo to a more naturalistic role for facial products—hiding imperfections rather than completely remaking. Creams, whose production began in the late Meiji period, saw a further increase in demand during the Taishō era, replacing *bintsuke-abura* (pomade) or *suki-abura* (combing oil) for use as foundation. Besides the safflower rouge, lipsticks made from synthetic dyes or synthetic pigments came into production in Japan in the early Taishō period and offered the choice of a variety of colours, which facilitated the ability to differentiate cosmetics according to age. The concept of make-up in keeping with age, with cosmetic companies classifying people as students, middle-aged, elderly and so forth, also signalled a more naturalistic approach to personal grooming.

In the early Shōwa era, women gradually integrated Westernized make-up with cream and face powder into their routines along with occidental outfits and hairstyles, though many rural and working-class women still dressed in kimonos and retained the ear-covering hair with customary puffed-out back. A make-up procedure at this time consisted of smoothing a vanishing cream over the face and neck as foundation; rubbing the cream into the skin; putting face powder onto a puff and applying it evenly; sweeping extra powder off and leaving the powder that adhered well, thereby producing a smooth texture. Presumably due to its convenience, the make-up method with the exclusive use of cream and face powder spread among women from the beginning of 1935, and it was practised even after the Second World War.[30]

In the early Shōwa era, the use of lipsticks percolated among ordinary women, coexisting with the conventional safflower-made *kyōbeni* (literally, Kyoto rouge). Women used to paint their lips to appear somewhat smaller than they really were, but they began to rouge the entire area of the lips around 1940, turning their individuality to their advantage, some seventy years after the dawn of the Meiji era.

In English we use two terms: cosmetics and make-up. Cosmetics is the older term by far, meaning the art of adorning. It comes via French from the Greek *kosmos*, meaning the universe as a whole. This meaning is still central to the essence of cosmetics, which tries to create an abstract unity in the face through symmetry and a framing of features. It implies that there is a correct way to be: a propriety and decorum, an outer appropriateness, towards which to strive. The aim is to confirm the order of things, as with dress. The appearance of the whole person should be fitting to social rank. In English there is also a second meaning of cosmetic, which implies a fear of duplicity and deceit. Cosmetics could be used to signal the elevation of a lower rank to a higher one, given the existence of anxiety amongst the upper classes that their ranks could be deceitfully infiltrated. Likewise, in terms of gender relations, through cosmetics a woman may deceive a man in rank, age and appearance, engendering general anxiety that men might be deceived by women. These issues of stylization and naturalism play themselves out in the Japanese experience.

However, on the whole, the Western practice of facial adjustment is one of formal ideals expressed through the face and through the clothes—of local compliance with a greater social order. This is done by controlling disorder, and by equating order with attractiveness, an idea already essential to Japanese culture before the influence of Western facial adjustment. When finding the balance between a geometric and abstracting crystalline aesthetic and an organic aesthetic, cosmetics pull towards the crystalline. Perhaps it could even be said that there is an underlying Western continuity symmetry implying a democratic, because balanced, moral aesthetic. Georg Simmel wrote about forms being more stable, and therefore classic and more resistant to change, when they were more symmetrical.[31] A balanced form is less likely, in Simmel's view, to change with fashions. Fashion in this view is the desire for visual newness, and when a form is more classical, the desire to replace it is lessened. Thus, in cosmetic practices, the basic principles are usually to achieve a balance, a framing of features, and a conformation of social norms.

The three reasons for the origin of cosmetics include a functional one, that of actual care for the skin and body; a social one, referring to the etiquette of social communication; an aesthetic one, that of conforming to an ideal of beauty. These reasons echo the origins of clothing; aesthetic facial adjustments are, like clothing, making bodily adjustments, in how the face is cared for, how it communicates and conforms socially and how it expresses an aesthetic ideal. There was, and still is, a social need for different female face levels of formality; and to a lesser degree, mainly in terms of facial hair grooming, there are also certain male face levels of formality. In the West, there was extensive male cosmetic use in the seventeenth and eighteenth centuries, as there was in Japan up to the Restoration. However, in the West, the gendering of the Victorian age ended, to a large extent, male facial adjustment other than beard trimming. Nineteenth-century female cosmetic use was also frowned upon at the height of Victorian morality. It was thought vulgar, and used by actresses and prostitutes, and it implied a disguise.

In the Crimean War, officers wore make-up to hide their fear from the foot soldiers and the Light Brigade charged in full make-up consisting of rouge and powder. A slightly stylized war paint, but war paint nonetheless. On the whole however, in the West, the nineteenth century heralded the beginning of an age in which the use of make-up was limited to women wearing it and men looking at it. Reinforcing femininity as a social role as well as a visual one was a Western cosmetic project. Japan came late to this project, male and female clothes and cosmetics being markedly similar in premodern Japan, but engaged in it in the early Meiji period. This is demonstrated most starkly by the sudden change in the use of the image of the Emperor, changed from that of a highly made-up, feminine figure to a masculine, martial image of highly-gendered, never-used-lipstick-in-his-life strength.

No social area has been unaffected by facial adjustments; they define class, gender, status, age and sexual availability. Female apes' lips turn red when they are in heat, suggesting a sexual reason for the use of lip-colours—common to both the West and Japan long before they met in the modern era.[32] However, there are more than just sexual reasons; make-up also confirms sexual identity, a social role and formality, and expresses the aesthetic ideal of symmetry.

The ideal has no irregularity—individuality is being erased. The more formal the occasion, the less the individuality that can be expressed. Geisha, present in the highest level of stylized entertainments, are made-up to erase their individuality, their faces covered in white powder, with the features painted over the top. Formality is not subjective—there is a ceremonial urge to order things, to move towards the purity of the ideal. The ceremonial face, as with ceremonial dress, is above the everyday. It seeks to create a divine ideal—to hide all blemishes and create an abstract unity through the texture of skin, the delineation of lines, the unity of and general symmetry. This is the same as the ideal of a perfect body as part of the project of clothes.

Modernity's visual revolution—which Nietzsche called 'the great disengagement'— began with the impressionists, who replaced solid, trustworthy objects with fickle subjective perceptions of them.[33] Japan used similar images and techniques to illustrate the same process. Nietzsche associated the pictorial technique of the impressionists with a moral attitude and psychological mood. This way of thinking makes such techniques transferable to similar moods in other places and at other times. In 1932, the critic Siegfried Kracauer, describing the edgy, nervous stimuli of life in Berlin, said that metropolitan existence was 'not ... a line but a series of points',[34] a sentiment echoed in Kishida Ryūsei's description of modernity in Japan as 'beauty of the quick glance'.[35] This new means of expressing modern experience was not Western as such, a complex cultural product intimately tied up with the growth of Europe and America, but a universally appropriate expression of this new existence. Clothing and cosmetics follow the same logic—it is not merely a Western imposition of forms, but a development from the same origin within modern experience. The importance of this point is that it shows that modern phenomena were present and could be directed towards ends to do with local, Japanese discourses, paramount among which was the redefinition of Japan after its relativization by the West.

Yet in the small urban group comprising the children of modernism, the aesthetic codes of the new age were second nature, and there could be nothing more central to a modern identity, even more so than clothing, than make-up and facial adjustments. The new face was sexual and naturalistic. Popular words and expressions from the late Taishō and early Shōwa periods offer a view of the aesthetic changes that defined this time of sometimes neurotic refinement and intellectualism that was the product of the great Meiji endeavour to encompass and catch up with the West: 'It', *shan*, 'mannequin girl', 'modern life', 'stick girl', 'casino' and of course *mobo* and *moga*. 'It' referred to the Clara Bow film, Bow being the archetypal flapper in American film. Flapper culture was to some extent an international phenomenon, and the *moga* and flapper developed in concert, born out of the same conditions: economic surplus, a growing desire for further emancipation and the growing influence of visual modernism. *Shan* is from the German *schön*. It is a masculine term referring to feminine beauty. Suddenly women had sexual power and the visual manifestations of that power in clothing, cosmetics and attitude were seen as aggressive and therefore masculine. Today, the term *oyaji-garu* (old man girl) refers to the same thing with the same insecurity. If a girl smokes, drinks, is loud, likes to joke and is sexually forward, she is defined, usually by other girls, as masculine. The mannequin girl is a particular kind of beauty, the fashion model. Though models had been used in advertising even before the earthquake, the modelling business really got started in 1929. From the spring of that year all the big department stores began using them. This form of beauty is distinctly modern, a blank canvas for promotion and the beginning of universal criteria for feminine beauty.

As with flappers in Europe and America, *moga* in Japan were both a feminist empowerment and a sexual challenge, presented by members of a generation that had known only the products of Meiji modernization and none of its hardships and struggles. The visual codes they adopted with regard to cosmetics were entirely modern. They stressed naturalism over artifice. Make-up hid imperfections but did not remake the face. The sexuality was overt, young and strong, if not aggressive. Make-up was used as a tool to enhance sexual attractiveness, and this purpose was not hidden or diluted; with Kantian fidelity the brush strokes were visible. There were elements of fashion too, and the trends demonstrated, deliberately, a cosmopolitan knowledge of the world, especially American movies. In Tanizaki's *Naomi*, the *moga* Naomi becomes seemingly Western, which amounts to the pinnacle of beauty in the eyes of her obsessed lover, when she alters her make-up.[36] The sexual power of this *moga* was an allegorical representation of the seductive power of modern, foreign aesthetics and the emasculation of Japan. However, modernity was not owned by any nation more than another. The modern principles of facial adjustment became universal: a shift from stylized forms to naturalism, make-up in keeping with age, the open disclosure of the intention of sexual enhancement, and the principles of symmetry, natural colour and harmony moulded to modern convenience and periodical trends. Cosmetics followed a progression towards a modern fashion system during the Meiji and Taishō periods that was much more consistent than that of clothing, but the results were identical. Modernism brought two conflicting systems, a political and philosophical as well as aesthetic desire for rationalism, simplification, functionalism and naturalism, and an economic system and accompanying aesthetic desire that stressed visual newness, trends and fashion. The history of Japanese cosmetics, like many of the crafted objects of modernity, was a continually readjusting compromise between the two.

Hairstyles: The First Experiments

In the very early Meiji period, it was a punishable offence for women to cut their hair without permission, indicating its significance as an element of the culturally constructed notions of feminine pulchritude. However, no such prohibition existed for men, and hairstyles became one of the earliest and most readily accessible ways to flirt with foreign customs and indeed with modern aesthetics—a means of reframing the face, valuing continual change and enacting individual visual self-actualization. In the popular fiction of the late Edo period, the barbershop, like the bathhouse, had epitomized the social space for engaging in the distinctly urban spectacle of display and observation. So it was fitting that this quite modern socializing space, already associated with the fashion spectacle, became one of the first settings for visual adornment in Japanese modernity.

Foreign dress was initially expensive and difficult to obtain, but the foreign hair-cut was not, nor did it involve complicated and confusing details and observances as foreign clothing did. Its accessibility meant Japanese men were able to take to it almost immediately. Women however, already burdened with being considered the embodiment of national cultural purity, and with early modernity's extreme division of gender, came to hairstyle experimentation more slowly—as a story about play-wright Hasegawa Shigure and her mother illustrates. Hasegawa Shigure writes of how she came home one day and found that she had a new mother. Her mother's eye-brows had always been shaved, so that only a faint blue-black sheen appeared where they might have been. Her teeth had been clearly black. 'The mother I now saw before me had the stubbly beginnings of eyebrows, and her teeth were a startling, gleaming white.'[37] Hasegawa's bewilderment reveals just how ingrained the details of cosmetic gendering were at the beginning of the Meiji period, and how difficult they would be to modernize. As already noted, the women of the Edo period shaved their eyebrows and blackened their teeth, and when Tanizaki became an advocate of darkness in his late years, he developed theories about the effect of shadows in the Edo period upon the spectral feminine visages created by these practices.[38] The Empress had ceased blackening her teeth in 1873, and this elite example of maquil-lage adaptation cleared the way for further feminine experimentation with foreign adornment styles.

The Meiji word for the most advanced and modern way of cutting the hair was *zangiri* or *jangiri*, meaning roughly 'random cropping'. The older hairstyles, for samurai and commoner alike, had required shaving part of the head and letting the remainder grow long, so that it could be pulled into a topknot. So rapid and popular was the male experimentation with hairstyles that as early as 1873, only six years after the Meiji Restoration, a newspaper reported that about a third of the men in the city had the new cropped heads.[39] The speed of this restyling can be accounted for by the abolition of feudal class structures and the insistence that samurai cut off their topknot. The very first barbershop offering new-style haircuts opened in 1869 in Ginza—the barber had learned his trade in the foreign community in Yokohama. His first customer, and thus the very first example of experimentation with foreign styles, outside of the travelled and political elite, was recorded as having been the chief of the fire brigade. This initially seems inappropriate, as firemen were reputed to be among the more traditional and conservative of Tokyo urbanites, noted for vivacity and valour, so it seems that in the Meiji period tradition and change were not at odds; the one demanded the other.[40] As yet there was no cultural resistance to change or any framing of it as the destroyer of cultural things Japanese. By 1880, two-thirds of the men in the city had randomly cropped heads. The figure reached 90 per cent a scant six years later, and by 1888 or 1889, only the rare eccentric still wore his hair in the old fashion.[41] The inroads of the Western barber were far more rapid than those of the Western tailor. However, it was not really until the day of the *moga* that women really began to take part in an equivalent experimentation with coiffures. Amongst liberated and more socially mobile Meiji women, the pompadour style enjoyed popularity; it was known as 'eaves' from its way of projecting outwards in a sheltering sweep. A few geisha and courtesans adopted foreign dress from the mid-Meiji period, and several wore what was known as the 'shampoo coiffure', from its resemblance to hair let down for washing and not put back up again. However, the vast majority of women remained very restricted in what they could do or express with their hair.

The vast majority of Japanese women in the Meiji era had worn Japanese traditional coiffures. With the construction, in 1883, of the Rokumeikan, the wives and daughters of the high officials, attired in their imported bustle dresses to imitate the prevalent European vogue of the time, started to adopt *sokuhatsu* (Westernized swept-back hair) in conformity with their new clothes. Though the Japanese versions of occidental clothing were fairly accurate, imitations of foreign hairstyles were evidently more difficult or less desirable, perhaps because of physical differences in hair, so they were rendered in combination with customary Japanese coiffures, resulting in swept-back varieties or a turned-up form called *yakaimaki* (literally, soirée chignons), which was a hybrid neither entirely Japanese nor entirely foreign in provenance.

In images from about 1902 onwards, common women can be observed with a low pompadour called a *hisashi-gami* (literally, eaves-hair) or *odeko-kakushi* (literally, forehead-hiding). This style was distinct in that the frontal hair was puffed out without the traditional separation between the front and the sides. During the Russo-Japanese War of 1904, the significant capture of the strategically crucial Nihyakusankōchi, a hill overlooking the Russian Port Arthur, coincided with the popularity of the new low pompadour style, and it was therefore nationalistically called the *Nihyakusankōchi-mage*. The hairstyle was so named because the front hair was projected, the back was tight, and the sides swept up into a high bun, the shape of which was apparently reminiscent of the Nihyakusankōchi hill. This style spread over the entire country, a trend perhaps driven by its patriotic association, and thereafter, swept-back styles became increasingly prevalent in Japan.[42]

In the early Taishō period, the fashion of swept-back hair or low pompadour remained prevalent; however, around 1920, this hairstyle became extremely Westernized, resulting in the vogue for *mimi-kakushi* (ear-hiding) hair, and hair waved with a curling iron. Considered highly modern, this *mimi-kakushi* hairstyle harmonized with both traditional Japanese costume and the then increasingly popular foreign clothing—evidence of the growing hybridity of Japanese adornment and taste. The curved lines obtained by waving long straight hair comprised a technical and aesthetic innovation much more significant and appropriate to modernity than the arbitrary change from the original Japanese coiffures to the occidental swept-back styles of the Meiji era. Though a target of censure in the 1930s, the permanent wave, the short, curled hairstyle, became the most basic symbol of modern Japanese femininity. It was introduced in 1921 by a photo in *Fujin gurafu* magazine. The first curling machine, brought to Japan in September 1923, was destined for Yokohama, but it was installed at the beauty parlour in Kobe's Oriental Hotel owing to the Great Kantō Earthquake. By 1931, permanent waves ranged in cost from 6 yen to 30 yen, and after 1934, when Japanese manufactured their first permanent wave machine, the process declined in cost and increased in popularity. In Tokyo alone, 850 beauty parlours offered permanent waves in 1939.[43]

As in Europe and America, *danpatsu* (literally, cut hair) or bobbed hair came into fashion in Japan around the end of the Taishō period as an emblem of sexual maturity and agency and the larger agenda of emancipation. Immediately prior to the fashion for bobbed hair, the ear-hiding style served as a precursor to the vogue of the smaller appearance of the head. The short hairstyle was an international trend, visually symbolizing the sexual, social and political emancipatory desires of women. However, the hairstyle did not gain prevalence among the majority of Japanese women, perhaps because of lingering conservatism and nationalist dictates of femininity, and thus it required strong determination to go against palpable social constraints.

Bobbed hair was popular only among film actresses and *moga*, who were socially and financially able to pursue the latest fashion trends and the dictates of a modern aesthetic. The *moga* were almost defined by their choice of hairstyle; it drew so much attention that journalists referred to them as 'cut-hair girls'. In 1920, F. Scott Fitzgerald wrote about this flapper-age dilemma in 'Bernice Bobs Her Hair', a story about a timid provincial girl for whom bobbing represents a transition between two periods of life and two historical epochs.[44] The new style ejects her from Madonna-like girlhood, in which she was protectively cocooned in tresses, and announces her sexual maturity. Bernice fearfully acknowledges the revolutionary antecedents of the process. Driving downtown to the men's barbershop where the operation will be performed, she suffers 'all the sensations of Marie Antoinette bound for the guillotine in a tumbril'. The French revolutionaries decapitated their bewigged aristocrats in order to remake an old world. Bernice, however, has her own hair chopped to fit her for membership of a new society: bobbing conferred erotic allure on girls who were previously dismissed as wallflowers. For flappers and *moga* alike, the agency they sought in this new erotic allure was not merely individual but collective—to elevate their entire gender from the status of wallflowers.

For Japanese women, bobbing their hair was a deliberately modern act of changing character, not only individually but also collectively as a nation. In Kishida Ryūsei's essay entitled 'Modaanjo' or (Short-Haired Missy), he claims that the aesthetic preferences of the modern girl are based on Western-style beauty.[45] He states:

> This is even if there are few modern girls in Western clothes and they mostly wear Japanese clothes, for the sense of the 'beauty' they express is Western-style. The face is that of a Japanese, but it is one which skilfully endorses Western-style beauty. It is certainly not something translated nor futilely imitated, as in the Europeanization of just one period before, but constitutes an extremely natural kind of beauty.[46]

Even before clothing did so, this fashion enacted the coming of a new era. This new 'natural' kind of beauty repudiated the aesthetic regimes of old Japan, wishing into being a new sexual freedom for women, as had been shown in American movies. To show the neck, in a country where there were such highly developed notions of provocative display, was a major move for young women. As with the suit for men, bobbed hair both displays and hides the human form. It is a form of millinery dissolved into hair—part of the artifice of the hat and its function of accentuating the face while also protecting and hiding it. While hats represented going out of the home, the new hair fashion represented not just leaving the home but leaving the Japanese notion of hiding the form; bobbed hair represented entering into a spectacle of display. Aesthetically, particularly in adornment, modernity tends towards a naturalism of form—following function—rather than a stylized construction.

The fashion spectacle, which is a mutually voyeuristic notion of displaying (wealth, sexual availability, beauty and so on) is at odds with the Japanese notion of a form that withdraws—the notion of shadows which Tanizaki discusses. Ryūsei argues that modern beauty has no 'stillness' and this is seen in the Western fashion spectacle. He goes on:

> Modern beauty is a busy beauty, a beauty for a quick glance. It is a beauty which strikes the eye and is not one for aesthetic observation. But the kind of beauty where the hair has a wet black look with a boxwood comb is one where the beauty appears the more you look at it. The beauty which catches your attention, the experience of short hair and a coiffure which covers the ears, gives no aesthetic pleasure. Such hair has no inherent beauty but only functions to accentuate the face.

This aesthetic of bobbed hair announces itself, unlike the beauty of which Ryūsei speaks, which withdraws and must be sorted out. Modernity has a productive aesthetic which everywhere seeks to manifest itself. It is an idea constantly in search of a form. The Japanese notion is a seductive aesthetic which is everywhere withdrawing from view. Its attraction is not the form which is seen, but the form which is yet to be seen.

The productive urge of modernity—the idea that fashion was leading us somewhere—was a highly gendered concept in Japan as it was in the West. The representation of working women, especially within the urban socialist movements, made use of Japanese dress, in contrast to the more international style of their male comrades, implicitly placing the women in a more localized and feminized context.

While urban working-class men's clothes took on the international functional form, which displayed the muscular and violent bodies of the male workers, urban working-class women's clothes remained localized and feminized, with much symbolic weight placed on working mothers. Anxieties about modernity and industrialization were expressed as anxieties about the bodies of potential mothers. This conceptualization is still a productive one, its object being the future soldiers these mothers will bear. Such hard rational thinking is part of the application of mechanized forms to all areas of life. This is the modernism of the modern boy. The modernism of the modern girl was more about display.

It is an often noted trait of the Japanese national character, in so far as any such generalizations can be made, that there is a love of all things new and faddish. This enthusiasm, however, includes an insistence that there must remain an essence that is never assimilated into foreign influences, and that things must be kept at arm's length and considered play rather than serious change. While nothing about culture is really immutable, the very fact that this attitude exists demonstrates a certain conservative bent and willingness to believe myths about Japanese uniqueness, myths that themselves have only recently been contrived.[47] The serious debate over something as seemingly trivial as hairstyles demonstrates this, and reveals the unique problem created by the lengthy Tokugawa isolation, the idea that every foreign visual influence, however small, could be seen as a threat to national identity. Hairstyles provided the first way for the general population to flirt with Western customs and modern aesthetics. Foreign clothing was initially expensive, but the haircut was not; nor was the ability, through shifting trends in hairstyles, to enter a modern visual fashion system. From the opening of the first barbershop in 1869 in Ginza, hairstyles became a method of enacting modern visual aesthetics on the self. As a cheaper and more accessible means than clothing of experimenting with, and displaying, a new aesthetic, the doors to which, after a long-enforced closure, had suddenly been flung open, as if centuries of visual creation had all at once been revealed, hairstyles were the first words in a whole new visual language. Again they represented a foundational choice between the traditional and the modern, a choice that had to be made before all other issues of style could be addressed, and they came to represent everything, from political modernity to sexual emancipation and social reform, as well as an obvious foreign aesthetic. They were the first new self that could be tried, and because of their patent insignificance, they pioneered the way for future adornment experiments with modern aesthetics.

Kimono Reform and Traditional Identity

As with *nihonga* (Japanese-style painting), which continued to develop alongside but independently or in rejection of the foreign-influenced *yōga* (Western-style painting), a parallel strand of clothing history existed, although it was very much in a minor key. This was the reform of, and changes in, traditional forms, materials and conventions of clothing. While in the modernization of Japan's clothing and clothing conventions the Japanese most certainly chose the path of adopting modern dress of foreign provenance and adapting it to their needs, rather than the alternate route to modernity—that of modernizing Japanese dress—this other route was still travelled, albeit in terms of minor sartorial needs, and exists today in the reformed festival clothing and other continuing indigenous styles that, while often believed to be ancient in their derivation, are actually the result of more recent reforms. The kimono was the basis of a fair bit of invented tradition. Also, the adoption of *hakama* (trousers) by women in education became a symbol of emancipation; and in general, the use of materials, colours and forms by classes of people for whom these materials, colours and forms had previously been economically and socially prohibited conformed to the gradual process of general embourgeoisement which led to a samuraization of tastes.

Time

More essential, though, in the process of indigenous clothing reform, was the erosion of the distinctions between festival and non-festival time—the end of a feudal, circular, agricultural notion of time and the beginning of a modern, linear, fashion-driven notion of time. As the entire temporal structure of the way life should be ordered was uprooted, with the sudden introduction of modern ideas and foreign cultures, so too, the way that temporal order was performed and signalled sartorially also changed. The idea of fashion, which relies on a modern notion of linear time, was introduced to the general public and had its first major manifestations in the department stores' promotions of major short-lived trends. The introduction of the economic mechanisms of capitalism and the introduction of a broadly accessible trend-based sartorial system were intertwined, and the clothing once used to delineate sacred and nonsacred time was now used to generate the demand for both economic and aesthetic modernity.

During the early part of the Meiji period, working clothing or livery, as well as the everyday dress of the rural population, consisted, even in winter, of layers of unlined hemp garments. The resilient robustness of rural farmers and fishermen and the shaping of their lifestyles around the elements, instead of relying on clothing constitute a major difference between feudal and modern consciousness. Cotton and cotton cloth had become widespread as early as the middle Edo period, around the eighteenth century; however, it did not trickle down to the working clothing of people outside the major towns for some time. It was only with the sudden development of spinning and weaving techniques during the Meiji period that the hemp garment began to fall rapidly out of use.

With the development of textile factories in the Meiji period, the thin pliant cotton turned out on machines replaced the stiff homespun that had been almost tiresomely durable. The new cloth took dyes easily and made more attractive clothing. It was perhaps the long-wished-for end of the history of the hand-loom that made the material most practical and most attractive to the women who would use it to make the nation's clothes.

Silk has been used in Japan from time immemorial, but throughout premodern history, it belonged exclusively to those who were not of the working class, being restricted by price and by sumptuary laws. Not until the Meiji period did it slowly spread, like rice, among the common people. Also during this period, muslin became fashionable, and the famous Yūzen Dye-works of the Tokugawa period became the Muslin Dye-works. Neither silk nor muslin, however, was used for work clothing. Both were treasured for gala dress, and in that sense, usage differed from later practices among women in the urban areas.

One great principle observed in the mores of premodern Japan, as in feudal societies everywhere, was a clear distinction between ordinary routine days and festive occasions. The time chosen to be sacred is generally a civilization-defining attribute and of the highest importance. The attitude of the Japanese people towards life was, in a sense, dominated by this distinction. It is evident from many old verbal expressions that in the minds of premodern Japanese, everyday clothing was a completely different thing from fancy occasional dress, as with food. Expressions such as 'everyday rice' and 'everyday rice container' were clearly used for distinguishing everyday food from food used on festive days. The latter was in many places called, literally, 'different food'.

Sechi, the old term for ceremonial days, appears to be etymologically related to the word that signifies the joints of a bamboo stalk. Festive days were thus probably thought of as dividing the year into seasons, just as the joints divide a stalk of bamboo into sections. This is the most logical division in a feudal society where wealth is based on the land and on agriculture. The usual yearly festival days were spoken of collectively as the 'annual activities' (*nenjū-gyōji*). They were by no means determined arbitrarily, and in general, the basis for them lay in agrarian life, with most of them occurring at the beginning or end of some phase of the annual farm work, when it was considered necessary to offer devotions to the gods for a successful crop. In addition to the 'annual activities', there were personal days of celebration such as the days of birth, marriage, coming of age and attaining a propitious age. These events also had a special status and hence a different sartorial code.

Despite religious prohibitions, there must always have existed an instinctive desire to carry over the gaiety and pleasure of the festive occasions into ordinary life. In the Meiji period, this became, in many instances, financially feasible, and with a loss of faith in the old gods and disconnection from the land due to urbanization, the ancient distinctions began to fade away. This began in the cities, where ideas founded on agricultural life did not have a strong hold anyway, and later gradually spread to the rural areas, thanks both to a strong Japanese tendency towards adulation of urban life and to increased population movements.

There were many variations in the material and cut of festive dress at the beginning of the Meiji era, and the government, bent on enlightenment, took a number of steps to encourage uniform modern standards. Decrees were issued intermittently, but few of them had much effect among the bulk of the population. Still, since festive dress was worn only rarely, and had little to do with the requirements of everyday life, it was comparatively easy to change, and it began rather quickly to show the influence of the new culture. The first Meiji regulation concerning clothing was the chancellery's proclamation of 12 November 1872, which ordered the substitution of Western dress for the ceremonial robe and crown hitherto worn by noblemen at court. There were, naturally, reactions among the more conservative against the adoption of foreign styles, but the tendency towards imitation of the occident proved irresistible.

At first both hemp and cotton were used for everyday clothes, but gradually the former was displaced by the latter. Until the Meiji era, the women in farming villages made thread and wove clothing for their entire families, but with the development of the textile industry and the importation of cheap cotton from abroad, the production of Japanese short-fibre cotton and fabrics made from it tended to decline. In many locales, the change resulting from manufactured goods came around the middle of the Meiji period. An interesting side effect was that the old practice of starching cotton fabrics until they were stiff—a remnant of the age of hemp—fell into disuse. From about the 1880s, it is said, rural women began to look soft and gentle even from a distance.[48]

After the Meiji Restoration the sumptuary restrictions were abolished, and in theory people might wear the gaudiest clothes within their means, but in the earlier half of the Meiji period, kimonos were relatively conservative, in line with a general samuraization of tastes. Men and women alike preferred dark blue or brown silks, usually with a quiet stripe or plaid. The emancipation of colour first became visible in the summer cotton kimono. Traditionally, this had been a very plain garment, but at summer festivals, when everyone dressed similarly and there was a celebratory collective identity, a bolder design could be selected. In 1905, the Mitsukoshi clothing department introduced ladies' silk kimonos with *genroku* designs, so called because they resembled the bold, flashy patterns popular in the Genroku era (1688–1703), and this proved to be a milestone. By the next year, styles that suggested the dazzling gold and silver of the Momoyama period were in favour, and brilliance had become the main feature in women's fashions. It is worth noting that women began to allow the border of the undergarment to show at the collar of the kimono, and this seemingly small touch came to be considered a very important part of their attire. Perhaps this was a result of the more general influence of Western clothing, in which a white shirt appears underneath the suit, or perhaps again a result of the process of undergarments becoming outergarments as formality began to fade away in modernity. The material was originally silk crepe, and the colours employed were red, purple, blue or yellow, the shades varying according to the age of the wearer.

These changes were largely confined to urban Tokyo, and, for that matter, to only a segment of the population there. Rural areas were inclined to imitate city life in many respects, but they held rather stubbornly to traditional apparel, for financial as well as cultural reasons. Still, the shifting fashions of the metropolis, kaleidoscopic though they were, reflected important cultural trends. Primarily, they illustrated graphically that the people were slow to take advantage of the new freedom resulting from the rout of the Tokugawa shogunate—samuraization was the preference in taste. This very probably means that colourful or luxurious clothing was so closely associated with festive days that it was not considered proper for ordinary wear until the distinction between special and routine days had well-nigh disappeared. Also, the confusion between Western and Japanese clothing was at its height during the late 1880s, the very period when the government was trying to decide between monarchy on the democratic plan and German Kaiserism à la japonaise. After the Russo-Japanese War, styles, like public sentiment, reverted to tradition. Extreme Westernization came in for a general reappraisal, and there was a strong trend towards clothing resembling that of the Momoyama period, possibly the most thoroughly Japanese, if there can be such a thing, of all epochs in the nation's history. The most pronounced change, however, was the collapse of the distinction between the festive and the ordinary, which had hitherto amounted to a strict rule of life and certainly of sartorial life. The mixing of these two concepts, the festive and the ordinary, even began to spread from the cities to the provinces, though not too rapidly.

In the Meiji period, Western dresses for women were fashionable only as formal attire for the elite. Women at work, either on the farm or elsewhere, wore more traditional clothing, especially for household work. In 1872, when the first Japanese textile mill was set up in Tomioka, Gumma Prefecture, the young girls employed as reelers wore men's striped *hakama* to work. This was a little strange, considering Japanese sartorial gendering, but it was difficult to work in long kimonos, and it would hardly have done to dress in farming apparel: new labour required a new dress code, and it must have seemed logical to borrow a garment from the sex that was traditionally associated with out-of-the-household employment. Subsequently, the *hakama*, which had until then been strictly limited to masculine use, was adopted by girl students as well as factory-working women, and became a symbol of—albeit limited—emancipation. It is still worn today at graduation ceremonies by young female graduates, while men wear Western suits. By 1900, a type of *hakama* that had no division between the legs had become very popular among women. In 1907, the following instructions were issued to teachers in the schools of Hiroshima Prefecture:

> The female instructors in primary schools will engage in physical training just as male instructors, and both in and out of school they will be expected to be quick and alert. Accordingly, on the school ground they will wear narrow-sleeved kimonos and *hakama*.[49]

This, incidentally, is the first example of clothing regulations for women teachers in the rural districts. During the last years of the Meiji period, women in urban schools, instructors and students alike, more often than not wore the *hakama*.

As for the Imperial Household and the aristocracy, they were aware of the importance of preserving traditional forms, albeit for new uses—no longer to define festive time but to forge a national identity—and the need for reform. Noting the history of top-down reforms in the history of Japanese women's clothing, the Meiji Empress made a proclamation advising women to adopt Western fashions but advocating the use of Japanese talents and materials:

> From olden times there have been imperial regulations regarding women's clothing. Some examples are the Taika Reform of 645 during the reign of Emperor Kōtoku [reigned 645–654], the guidelines for imperial court uniforms during the reign of Empress Jitō [690–697], and the taboo against wearing clothing folded left over right during the era of Empress Genshō [reigned 715–721]. During the reign of Emperor Shōmu there was an ordinance especially for women to wear a new style of costume. At that time women's clothing consisted of two parts, the kimono [or outer jacket] and the skirt. Some women wore many layers of skirts and an ordinance was issued prohibiting this practice. As a result women in town and countryside generally wore a single red skirt until the medieval period. From the Nambokuchō period [the mid-fourteenth century], a time of warfare, the kimono was worn for convenience without the skirt; the outer jacket was simply lengthened to cover the legs. More recently, during the Empō period [1673–1681], the obi became wider, paving the way for today's clothing style. However, it is not normal to wear only tops without skirts. From olden times the progress of culture depended on conforming to the old order. Now we can no longer restrict ourselves to bowing from a kneeling position, but will have to observe the Naniwa [Osaka] style of bowing while standing. Moreover, if we look at contemporary Western women's wear, we find that it combines a top or jacket [kimono] and a skirt in the manner of our ancient Japanese system of dress. This is not only suitable for the formal standing bow but is also convenient for action and movement and makes it only natural to adopt the Western method of sewing. In carrying out this improvement, however, be especially careful to use materials made in our own country. If we make good use of our domestic products, we will assist in the improvement of techniques of manufacture on the one hand, and will also aid the advancement of art and cause business to flourish. Thus the benefits of this project will reach beyond the limits of the clothing industry. In changing from the old to new, it is very difficult to avoid wasteful expenditures, but we can certainly achieve our goal if everyone, according to their abilities, makes a special effort to lead a frugal life. These are my aspirations for the reform of women's costume.[50]

The Empress's aspirations did not come to full fruition for many decades, and not in the form she imagined, either. Most Japanese retained Japanese styles, and even the women of the aristocracy returned to them after a brief flirtation with foreign styles in the early Meiji period. Also, the industrialization of clothing production and the rise of modern methods of sales and advertising in a demand-driven, modern capitalist economy militated against her perceived need for thrift. However, as a statement of the general principles of Japanese modernization, the proclamation is quite accurate. The principle of just taking what was needed from Western cultures and adapting it to Japanese needs was the model for much of the clothing reform that actually took place over the long term.

As the early Meiji elite knew, Japan had very suddenly jumped from feudal to modern times, without the centuries of enlightenment and reforms that Western populations had had to soften the process. The principal means for ordering time and hence clothing had been agricultural and—as Shinto is, arguably, principally a nature cult—religious. With the Meiji era's rapid secularization and urbanization, the old framework for ordering life was eroded and broke down. The festive clothing once reserved for special times was soon demanded as means and wants dictated, rather than as seasons did. The ever more porous distinction between sacred and nonsacred time meant that the ordering principles of life and clothing dissolved. However, rationalization movements, which debated what the most rational shape and style of clothing should be in the West, were severely limited by the speed of modernization in Japan. Without centuries for clothing to evolve a simplified structure, the greatly increased production capacity and financial means of early-modern Japan meant that what was demanded was not, on the whole, a new rationalism in clothing, but the best of what the Japanese already knew. This meant that samurai tastes, finer cotton materials and festive styles constituted the direction of most Japanese clothing desires in the Meiji and Taishō periods. In terms of both fabric and fabrication, the mass of the population acquired—or perhaps more accurately, were at last financially and legally empowered to demand—the taste for samurai clothing. The samurai class had been abolished, but now Japan had a whole nation of samurai. As an accompaniment to the deliberate indoctrination of Bushido values, there came a desire for Bushido clothing. As the ordering principles of the agricultural calendar, with its circular movement of time, gave way to a modern linear notion of time with the values of progress and development, so too came the introduction, in Japan, of a fashion system.

The rapid change in the availability of materials, especially cotton, allowed the kimono to become a much more common item, and the embourgeoisement of the population allowed more and more people to afford it. Wealth brought traditional tastes, and while new ideas were making the money, it was being spent on traditional clothes—the home and work division, in clothing and values, is one that remains in place today. The process of change in the Meiji period involved a great deal of invention of tradition, as part of the larger project of creating a national identity which could be used for the benefit of the State. The example of the *hakama* as a symbol of female emancipation and education seems to be anomalous—indigenous clothes were mainly used for reinforcing traditional values. But by the Taishō period, the department stores started the marketing of trends in kimono designs, and what was once a symbol of tradition became part of the system of capitalism and the artificial creation of demand that is the modern fashion system.

–5–

Conclusions: A Theory of Costume
for Japanese Modernity

This chapter uses the narrative so far constructed of the history of Japanese clothing modernity to investigate how far generally established theories of fashion do or do not apply in the Japanese context. The question of how Japanese sartorial modernity differed from European and American sartorial modernity and how it was similar is perhaps best answered by privileging the aesthetic discourses of modernity over other discourses—such as class—in the practices and fashions of Japanese clothing in the early modern period. Other considerations in the explanation of fashion, such as conspicuous consumption, a dialectic of imitation and deviation, or inorganic cycles of repetition, are still in varying degrees applicable. But in the Japanese circumstance, the formal structure of clothing and how it changed was governed, to a degree perhaps greater than elsewhere, by adherence to, or rejection of, the aesthetic dictates of modernism. Naturally, not all elements that can affect the fashioning of sartorial form operate to the same degree and at the same time. While modernity is ubiquitously equated to the spread of individualism, the destabilizing of religious epistemology, and alienating technological acceleration, the late entry of Japan into these processes meant that they collided with certain sartorial forms at entirely different points in the process from that of the West, and the resulting sartorial hermeneutics and applications are thus also radically divergent from their Western models. The Japanese example of the development and operation of a fashion system is unique and useful because it challenges many of the assumptions upon which modern fashion theory is based—modernity before industrialization, dissimilar class systems, practices of performing gender and visual sexual exchange, entirely distinct conceptions of self and community identity and intellectual traditions. This book has aimed to test the canon of fashion theory by using the Japanese experience and to draw attention to an ignored aesthetic component in fashion's governing dynamics, which the particular modern dress history of Japan accentuates.

The cat in Natsume Sōseki's satirical novel of middle-class Meiji society and the aping of Western customs, *I Am a Cat*, says, 'Man without clothes is not man.'[1] As he also says, the history of human beings is the history of clothes, not that of flesh and bones. Mankind is, for the cat, the wrapping rather than the substance, as this is where agency is situated. To extend this abstraction, it is the fashion that defines the man rather than the clothing objects themselves. Fashion is what defines, rather than clothing itself, and fashion is essentially a process of aesthetic change. It is about judgement. The history of the objects themselves—Japanese clothing—as opposed to the ideas, values and meanings—the fashions—that get encrusted onto them over time is obviously unintelligible without a discussion of the hermeneutic structure of fashion in which it is situated. Jacques Derrida argues that even a history of madness would have its own idiosyncratic reasons, its own governing logic, whether we can fathom it or not: 'That all history can only be, in the last analysis, the history of meaning, that is of Reason in general . . . '[2] And as Roland Barthes argues, history no longer documents 'the real' but produces 'the intelligible'.[3] Fashion is what makes the aesthetic changes in clothing, and other forms, intelligible over time, and this book has therefore been an examination of that conceptual structure rather than of Japanese clothing itself.

The other broad conceptual framework that has provided a structure of meaning for this examination of the forms of clothing is modernity. There are broad congruities between the periodization of the development of Meiji culture and that of Meiji modernization. They are seldom identical, but both find their wellspring in the flood of Western influence to which Japan had to respond. One useful metaphor is that of a wave that might break at different points along the shore, in response to the features of the land and the resistance it encounters, but is nevertheless one single wave. And that wave is overwhelming. As Irokawa Daikichi has phrased it, 'The influence of European and American civilization on Japan during the 1860s and 1870s was traumatic and disruptive to a degree that is rarely found in the history of cultural intercourse . . . For a time, any thought of defending traditional culture was scorned as an idle diversion from the critical need to respond to the urgency that faced the country.'[4] Kon Wajirō has said that the sole cause of the thoroughgoing change in Japanese culture was the arrival of the American *kurofune* (the black ships): 'The *kurofune* frightened the Japanese into thinking that Japan might be occupied unless she completely renewed her military defence and shocked them into thinking that they had to change their clothes too.'[5] Clothing was a central part of this original political imperative. It had to be modernized, as a sign of a capacity for rapid change, as a demonstration, to the foreign powers imposing unequal treaties, that Japan occupied one of the highest ranks of civilization, and as a tool for effecting genuine reform in the mindset and daily practices of the populace.

H. Suganami has argued that although two hundred years of domestic peace had made the samurai aristocracy largely redundant in terms of their original function as warriors and turned them into civil administrators, they maintained their traditional mode of thinking as military experts, separating strategic and tactical objectives: this helped the Meiji leaders to rule out strategically irrational options in responding to the Western threat, and consequently they understood the importance of technology, which they had no qualms about importing. China, with a civilian mandarinate, in contrast, had almost no interest in military and technological matters and even disdained them.[6] In one of his conversations with Chinese general and statesman Li

Hongzhang in 1876, Mori Arinori, then the Japanese Minister to China, justified the Japanese adoption of Western clothes by saying that the old Japanese clothes were loose and comfortable, suitable for those people who wanted to live peaceful and uneventful lives, but they were totally unsuitable for those who worked hard.[7] The flexibility of the Japanese elite, for whatever reason, made it possible for clothing to be considered as a tool in the early Meiji period, rather than as an expression of essential identity, and thus it was liberated from the conceptual framework that governed its use, with the result that it could also be used for aesthetic expression.

'Multi-functional and multi-meaning as the clothes may be, it is not the case that all their functions are equally important; at a certain time one function may dominate others. The same is true of the signs expressed by clothes; a certain sign is regarded as most important during a certain period.'[8] In the early Meiji period, the principal discourse in the adoption of new clothing was between Japan and an imagined monolithic West, and it was primarily political, without regard for the later discourses, such as those of class or gender or group imitation or aesthetic expression, that the first discourse would inevitably spawn. In the early Meiji period, clothing forced a foundational choice on each wearer—though this was limited to those with the capacity to make such a choice and it excluded, for the most part, those who were not male, wealthy and urban—between accepting modern, Western clothing or rejecting it. Immediately after the Restoration, the urban political elite, embracing foreign clothing, formed a politically motivated avant-garde in clothing, ahead of groups such as artists, writers and intellectuals who might normally constitute such an avant-garde movement. And this was because it was understood to be a military and political imperative, for the very survival and independence of Japan, to simply imitate modernism in all its forms without necessarily understanding it or examining all the consequences that such a rapid change might bring.

The avant-garde actions and clothing of early Meiji politicians stand in contrast to the world they created. Meiji cultural leadership by a dynamic elite was intentionally succeeded by a formal bureaucracy, which would make impossible the kind of leadership that accomplished the Restoration. By the end of the Meiji era, the radicalism was replaced with conservatism, and by the Taishō period, a substantial cleavage existed between the modernizing State and the modernizing society. The tension between embourgeoisement and the statist claims of imperial Japan resulted in the transformation of the distinctly political, and the emergence of the concept of society as an autonomous structure. Taishō-period thought and action appeared to reject the political, and as with so much else, inclined to cosmopolitanism. Harootunian argues that the belief in the perfectibility of the aesthetic and rational faculties of the individual independent of political conditions forged a new conception of personality in Taishō Japan. The resulting rejection of politics, implicit in the veneration of culture and creative personality, led not simply to indifference but to the deployment of culture as a surrogate for politics. The uses of clothing were an implicit demonstration of this; they were used as essential vocabulary for the visions afforded by modernity in Japan: visions both of the cosmopolitan future of the social and the fascist future of the State.[9]

Through the course of the seventy-odd years of the Meiji, Taishō and early Shōwa periods, the Japanese consciousness was transformed from feudal to modern. Early on, perceptions of self were altered—partially deliberately by the State—through changing attitudes and relationships with the body. The body had been conceived as a form that had to be wrapped and hidden, but Western clothing introduced a new understanding and way of looking at the body. Western principles of hiding and displaying the human form in equal measure were an obvious metaphor for, and element of, the coming rise of individualism and dynamic modern life. The change in attitude and perception of the body through clothing forced an artistic reevaluation of the human form and of artistic representation in general—a process that Western arts had been engaged in since the Renaissance—and the installation of man and the human body as the measure of all things.

For the still largely feudal consciousness of the early Meiji Japanese, this presented a profound challenge, spearheaded through clothing, but the Japanese elites had been to the world fairs and expositions and had taken on board the lessons of Darwinism that were so greatly emphasized by the anthropology and science of the period. To Western eyes at the time, clothing represented a civilization's level of evolution. The world's first international exposition was held in London in 1851, and in 1859, Darwin's *Origin of the Species* was published, with both the book and expositions being introduced to Japan within about twenty years. Ōkubo Toshimichi utilized expositions to exhibit the products, and their advantages, of his policies of industrialization and thus accelerate the process, and Darwinism was popularized as an organic theory of social evolution and did its part to impede political liberalism.[10] We can only speculate about the degree to which the new Meiji leadership actually believed in the Darwinist schemas of evolution, rather than simply acting in accordance with a strategic conceptual framework, simply seeing the sartorial transformation of the army, leadership and people as a means of visually demonstrating their racial equality to the West. It was a survivalist act, initially. Whether they believed in the science or not, they came to see the transformation of clothing and simple customs as a tool with which the State could infiltrate and reform everyday life, and through these simple everyday changes, whose recent invention would be easily forgotten, transform the population from a passive, feudal populace into an active, modern citizenry.

The programme of enlightenment, as advocated by the early Meiji State, was an attempt to accelerate the growth of concepts like individualism, reason, enterprise and civic responsibility in the European mould. The collective sloth of feudal Japan had to be shaken off, and all citizens were required to take part in the creation of the new State. State-led modernization was not simply economic and political but involved many painful cultural transformations, such as the transformation in clothing, and a process of profound contradiction and conflict. The people were not simply passive victims of the cultural transformations engineered by the State. Some of them volunteered to participate in the process, and many others, perhaps unwittingly, resisted it. But they did so within the broad framework dictated by historical conditions, in which the non-West had to take the West as its model in order to resist it.[11] In the imperial mandate of 1871, the Emperor reasoned that modernization was imperative in order to maintain the independence of the state. There was a great contradiction in Japan's adopting Western culture to fight against the West. Meiji Japan was a typical case of antagonistic acculturation. The historian Arnold Toynbee characterized Meiji Japan's attitude towards Western civilization as 'Herodian', as opposed to the 'zealot' attitude towards other civilizations.[12] Wearing Western clothes was in harmony with the 'getting out of Asia and entering Europe' (*datsu-a nyu-o*) policy.

The notion that the change to Western clothing constituted an enlightenment with regard to their nakedness was a culturally condescending notion for the early Meiji Japanese, with the sudden framing of indigenous clothing as backward and primitive. This perception righted itself as Japan gradually became more culturally and politically confident through the Meiji era, and as indigenous styles themselves went through a process of reinvention and modernization. The introduction of the new stimuli of both Western eroticism and Western prudery created both confusion and a fusion of values and styles with regard to clothing and its sexualization. The general enrichment of the population also led to the widespread dissemination of samurai tastes and morals, which were generally conservative with regard to the body and the way it was covered. There was a desexualizing of the body by showing it, and the change, often commented upon, from a seductive aesthetic of hiding to a productive aesthetic of showing. But the Japanese regulated this serious challenge to their bodily and sartorial identity through inner and outer conceptual barriers, wearing Western clothes in the street but kimonos at home, or through a reduction of Western styles to play, insisting that they were not a serious challenge by treating them with a faddish, playful, enthusiasm rather than with the reverence reserved for native styles. Even today, though it is barely defensible, the argument of an unchanging Japanese sartorial essence and an outer changeable Western veneer is still regularly put forward, even though many of the styles claimed to be evidence of the immutability of the Japanese people were in fact Meiji inventions or adaptations. The argument echoes the idea that the Emperor, symbolic of the nation, contained the duality of a dynamic, modern, changing nation and a transcendent, unbroken, link with an eternal Japanese past.

The materials with which to make clothing changed greatly through the Meiji period as a result of the opening of trade, industrialization, and the lifting of restrictive sumptuary laws. The importation of wool was essential for the spread of Western styles, through uniforms and through suits. The drastic reduction in the cost of cotton, imported from China, and silk, newly spun on machines, greatly increased the availability of these materials, though they, as well as wool, were initially utilized mainly for kimonos and native styles, so that the first real widespread modernization of Japanese clothing was a revolution in fabrication and texture rather than in form. The introduction of new colour dyes, outlawed in the Tokugawa period, led to an explosion of colour, especially in rural areas, and the introduction of fashion plates brought a knowledge of Western patterns and styles, though this was restricted to the wealthy. Later, the introduction of the sewing machine greatly increased the speed at which clothes could be produced and the level of experimentation that could be attempted.

The real material story was one of consolidation: luxury items, silk and cotton, once reserved for the samurai, became more readily and cheaply available throughout the nation, while the use of hemps and worsteds died away. In the main, this happened within the forms of indigenous styles, with the spread of Western forms, mainly popularized by the army and school uniforms, coming later. In general, the Meiji period saw a samuraization of tastes on the whole, with only a small, rich avant-garde experimenting with Western styles.

When the more general demand for Western clothing did come, it was motivated by the time men spent in military service, developing a taste for Western materials, for Western clothing structure and flexibility and, at the physical level, for Western furniture. Education also stressed a Western focus and had a Western model and idea at its core, thus orientating Meiji youths towards a taste for Western things. The new clothing was in many ways impractical until the lifestyle was lived and the stages for that lifestyle were built. Western chairs, desks, cafés, department stores, vehicles, sports and footwear protocols were all things that altered the way the Japanese worked, consumed and relaxed, requiring new forms of clothing, but these things took time to establish, and so the change was gradual and often involved sartorial dualities. Thinkers and writers responded to Japan's modernity by describing it as a doubling that imprinted a difference between the new demands of capitalism and the market and the force of received forms of history and cultural patterns. Although this doubling was frequently seen as a unique emblem of Japan's modern experience, its logic showed that modernity everywhere would always result in what Watsuji Tetsurō and others called a 'double life' (*nijū seikatsu*) and what Ernst Bloch, commenting on German life in the early 1930s, described as the 'synchronicity of the non-synchronous, the simultaneity of the non-contemporaneous'.[13] The Japanese lived this sartorial dualism for a century, differentiating their public and private lives through clothing. However, as the Western clothes worn in public became more or less standardized, and as the schoolboy's uniform spread from the public to the private school, the standardization of clothes began to penetrate people's private lives.[14]

The primary motivators in the change from native to Western dress were often disasters. The wars of the Meiji era increased the size and influence of the military and spread knowledge of, and preference for, divided garments throughout the male population. The various fires in Tokyo and other urban centres emphasized the need for women especially to adopt clothing that allowed for greater freedom of movement; the Great Kantō Earthquake destroyed much of what remained of Kantō's traditional clothing, and the reconstruction fuelled a great demand for Western clothes, which by then were being machine-made. The disasters of 1923 and 1945 both brought about sudden increases in the frequency with which women wore Western dress— although the victims of the 1932 Shirokiya fire were still in Japanese dress. In the postwar years, Japanese dress became so uncommon that it also became uneconomical. Low demand eventually led to high prices. Old weavers died, old techniques fell into disuse and those who had to have Japanese dress, such as geisha, had to pay high prices for superior pieces, as did those preparing marriage trousseaux.[15] The Second World War was also a catalyst for great sartorial changes. The reconstruction that followed the disastrous bombing of Japanese urban centres brought about the final wave of clothing change that reduced the regular use of kimonos in daily life to the level it remains at today. The various crises accelerated the rate of change at certain points, rather than being the sole reason for the change, and the media and the State played a considerable part in using these events to effect change.

The other party interested in the switch from traditional clothing styles and consumption to Western clothing and consumption was capital. Once manufacturers and retailers began to understand the profits to be made from a fashion system that regularly changes styles, and from a broad and unrestricted availability of products, they pushed the Japanese along the path towards modern materialism by a range of methods. The democratization of consumption that the rising department stores allowed was perhaps the major factor in the modernization of women's dress, along with the parallel rise of advertising. As Weber argued, a principal element in the evolution from a feudal to a modern consciousness was the creation of demand and of new motivations to work. Originally, in Japan, the motivation was not Protestantism, as Weber claims was the case in the Low Countries and in England, but the imminent threat posed by the vastly technologically superior military forces of the West. Later, the motivation became the culture of materialism and mass consumption fed by advertising. The principal commodity of early Japanese capitalism was clothing, and the fact that department stores could market both Japanese and Western styles aided in the creation of a seasonal fashion system and market. The Japanese local media, newspapers and magazines, always enjoyed some of the highest readership rates in the world, and were a major factor in pushing new clothing agendas.

In the spirit of the Fukuzawa books, Japanese magazines tended, and still tend, to be more instructional than their Western equivalents, which often have a class agenda and rely on exclusionary envy. The Japanese lack of exclusion can perhaps be explained by a particular feature of Japanese class development that has led to certain peculiarities in fashion. Since Japan went from rigidly sartorially coded feudalism straight to modernity without any of the Enlightenment and preindustrial stages of Europe, the aristocracy never developed a fashion system of exclusion— which involves, as Veblen theorized it, fashions changing fast enough to distinguish ruling-class clothing from middle-class clothing. The bourgeoisie rose so fast, after the long period of isolation, that the ruling samurai, now officially abolished, did not have enough time to develop social and dress structures that might have stopped the bourgeoisie's rise and allowed the samurai to differentiate themselves. Thus today, while Prada and Louis Vuitton signal in the West that you are different because you have something exclusive, in Japan they just signal luxuries that are universally available (40 per cent of all women aged fourteen to fifty-nine own at least one Louis Vuitton item). Luxury is something almost everyone can access. This instruction provided by magazines, based on a playful and interchangeable approach to fashion rather than on one that reaffirms social status through exclusion, fits well into a middle-class sensibility in which conspicuous consumption is more subtle than it is in an aristocratic sensibility. The Japanese merchant class still follows the principle of class-based sumptuary regulation. Finery is in the details, understated and subtle, in a semiotic sartorial efficiency which is better suited to the social interactions of trade and in which the middle class defines itself against the overt, flamboyant and aristocratic samurai sartorial codes.

The role of clothing in visual gendering was greatly transformed in the period of modernization in Japan, as it was throughout modernizing Europe. Masculinity is signalled through form as well as colour, and increasingly through metaphor: dark colours to indicate the seriousness of men in society and brighter colours to indicate the ornamental role of women; streamlining to indicate stoicism and agility; tailoring to indicate a modern relationship with the body, displaying and hiding it in equal measure—balancing the twin psychological urges of exhibitionism and modesty. It was a kind of Freudian reasoning applied visually. All these visual discourses of gendering and finding sexual forms appropriate to modernity are replays of, or played at the same time as, Western discourses and are thus always infused with the other central issues of cultural appropriation, national identity and aesthetic integrity. Japanese women's clothing in the Meiji and Taishô periods plays out these anxieties, returning to indigenous styles and becoming a symbol of Japanese national essence. This replays the nineteenth-century Western extremes of gender differentiation in dress, with male clothes ruthlessly stripped of decoration and female clothes at their most ornamental. The Meiji state had much more power than its predecessor, the Tokugawa shogunate, to impose the gender asymmetry that characterized the new comprehensive vision of national development in Japan. Neither orthodox Neo-Confucianism, nor Bushido, nor some amalgam of this with forward vision, advocated a public role for women, however, Tokugawa Japan imposed its will on women quite unevenly, while the Meiji state could be much more thorough.[16] The rise of a modern bourgeois sensibility saw the end of culturally sanctioned male vanity, flamboyance and insouciance: and the ceaseless mercantile effort to prove one's wealth diverted ambition from more luxuriant forms of self-expression in menswear. In Japan, as in the West, the civilized centre became the governing principle of male dress, defining itself against the extremes of decadent aristocracy and dishonourable poverty; against the underdressed working class and overdressed Dandyism; and against ornamental and nonfunctional femininity.

As well as the desire to display gender and personal wealth—both internally driven motivations—there was also the pull from the supply side, the profit-driven advertising of modern clothing and the system ensuring its constant replacement—fashion—and its promotion by department stores and elsewhere. This part of the awakening of a new modern consciousness, which freed people to think that they could change their material conditions—class, employment, attractiveness, status—through reform of their ways of life, gave rise to a more fluid, visual culture, of which clothing reform was an essential part. Essential to the process of clothing reform was the erosion of the distinction between festival and nonfestival time—the end of a feudal, circular, agricultural notion of time and the beginning of a modern, linear, fashion-driven notion of time. As the entire temporal structure of the ordering of life was overturned with the sudden introduction of modern ideas and foreign cultures, the way in which the temporal order was performed and signalled sartorially also changed. The idea of fashion, which relies on a modern notion of linear time, was introduced to the general public and had its first major manifestations in the department stores' promotion of major short-lived trends. The introduction of the economic mechanisms of capitalism and the introduction of a broadly accessible trend-based sartorial system were intertwined. The clothing once used to delineate sacred and nonsacred time was now used to generate the demand for both economic and aesthetic modernity.

The spaces in which life was lived also influenced the speed and direction of sartorial change. Early on, the civil service switched to Western-style desks and chairs, thus making their frock-coat suits more suitable for the workplace. However, it was not until the Taishō period that all the social spaces—cafés, department stores, toilets, trains and houses—started to adopt Western seating and other features that make Western clothing more practical and Japanese clothing less so. Unlike houses, clothes cannot easily be combined with others of a different style.[17] While the modern Japanese house is a rather grotesque mosaic of traditional and Western parts, the dress worn by the modern Japanese is either totally traditional or almost completely Western.[18] Once even part of the clothing is changed with the adoption of an imported foreign element, a change in the clothing as a whole is inevitable. When this happens, the sign conveyed by the clothing also changes completely.[19] It is interesting that the very bodies lived in by Japanese men and women also changed as modernity brought better nutrition and exercise, with women especially becoming taller, bustier and curvier and better suited to Western fashions, at the very same time that the physical environment also became better suited to the wearing of such clothes.[20]

The intellectual environment, the sudden dawning of a modern consciousness directly out of a feudal one, without the centuries in between that were experienced by Western nations, had profound consequences for aesthetic sensibilities. There was in effect a sort of reversal of the aesthetic change under shogun Yoshimasa (1435–1490), from the seasonal and ever-changing beauty of the eleventh-century *Tale of Genji* to the Zen-influenced aesthetics of the thirteenth to the fifteenth centuries, with their emphasis on impermanence in beauty. The first was idealized in seasonal gardens and blossoms, the second in rock gardens—idealizing not renewal so much as orderly decay. This is a simplification, of course, but the issue of narrative and progress in form is at the centre of modern aesthetics, and it remains a useful comparison. Such fixed aesthetics had suited feudal Japan, but with the arrival of Western ideas and the dawning of a modern Japanese consciousness, aesthetics were once again thrown into flux and that central element of modernity—a fashion system—was set in motion. Change and newness became values in themselves, and by the Taishō era, this was understood and acted upon implicitly by the young.

Harootunian argues that Japan was, by the first decade of the twentieth century, a modern society. An older model of society, which had achieved its goals, was failing to satisfy new demands and new needs and to accommodate new social constituencies, which the success of earlier policies had now made possible. Meiji society had created the conditions for its own disconfirmation. Meiji civilization summoned purpose and goal—self-sacrifice and nationalism—whereas Taishō culture, as it was conceived, evoked new associations with the nuances of consumers' lives, associations with individualism, culturalism (*bunkashugi*) and cosmopolitanism. It also marked profound changes in modal personality types, from what men during the Meiji period celebrated as *shūgyō* (education) to what men during the Taishō period cherished as *kyōyō* (cultivation). The former meant a commitment to discipline, practical education and self-sacrificing service. The latter stressed personal self-cultivation and refinement.[21] Nishida Kitarō's search for the pure and unmediated experience[22] and Kuki Shūzō's disclosure of style (*iki*)[23] and sensibility as the central elements in culture reveal the individualism in cultural consciousness that separated Taishō Japan from what had gone before.[24]

The Taishō plunge into pleasure represented a form of Dandyism, which did not simply summon traditional associations with Tokugawa *tsū* (connoisseurship) and merchant culture but represented a repudiation of the social conformism which government in the late Meiji period was trying to establish. It brings to mind Baudelaire's famous defence of dandyism as the 'best element in human pride,' which, in its struggle with social conformism signals the need 'to combat and destroy triviality'.[25] Takamura Kōtarō, in accepting the division between politics and culture, set the tone for Taishō culture when he wrote, in 1910, that in the 'psychological conditions of creativity there is only the humanity of one individual'.[26] Politics was unimportant. Only culture, manifested in the universalization of beauty, could claim the serious attention of the artist. This was the final metamorphosis of *shūgyō* (education) into *kyōyō* (cultivation). One of the defining features of modernism—progress: the idea that things are constantly getting better and that change is therefore inherently good—was absorbed by the wealthy youths of Tokyo and elsewhere, whose clothing reflected the idea that they knew how to 'do modernity' even if they knew nothing of the cultural and aesthetic discourses that had given birth to it.

The freedom and decadence of the Taishō period, which was comparable to the Edwardian period in Britain, both coming between two periods of austerity and seriousness, allowed many modern ideas to flower in clothing. Harootunian argues that individualism and success also offered new lifestyle choices and new modes of criticism of the existing arrangement of things; clothing was a radical tool of change.[27] A modern productive aesthetic brought into view an individualism and a visualization of sex, as well as a naturalism of clothing form and of facial adjustment. Processes of abstraction of sartorial forms became more dominant than processes of ornamentation. By the late Taishō period, the agendas of dress were in concert with those of the West, and modernism itself became more important than the demonstration of modernism. Avant-garde leadership in clothing reform, which in the Meiji period had belonged to the political elite with an agenda of rapid modernization, switched to the modern boys and modern girls of the Taishō period. Few in number though both groups were, they came to lead, often by decades, the clothing directions of Japan, through an understanding of both modern sartorial forms and the systems which governed their popularity and their appropriateness to the times. Thus, by the Taishō period, the agendas of Meiji modernization had been fulfilled to a certain degree, though modernism had become a self-sustaining phenomenon rather than a means to political and military equality.

Natsume Sōseki noted in his diary in 1902 that 'people say that Japan was awakened thirty years ago, but it was awakened by a fire bell and jumped out of bed. It was not a genuine awakening but a totally confused one. Japan has tried to absorb Western culture in a hurry and as a result has not had time to digest it.'[28] In Meiji times, all the cultural and social conflicts and discourses being played out in Western clothing had little or no meaning to the Japanese that adopted them. The meanings with which they invested Western clothing were different, and essentially concerned cultural equality and the demonstration of national ability. Historian Ienaga Saburō maintains that the Westernization of modern Japanese clothes was necessitated by the modernization policy of the State, and even comes close to saying that the Westernization of clothes *was* modernization.[29] Ienaga argues that any cultural change is motivated by cultural necessity. Either way, Japan came into Western clothing history in the middle, and it wasn't until the reflexive modernity of the Taishō era that the meanings of Western and Japanese clothing began to be the same. By then, the issues of appropriation, ownership and cultural integrity were as resolved as they would ever be, and young Japanese no longer had to make the choice—the foundational choice—of Japanese or Western style, before they made any other choice, in regard to their outward appearance. It was Fukuzawa Yūkichi who said that a civilization begins with 'doubts generated from within oneself'.[30] It was in the Meiji period that these doubts were so suddenly implanted, but it was not until the arrival of the *mobo* and *moga* that a knowing confidence returned.

For those not part of the clothing avant-garde groups, the story of modernization is essentially one of embourgeoisement and the samuraization of tastes, which
slowed down widespread sartorial modernism with the persistence of elements such
as Confucian ideals for women. Ienaga argues that as women needed no new clothes
to meet their daily needs and were backward in modernizing their clothes, they were
not liberated.[31] But the wave still broke across the entire sartorial beach eventually,
and it did so much faster than in many other nations. The change from passive, feudal
subjects with a highly coded dress system to an active, modern citizenry with the
desire and ability to signal multiple identities through clothing was rapid in Japan
and was less tinged by class-based conspicuous consumption—creating dress codes
of exclusion—because the speed of the transition did not allow aristocracies to
establish a system such as they did in the West. Thus, through the modernizing era
in Japan, the role of clothing was much more about actual aesthetic modernity than
about religion, class or aesthetic conflicts, such as the conflict leading to the victory
of the classical over the baroque that dominated Western clothing history. And so,
for Japan, clothing became part of the vocabulary of modernism in the higher arts,
and part of the detail that made up modern Japan, as a foundational element rather
than a latecomer. It was also part of the modern consciousness and modern aesthetic
sensibility that eventually, far from just being a signal of modern Japan, *was* modern
Japan.

The Economics of Aesthetics

> When observed across the span of a century things appear vivid and clear, just as our
> globe seems a beautiful blue when it is seen from the moon.
>
> —Irokawa Daikichi

What then are the particular implications of Japanese fashion modernity for the canon
of fashion theory in general? The several historical idiosyncrasies, which run counter to most other encounters with modernity, in the Japanese experience allow certain strengths and weaknesses to be highlighted within what is understood about the
operation of fashion and the scope of its relevance. Far from being a hit-and-miss
sideshow in the great circus of human thought, clothing fashions operate in such a
way as to recapitulate the larger mechanisms of aesthetic change, and thus they have
a much broader application in the examination of modernity. The heading of this
section is deliberately intended to be interpreted in a number of ways and to hint at
the conclusions which will be drawn. Firstly, and obviously, it implies that clothing fashions constitute an aesthetic, which has implications beyond arbitrary taste
and systems of imitation of the arbitrary. By using the word 'economics', I mean
to imply that fashion operates on such a large scale as an aesthetic practice that it is
understandable only through patterns which exist across it and through tendencies

often revealed in the myriad rejections of it. The heading is also intended to imply that within the discipline of economics, fashion, a phenomenon rarely examined, governs a great many economic choices of production and consumption at a level not explainable by rational laws of supply and demand. Economics does not explain how tendencies in form—fashions—shape economies beyond rational questions of price and exclusivity.

The patterns that can be discerned in forms over time, and the major pattern that is described by this research—modernity—are aesthetic rather than social or economic, and the sovereignty of aesthetics over other motivations in the creation and appreciation of objects, sartorial or otherwise, is also something that this study has sought to establish through an examination of modernity in Japanese fashion. Technology and political change were required, but it was aesthetics that did the shaping, while these other factors simply provided the circumstances. In a manner analogous to Newton's reduction of the multiplicity of celestial phenomena to the single principle of universal gravitation, aesthetics searches for universal rules behind human feelings, in the human responses to the world where these feelings are best exteriorized and expressed in an observable way, in artistic objects. Because of its separation from but also unique relationship to European costume history, Japan provides a distinct example of dress motivations and responses to the material and abstract conditions of modernity.

An examination of the cultural order in terms of nations, rather than in terms of other possible groupings or patterns across objects, is something that Japan, because of its particular geography and continual insistence on uniqueness, forces upon studies of its modernity. While arguments of inherent national qualities or uniqueness are undoubtedly flawed, it is nevertheless necessary to engage with them on some level, as they were so widely accepted within Japan during the modern period and were a crucial element of individual and national identity.[32] This has necessarily engendered a particularly Hegelian structure of history as a critical exegesis. Because of this structure, a theoretical cleavage is created between the subject and object of knowledge: mind and nature, self and other, freedom and authority, knowledge and faith. And following Hegel, a coherent interpretation of these contradictions and tensions is that they consist partly of a comprehensive, evolving rational unity. The monolithic others which Japan, in its isolation, always imagined, are eminently suitable for a dialectical understanding of history. 'The image of a monolithic West replaced an earlier interpretation of China as the 'other'. Japan's conceptualization of the West affirmed a theory of militant and articulate revolt against the other, usually imagined as a collective threat to Japan's national independence and cultural autonomy. The construction of the other required that it be portrayed as the mirror image of the indigenous culture. It was this representation of the other that clarified for the Japanese the essence of their own culture.'[33] Japan, as an idea, is constantly manifested in contradiction and negation; identity is formed in difference. And from this theoretical structure, the Hegelian conclusion that nothing is completely real except the whole, especially in examining a pattern of form such as clothing fashions, is particularly appealing.

Michele Marra argues that in the Japanese context, aesthetics was 'a modern mechanism that is responsible for a number of hermeneutical strategies directly related to the production of subject and state'.[34] And certainly the major role played by aesthetics in the formation of judgements could not be underestimated at a time when the Meiji politicians were searching for new ways of eliciting agreement within and between communities. How could any agreement be reached without first devising a mechanism that would allow one to ground the immanence of subjectivity in some kind of transcendent objectivity? Once religious hermeneutics had lost credibility after the close scrutiny of the Enlightenment, or at least in its state-sponsored Japanese equivalent, a new bond was required to keep communities together. A secularized version of the divine could be found in the cult of 'beauty', whose inscrutability, rooted in the depth and mystery of a person's innermost feelings, was as profound as any path leading to God or the divine. Belief in the potential of art to bridge the final actuality and the infinite freedom of reason—metaphysical universality and the determinateness of real particularity—made the work of art an epiphany of the Absolute Spirit in front of a newly constituted assembly of believers (the art critics and the appreciators of art) who filled with aesthetics the void left by theology.[35] Clothing fashion acted as a democratic extension of this: through dress, everyone, not just artists, could achieve an aesthetic self-actualization. Modern fashion allowed all people access to the epiphany of the Absolute Spirit through the medium of their clothes.

The hermeneutic position of Immanuel Kant on the issue of taste is absolutely central to understanding the interest that Meiji politicians showed in the notion of the intersubjective validity of the category of taste as a common response to beauty. Kant questioned the paradox of the antinomy of taste: how to reconcile the alleged universality of aesthetic judgement with the particularity of the subject pronouncing that judgement? In answer to this, Kant proposed two types of judgement: determinant judgement (of cognition) and reflective judgement (of taste). Kant argued that judgement presupposes an indeterminate horizon of expectation, or principle, to reflection. Aesthetic satisfaction is felt when the reflective subjects observe an agreement between the real and their expectation—between what is and what ought to be, a reconciliation of sensibility and intelligence.

Kant's major philosophical achievement was the organization of knowledge along the lines of logic (true and false), ethics (good and bad) and aesthetics (beautiful and ugly). The ultimate point, however, remained the formulation of judgements (right and wrong). Unlike premodern times in Europe, which were ruled by religious beliefs in which the three spheres (ethics, aesthetics and logic) were interdependent—so that beauty could not be false or ugly—modernity grounded its distinction in the notion that set each sphere as independent from the other. This was made possible by a belief in the inherent value of each type of knowledge, which resulted from the crisis faced by the very notion of belief: a single authority in charge of the process of legitimation. Markets, on their way to development, needed different justificatory devices for actions that could be profitable (true) but ethically questionable (bad) and aesthetically unacceptable (ugly). Truth had to be found in what used to be considered false (evil and ugliness), so that beauty could also be spotted in what was perceived as morally reprehensible and logically absurd. This has enormous implications for forms that clothing could take and how it could be used as an expression of self. Fashion is a result of this distinction, existing with autonomy from logic and morality. Since judgement in the modern world was the result of putting into brackets concerns that belonged to a different sphere of knowledge, the judgement of taste required that ethical and logical notions such as goodness and truth be dropped from the process of judging. The displacement of reality into the aesthetic realm frees the modern participant in the fashion system from the feelings of self-blame to which rational thoughts would inevitably expose him, while providing pleasure in the possibility of aesthetic evasion.

The construction of a community based on the universal communicability of sensation, and ruled by notions of taste, had tremendous political consequences with regard to the burgeoning modern Japanese State. 'The satisfaction of aesthetic contemplation, or the pleasure of a finality without an end ... turned into principles of spontaneous consensus, so that beauty became the internalization of a moral imperative—a sort of pleasant repression.'[36] By the time a modern fashion system was really established, in the early Taishō period, the estrangement of the social and the state reflected this. H. D. Harootunian points out that

> Miki Kiyoshi, an early adherent to Neo-Kantianism, proposed that literature and philosophy, found in the ideal of self-cultivation, were essential to a science of culture, whereas physical science and technology belonged to material civilization. Clearly 'civilization' became a pejorative concept in the 1920s and came to mean material progress and human debasement, whereas culture was associated with creative self-realization. The important implication of this polarization of civilization (*bummei*) and culture (*bunka*) was the belief that individual self-cultivation could not be reached through capitalism and technological industrialism.[37]

The agenda of the Meiji State, to use aesthetics, in the absence of theology, as a means of establishing a national identity and consensus on modernization, had been completed by the 1920s, and yet its twin dialectical formations remained: Japanese and foreign, and particularly, old and new.

As a means of establishing an individual identity, rather than a national identity, the dialectic of old and new remained potent in the form of neomania (which René König refers to as 'neophilia').[38] Roland Barthes argues that

> Fashion doubtless belongs to all the phenomena of neomania which probably appeared in our civilization with the birth of capitalism: in an entirely institutional manner, the new

is a purchased value. But in our society, what is new in Fashion seems to have a well-defined anthropological function, one which derives from its ambiguity: simultaneously unpredictable and systematic, regular and unknown.[39]

This function, even when the new is not genuinely new but summoned from an idealized past, provides the necessary fluidity in the system to make fashion a tool of empowerment and aesthetic actualization. Change as a value in itself was, from the European Enlightenment, the epistemological reordering that centralized the continual questioning of the authority of forms—and thus their continual refashioning with greater and greater sophistication.

Fashion, as a structure that esteems the continual reevaluating and restyling of things and the speed of this change, is at the heart of modernity. Herbert Blumer stated that 'Fashion is an outstanding mark of modern civilization.'[40] Giles Lipovetsky agreed: 'While clothes are almost universal, fashion is not. Fashion does not belong to all ages or to all civilizations; it has an identifiable starting point in history.'[41] And Jean Baudrillard too has argued that

> Fashion only exists in the framework of modernity . . . In politics, in technology, in art, in culture, modernity defines itself by the rate of change tolerated by the system without really changing anything in the essential order . . . Modernity is a code and fashion is its emblem.[42]

For Baudrillard, fashion is one of those institutions that best restores cultural inequality and social discrimination, establishing them under the pretence of abolishing them.

The Japanese experience of modernity, and the adoption of fashion as the system that governs the reordering of the creation and appreciation of things, comes with a particular and distinct set of class arrangements, artistic practices, social structures and the history of previous isolation, in the context of which, as has already been mentioned, certain key theories in fashion apply or do not apply in degrees that are different from those of their assumed application in the areas and times of their creation. This difference allows for a better measurement of the worth of certain explanations.

The Recurring Problems of Fashion

Despite an abundance of literature and social science devoted to the problems posed by clothing and the system which governs its production, distribution, consumption and appreciation, unanswered issues and unresolved complexity remain with regard to ways to understand fashion. The established pillars of the canon are largely unconnected. In general, the sociological elements of fashion are privileged and art historical elements excluded. While the designing of clothing is sometimes sanctioned as an artistic practice, the mere wearing of it is almost never so sanctioned. The rather simple challenge to this established order, of deeming an individual or collective act of clothing choice to be an act of aesthetic creation and self-actualization, is not a particularly large leap of reasoning in the age of postmodern interpretations of what can be thought of as legitimate artistic practice. Beyond the political, material and technological reasons for clothing change in Japan, there seemed to be a very clear desire to perform modernity with whatever medium possible, and the most readily available medium and the one most closely aligned to the self was the fleeting fabulousness of clothing fashions. In a way, the continuing attempts to explain sartorial reasoning are, in many cases, foiled by their subject—the very nature of fashion, preferring novelty and transformation, thus escapes fixed models; there are fashions in theory too. The attempt to establish aesthetics as a sovereign, though certainly not exclusive, means of answering the recurring questions of fashion in the Japanese context is a modest attempt to add a theory of synthesis to traditional theoretical explanations of fashion. Herbert Blumer identified traditional and current explanations of fashion as generally falling into two broad categories—functional and dynamic—and it is perhaps possible to add to these a category of synthesis—the aesthetic, that clothing has a function, autonomous and predominant over all others, that is essentially a means of expression in and of itself.[43]

Functional Explanations

Social consequences are the focus of functional explanations of fashion. Functional arguments assert that a phenomenon such as fashion can be understood in terms of what it does in a society, rather than in terms of its origins or causes. The essential question, for this body of theory, is not how fashion begins and spreads but what functions it serves, what purposes it fulfils, and what consequences it has. These consequences may be identified as primarily individual, institutional or societal. The consequences are not confined to one level of social reality, of course, but such explanations tend to emphasize the functions of fashion at a particular level. Functional explanations are particularly important for the early period of Meiji clothing change, as the sartorial reasoning was often clearly articulated. Western clothing became compulsory for government officials in November 1872, when a directive established Western clothing as the official ceremonial dress. In 1876, frock coats were decreed as standard business attire.[44]

When Western value systems came into contact with Japanese values, there were three possible outcomes: the two could conflict; the Western values might be adopted without change; or they might be altered in the process of being accepted. At first the adoption of Western clothing would seem like a total adoption without conflict or alteration. The unequal treaties concluded by the *bakufu* (shogunate) in 1854–1858 were inequitable and undeniably humiliating: Japan was forced to relinquish tariff autonomy and concede extraterritoriality to foreigners. To obtain equal status with the West, the early Meiji government would first have to prove, on foreign terms, that Japan was a 'civilized' country, deserving equal status and treatment. Early clothing legislation would seem to have had this clear political objective. It was to serve a symbolic role with regard to Western powers, and to be part of a genuine belief that such clothing was more modern and would aid Japan's transformation into a modern power. The Meiji Restoration completely altered Japan's political leadership, and strengthened the resolve to learn from the West that was already forming by 1868. The most important of all the official missions sent to study foreign powers with a mind to imitating them followed the Restoration. In December 1871, the new Meiji government dispatched Ambassador-Plenipotentiary Iwakura Tomomi to America and Europe. The public celebration and influence of this mission demonstrated that xenophobic extremism had spent its force in Japan, and foreign dress and influence was accepted in the mainstream. However, on a similar mission, ten years earlier, the antiforeign sentiment had evidently been much stronger. The captain, Katsu Kaishū, on returning to Japan, playfully displayed a Western umbrella he had bought over- seas. When he asked, 'What would happen if I tried to use this in Japan?' other mem- bers of the delegation cautioned him not to invite assassination.[45]

Thus, a functional explanation would seem very suitable here—clothing plays a clear role in society and in political movements to change society. Clothing symbol- izes modernity for reformers and invasion for xenophobic extremists. But this line of argument on where clothing originated ends in unproductive conclusions about ethnicity as the starting point of culture.

Meaning and Identity in Fashion

A second major body of thought in the analysis of fashion is presented in terms of its functions for the individual or nation seeking to construct meaning in existence, or striving to establish identity. Orrin Klapp argues that both fad and fashion 'symp- tomatise a restlessness about identity which is becoming characteristic of much of the modern world'; even in fashion's 'most frivolous and desperate searches for novelty', we encounter 'not mere sensationalism but a search for meaning'.[46] Klapp's ideas correspond to the notions of *Geist* in German thought—a spirit of the times restlessly trying to manifest itself through imperfect materials, or a person's inner nature being expressed in an outer form. For Klapp, people consume and wear fashion because they are attempting to construct significance in their patterns of life. The term that the present book has employed—aesthetic self-actualization—is an extension of Klapp's idea that has been used to describe the manifest desire in Japan not to just live in modernity but in some way to perform it as well. Japanese individuals who expressed this desire strove to discover who they really were, and to express their real selves in various ways, including the expression of self through the selection and wearing of fashion. This interpretation of fashion assumes that humanity has a decorative urge, fundamental to the psychological make-up of the self. Japan's encounter with modernity fits this idea of restless identity searching for form. Underlying this characterization of clothing fashions is the problematic nature of individual identity in mass society. Klapp argues that with modernity and the advent of a mass society, the function of fashion has shifted 'from class maintenance by status symbols to identity seeking by ego symbols'.[47] The different nature of class distinction in Japan—initially more feudal than bourgeois—means that the function of national identity is more central in clothing than class differentiation. The process might even be argued as being more valid, in the sense that the end of the Meiji period was equated by Kamishima Jirō and others with the formation of individualization and privatization, and thus within that process, fashion used as a tool in the construction of new individual identities was even more applicable.[48]

The functional significance of fashion for the individual was emphasized by Georg Simmel and Edward Sapir. Simmel's 'trickle-down' theory of fashion was based on the assumption of two opposing tendencies in human life—the need to conform to the group and the need for individual expression.[49] The need to conform, for Simmel, is maintained by imitation, and since fashion always involves imitation, it satisfies our need to conform. At the same time, it satisfies our need for individualization. It marks us as conventional members of a particular group, while it simultaneously differentiates us from those who are outside that group—those who do not adopt the same fashions. Simmel's model of fashion is not dialectical, as it envisages no final, sublime form. Japan's use of fashion, however, often seems to reveal a purpose behind the clothing fashions and behind the adoption of progressive forms in general, be they legal, political, industrial or sartorial. The conscious purpose of the use of modern clothing in Japan was to become equal to the West, and thus fashion thought of in this way is more intertextually consistent with Hegel than with Simmel. It had a sublime form, that of its model.

Simmel's characterization of fashion is premised on a situation already akin to modernity, and there are thus a number of historical instances where Simmel's two opposing tendencies may not be present. In such cases, Simmel argues, there can be no fashion. For instance, in isolated, preindustrial societies there is a 'deep-rooted distrust' of anything novel, and little or no interest in individualization. Such societies lack fashion. On the other hand, the nature of modern society increases the need for fashion and facilitates the continual changing of fashion. Premodern Japan, while often said to have had a sense of individualism that was less developed than that of Europe, did have some elements of a fashion system before the end of its isolationism, and even examples of catalogue-style advertising to display the next season's kimono patterns. There was deep-rooted distrust, not so much of things new as of things considered foreign. Even so, this element of Simmel's argument appears difficult to apply in this case. The premodern Japanese system of time was classically cyclical, rather than historical. New kimono patterns marked cyclical time rather than linear time—the new styles were within a very rigid framework, and symbolized renewal more than the new. The process of creating demand through novelty—inverting regular economics of supply and demand with the non-price element of fashion—is part of premodern fashion, as is status differentiation, but without the element of a concept of linear time, Simmel's analysis functions only partially.

Simmel presented a further argument concerning the origin of fashions. He argues that 'people like fashion from outside, and such foreign fashions assume greater values within the circle, simply because they did not originate there. The exotic origin of fashions seems strongly to favour the exclusiveness of the groups which adopt them . . . This motive for foreignness, which fashion employs in its socializing endeavours, is restricted to higher civilization.'[50] This position is clearly applicable to the fashion of Japan if viewed from a national perspective. The political elites of Meiji and the *mobo* and *moga* of Taishō valued the exclusiveness and potential for renewal that foreign sartorial forms could be used to represent. The value of foreign clothing was that it came from outside traditional visual discourses and could therefore be used to perform something radical within the group it was brought into, rather than between it and its foreign model.

In contrast to those of Simmel, Edward Sapir's arguments focus primarily on one function of fashion for the individual—its symbolic significance for the expression of the ego.[51] Fashion, according to Sapir, functions as a symbol either of 'personal distinction' or of membership in a group that has distinction. Thus individuals use fashion to enhance themselves and their attractiveness to others. Whether the particular fashion in question refers to clothing, art, recreation, morals or something else, there is, for Sapir, a close, intimate linkage with the ego. The often-mentioned lack of emphasis on individual identity in Japan makes Sapir's arguments harder to apply in this case. Individualism is an element of the end of supernaturalism, which is part of modernity but also a result of alienation in the new social. Fashion is only identifiable across forms, and so Sapir's alignment of it with the individual ego is very limiting, especially for this analysis of Japanese fashion, which is structured, for better or worse, around a particular national experience. Furthermore, Sapir does not adequately explain why alignment with a certain aesthetic would equate to enhancement and attractiveness and only to these. The desire to be modern, to perform modernity, seems to function at a higher level than Sapir's explanation of personal distinction.

René König also presents a thesis which places the role of fashion in the creation of meaning in an individual's life.[52] König argues that a number of aspects of human nature underlie the potency of fashion as a social phenomenon. These basic aspects of human nature, however, can be seen in terms of the individual's pursuit of identity and meaning. For König, human nature is disposed to display the body in order to make it attractive to others, to present itself in a way that will gain it recognition, and to secure the awareness and approval of its individuality by others. Individuals use fashion in the ongoing effort to establish their own identity, delineate their own distinctiveness and enhance the meaning of their lives. König also hints at an aesthetic element, though this is always secondary. König's formulation is once again an approach grounded in the individual, whereas the assumption of the present study is that fashion can only exist as a collective structure. No single element in a network as complex as that of Japanese fashion in the modern era should be regarded as the cause of fashion: not the dress taste of individuals, nor the sum of their desire for distinctive attractiveness. Fashion quite clearly in the Japanese experience was something in which a structured collective being preceded, and provided the foundation for, an individual being.

König argues that the contents of fashion are always a manifestation of their epoch; that fashion's structural form as a special kind of controlled behaviour incorporates certain constraints which decide initially what fashion is.[53] However, König configures collective being as merely a constraint to the predominant individual motivations, and this is why his explanation can be classified as functional. He conceives of fashion as a tool of individuality, used to enhance the likelihood of that individuality reproducing. What is overlooked when this essentially psychological explanation is applied in the case of Japanese clothing is the coherence exhibited by the clothes inside the groups in which they circulate, as against the great variations in clothing styles that exist from one group to another. The only way to account for this is to make the group structure, the social system, into the major determining factor in the constitution of Japanese clothing in modernity.

The Japanese example would show that fashion is a social phenomenon. This is particularly true when considering its sudden origin in a moment of appropriation. Many explanations of clothing rely on an evolutionary or phylogenetic method in which clothing, and indeed social life in general, is regarded as a collection of individual traits, each with its own evolutionary pathway into the present. Clothing, in this model, is seen as a set of garments that have acquired their present form because of their past. Roland Barthes criticized this model, and his criticisms are especially well illustrated in the Japanese experience by the rapid adoption of entire systems of clothing, not out of indigenous motivations and frameworks but from another place entirely. Barthes argues that collective life cannot be accounted for in terms of the psychological dispositions of the individuals that make up the group. 'All such discussions fall victim to an illusory psychological explanation: that is, they define a social fact such as clothing by way of the sum of a certain number of psychological instincts, conceived of at a strictly individual level. These are then simply "multiplied" by a group factor. This is a problem that sociology would want to explore more thoroughly.'[54]

Emile Durkheim insists upon the reality of social facts: 'a cultural or structural characteristic of a social system which we experience as external to us and having an influence and authority that amount to more than the sum of the intentions and motivations of the people who happen to be participating in those systems at a particular time'.[55] Fashion as a social fact can't therefore be simply a tool of individual expression. Identity is collective as well as individual, and therefore any search for it has to be in a form far more complex than a simple amplification of individual motivations. More importantly, it could not have evolved out of individual motivations. In Japan, modern identity was inseparably linked to a dialectic between native and foreign, not just to a dialectic between the present and the past. Modernity's sudden arrival in Japan represents a disjunction with the past such that it could not have simply evolved out of the past. The general appropriation of sartorial forms in Japan would indicate that far from signalling an identity, fashions at this point represented a general experimentation with form. They had nothing to do with identity—they were in fact totally alien—and they were rather a conscious reaction to new material and social conditions. Modernity was not just incorporated into an identity but performed, and thus had an element that was not just functional as an identification, but aesthetic in that it was done in and for itself.

The Struggle for Status in Fashion

A second body of theory maintains that fashion is functional both for the individual and for groups, in terms of social and sexual competition—the struggle to enhance one's status. A number of theories have analyzed fashion as a tool that is used to gain advantages over others in the competition. This is undoubtedly true; however, it does not explain patterns of forms throughout groups and over time. J. C. Flügel argues: 'there can be little doubt that the ultimate and essential cause of fashion lies in competition.' This competition is both social and sexual, with the social elements being 'more obvious and manifest' while the sexual elements are 'more indirect, concealed and unavowed, hiding themselves, as it were, behind the social ones'.[56]

In analyzing fashion as a competitive phenomenon, Flügel also emphasizes the way in which fashion becomes involved in the struggle between social classes. He argues that it is a fundamental human trait to imitate those we admire or envy. Normally, that means we imitate those who are above us in the class hierarchy. And what is 'more natural, and at the same time, more symbolic, than to start the process of imitation by copying their clothes, the very insignia of the admired and envied qualities?'[57] But those in the higher classes are not willing to have their symbols of superiority appropriated by those beneath them. They can maintain their insignia of superiority in two ways: through sumptuary laws or by abandoning the styles that are being copied by the lower classes. In Japan, sumptuary laws were no longer a viable option after the Restoration. The upper classes therefore adopted new styles in order to maintain the distinction between themselves and those beneath them. 'And thus fashion is born.'[58]

During the Edo period, with the development of cotton production and indigo dyeing, the more common clothing shifted 'from hemp to cotton', and, according to Yanagita Kunio, through this experience of 'the fragrance of deep blue and the feel of cotton', this development fostered in Japanese men and women a keener sensitivity to things and thus a modern transformation to a social system where social relations were mediated through commodities.[59] The development of indigo dyeing in particular proved beneficial in bringing to fruition a sensitivity to colour that was developing among the masses. The free use of colour was forbidden by the Edo sumptuary regulations, but these were removed at the beginning of the Meiji period. After this, people's powers of imagination regarding colour developed to a dazzling degree, as did their ability, Yanagita argues, to involve themselves in a materialist system of class competition through fashion. Flügel argues that fashion had developed because of the particular society and culture of the West. In agreement with this, in earlier chapters it has been argued that the particular history of Japanese class structures did indeed mean a different use of clothing in regard to class competition.[60] This is not to say that clothing was never used as an indicator of social division in the way that Flügel outlines, but the emphases in the uses of clothing in Japan during the early modern period were certainly different on the whole, and thus the validity of Flügel's explanation for fashion is reduced.

Flügel is reiterating, with new elements, the 'trickle-down' theory of fashion which can be traced back to Spencer, Veblen and Simmel. Spencer argued that fashion is 'intrinsically imitative', and that imitation can arise from two different motives: 'It may be prompted by reverence for one imitated, or it may be prompted by the desire to assert equality with him.'[61] Spencer believed the net effect of fashion was to enhance egalitarianism in the society. 'Serving to obscure, and eventually to obliterate, the marks of class distinction, it has favoured the growth of individuality; and by so doing has aided in weakening the ceremonial, which implies subordination of the individual.'[62] Though Spencer was writing at the very moment when Japan was shaking off the restraints of feudalism, and the system he wrote of was a bourgeois one, the elements of imitation are interesting for the purposes of the present book when applied at a national level. Japan as a nation had a political agenda of obscuring and eventually obliterating the marks of distinction between it and the West, for which it used the tool of clothing. Spencer's notions of equality imply an end where distinction would no longer be necessary in clothing and fashion would end—a sublimely Hegelian moment when the dialectic would complete itself.

Spencer's stipulation was that fashion required a certain degree of mobility and fluidity within a society; imitation had to be permitted by authority.[63] This was, interestingly, reversed in Meiji Japan, by an elite that deliberately set out to provide universal examples of clothing, rather than to create codes of exclusiveness. Imitation was not just permitted but encouraged. The competition was on a national level, not just on a class or individual level. The freedom from sumptuary laws that came with the Meiji era, coupled with general embourgeoisement and enrichment through the industrialization of the clothing industry and the opening of trade in cheap cloth with China, resulted in a samuraization of tastes. The desire for samurai clothing was no longer the result of an attraction to the style of the higher classes but a return to the sartorial tastes of a class that no longer existed. This may have occurred for reasons of alienation from the processes of modernization and the resultant desire to reconstruct an idealized past through clothing choices, not necessarily for any reasons of class imitation.

Thorstein Veblen, whose theory contradicted Spencer's and is perhaps also invalid in the case of Japanese sartorial modernity, saw clothing styles as maintaining rather than diminishing class distinctions. Veblen tied in dress with his ideas about conspicuous consumption among the leisured class. He argued that, in the most advanced societies,

> . . . it has (ideally) become the great, peculiar, and almost the sole function of woman in the social system to put in evidence her economic unit's ability to pay. That is to say, woman's place . . . has come to be that of a means of conspicuously unproductive expenditure . . . 'Dress,' therefore, from the economic point of view, comes pretty near being synonymous with 'display of wasteful expenditure'.[64]

Furthermore, the display of wasteful expenditure can be achieved not simply by expensive clothes but by the continual adoption of new styles of expensive clothes: in other words, by fashion changes. Fashion for Veblen, therefore, is built upon the principle of conspicuous waste. The upper-class individual uses fashion to maintain class distinctions. The lower-class individual tries to emulate the lifestyle of the upper classes but is inevitably thwarted by a lack of resources and by the constantly changing styles. The Japanese construction of clothing into modern and traditional categories, with modern clothing being encouraged by the elite, was far more dominant than any discussion of class. Japanese literature, women's magazines and education were almost always concerned with the separation of traditional and modern clothing, and thus displays of, or sartorial systems of, class were simply not an issue. Veblen and class-based imitation theory in general is therefore largely inapplicable in the case of Japanese modernity.

Interestingly, Veblen commented directly on Japanese development from his vantage point in the very early twentieth century. He argued that borrowed industrialization did not have the same solvent effect on 'archaic' social institutions as the original industrialization in England had had. An 'unstable cultural compound' resulted. Veblen assumed that this was a transitional phase and that in the end, social institutions would adapt to conform to new technologies.[65] The continuing differences in the use of luxury symbols, and in the general structure of women's magazines, would perhaps lead to the conclusion that the distinct history of class structure in Japan has a legacy even today.

'Attempts to understand the dynamics of fashion have been mostly dominated by variants of imitation theory that start from the presumption that fashion is an essentially hierarchical phenomenon prescribed by some identifiable sartorial authority. Sartorial power is most often conceived as residing with some dominant social group or class whose decisions on what is fashionable are then emulated by successive layers of the social hierarchy.'[66] Yuniya Kawamura presents a more general understanding of imitation, which is more open and therefore more applicable to the Japanese example. Sartorial power was generally vested in the political elites and in the wealthy urban population. Yet fashion was not used as a means of reinforcing or amplifying the social position of elites; it was used for other agendas. Whereas immobility in the distribution of vestimentary signs always corresponds to immobility in social structures, in Japan both were relatively fluid, and clothing was put to other uses other than making unequal social relations look natural.[67]

The Economics of Fashion

The economic approach to the study of fashion focuses on its functional significance and sees fashion as a system of provision which intervenes and arbitrates between producers and consumers using capital and information to effect a profitable reconciliation between the capacity to produce and the desires of consumers. Some theories have characterized fashion as essentially, and sometimes exclusively, an economic phenomenon. Werner Sombart argues that 'Fashion is capitalism's favourite child,'[68] and he denies that the consumer plays any part in creating fashion. For Sombart, the wearer of clothing has to accept what producers offer, and he stresses that it is the producer that shapes fashion while the consumers merely acquiesce in the styles offered to them. The Japanese example, however, negates this argument almost immediately. Initially, there was no economic advantage in Japanese adoption of foreign styles; new modern clothing had to be made to each customer's specifications in the early Meiji period anyway. The desire to look modern was made more actually accessible only by capitalist provision; this also made indigenous styles more consumable through increased availability. Certainly department stores and avant-garde design boutiques such as Shiseidō provided new means of entry into sartorial modernity, but to deny the role of the collective reception of forms is patently unsound in the Japanese instance. Aesthetic judgements about commonplace objects were a preoccupation at all levels of the modernizing Japanese consciousness, and to imply that these had no influence on the forms that producers provided is manifestly untrue.

Veblen also gave an essentially economic interpretation to fashion. As already noted, he regarded fashion as one of the means by which a leisure class could demonstrate its affluence. The clothing worn by those in the upper classes was not only expensive but was also dysfunctional for any productive purposes. In other words, for Veblen, the elite not only showed how much they could spend on clothing but also demonstrated the fact that they did not have to engage in common labour. The things that people defined as elegant or 'charming' in fashion were those things indicating 'that the wearer cannot when so attired bear hand in any employment that is directly and immediately of any human use'.[69] Exemption from labour was an element in the sartorial judgements that were made in modernizing Japan, yet these did not always carry the same class implications that their foreign models did. Complicating things was the fact that the moment when Japan began to reproduce foreign clothing forms was also the moment when male clothing was removing itself from impractical displays and retreating into an aesthetic of usefulness. From the end of the eighteenth century, the bourgeois male in Europe and America underwent what has been called the 'great masculine renunciation', which Flügel describes as 'the most remarkable event in the whole history of dress'.[70] Elite men abandoned their claim to be beautiful and aimed at being only useful.

This process was gendered for Veblen; affluent men showed their wealth by displaying lavishly dressed wives. Such women were, of course, totally dependent in an economic sense upon their husbands. This, argued Veblen, meant they were the property of their husbands, who used them for display. There was, for Veblen, a displacement of the social relations between men onto the clothing of women. 'The homely reason for all this conspicuous leisure and attire on the part of women lies in the fact that they are servants to whom, in the differentiation of economic functions, has been delegated the office of putting in evidence their master's ability to pay.'[71] The net economic effect of fashion for the entire society, therefore, was negative. Fashion, like many other pursuits of the leisure class, diminished efficiency and helped maintain social inequalities. For Japan, these factors were transcended in the Meiji era by the insistence that women also represent the traditional. In cultural conflicts, the clothing of women was initially a space contested by modern and traditional clothing aesthetics, and it could therefore not take on the displacement of male social relations until the synthesis of modernity in the Taishō period as part of, rather than a challenge to, Japanese identity. The preeminence of that identity, surpassing class and other considerations, made Japanese clothing history unique for a persistently long period and negates the application and validity of many theories of fashion in the early modern Japanese context.

In spite of many radical critiques, and the obvious bearing of fashion on the economy, economists have dealt very little with the economic consequences of fashion.[72] One economist who has, Dwight Robinson, pointed out that fashion has some unique economic ramifications. Unlike any other kind of demand, fashion exploits the 'versatility or partial fluidity of the factors of production in order to demonstrate command over currently disposable factors of production'.[73] In other words, fashion means that the consumer pays—willingly—for impermanence, for the stamp of recency upon goods. Consumers choose to believe that it is fashion they are wearing and consuming, not clothing, and that fashion is not a material product but a symbolic product, which has no content substance by or in itself. This comes very near to what Veblen argued. In fact, Robinson asserts that people value scarce goods for their symbolic value, and that an important factor in purchases is the extent to which goods can be conveniently displayed. But where Veblen viewed the phenomenon of fashion with contempt and with dire statements about its undesirable consequences, Robinson simply says that economists may find themselves undergoing a kind of quasi-Copernican revolution if they begin to take fashion demand seriously.

In the Japanese context, Robinson's theory of valuing impermanence and recency was certainly in accordance with trends. König argued that human receptiveness for anything new or 'neophilia' is essential to fashion-oriented behaviour.[74] Japan certainly had this tendency in abundance. Newness in sartorial form was valued in itself, without necessarily representing a superior economic capacity. But whereas economics could certainly benefit from an examination of fashionable behaviour, an examination of fashion in early modern Japan doesn't really gain that much from a purely economic insight, as the basis of economic knowledge—how consumers behave—doesn't really address why they do so. The judgements behind certain economic trends are aesthetic, but aesthetic judgements have no basis in economics.

Perhaps some exceptions in which economics might explain fashionable behaviour are to be found in the area of information cascades—an information cascade being a pattern of matching decisions which can occur when people observe and follow the collective. This can be rational if the information revealed in others' earlier decisions outweighs the individual's private information. There may, though, be noninformational factors that produce conformity in social interactions. John Maynard Keynes argued that 'worldly wisdom teaches that it is better for reputation to fail conventionally than to succeed unconventionally.'[75] In judgements about modern clothing, Japan chose to conform to foreign notions of how modernity should look sartorially, rather than to modernize its own indigenous clothing. Adam Smith was perhaps arguing in a similar vein when he wrote that the 'beauty of each species, though in one sense the rarest of things, because few individuals hit this middle form exactly, yet in another is the most common because all the deviations from it resemble it more than they resemble one another.'[76] What makes a member of a species beautiful is the most customary or average form rather than the most unique. For Smith, Japan's sartorial modernization involved the discovery of a new global average, towards which the Japanese sense of beauty in clothing necessarily had to gravitate and to which it had to adjust.

Keynes also argued, in his Beauty Contest Theory, that when we make decisions about what is beautiful, we do not do so based solely on our own perception. What actually occurs, he argued, is that the consumers' strategy is extended to the next order, where they attempt to predict what will be an average perception. This is not just based upon what others consider beautiful but predicts what others will consider beautiful. Keynes called this the third degree, where we devote our intelligences to anticipating what average opinion expects the average opinion to be.[77] This could be applied to Japan, in that Japan did not wear clothing it considered to be modern, but adopted and refined its clothing based on what it thought foreign powers would perceive as modern.

Fashion as Communication

Economic theories shaped a legacy whose central idea was that human activities were not random and did not originate from within the individual. Roland Barthes extended this idea and argued that no single element in a network can be regarded as the cause of fashion; not the dress taste of individuals or groups, nor the forms of clothing. Barthes argued that fashion was a system where structured collective being preceded individual being, where a totality of social relations and activities was required for individual being to come into existence. Barthes thus argued that clothing fashions could be explained through the methods of structural linguistics. This was essentially a functional explanation, as it sought to make fashion intelligible through ascribing to it a collective use—communication—and examining that.

Barthes asserted that clothing resembled language in a number of ways, firstly, in the sense that it was, like language, a preeminently collective activity. Like language, it was an authorless system, not contingent in its operation on the conscious will or intention of any individual. As in their use of language, individuals wear clothing within a set of forms or grammar. Further, individuals never just talk or just dress: both are highly structured by accepted, but arbitrary and therefore changeable, norms. Finally, clothing seems to resemble language in that it displays a synchronic density but at the same time also has a diachronic dimension—a history—so that it exhibits the dual aspects of system and process, structure and becoming.[78]

Barthes established a system identifying the different modalities that clothes assume in their journey across the fashion system, in the production, distribution and consumption of clothing. He calls these modalities the real, represented and used garment. Barthes maintains that the represented garment, the context for which is linguistic, is the point where fashion exists at the level of language, not as the physical garment itself. 'Clothes are always a combination of a specific signifier and a general signified that is external to it (Epoch, country, social class); without being sensitive to this, the historian will always tend to write the history of the signified . . . there are two histories, that of the signifier and that of the signified and they are not the same.'[79]

All of this can be demonstrated in the Japanese experience, mainly because the signified is often completely different in Japanese use from the signified in the context on which it was modelled. Thus, Barthes's methodological sophistication is shown to be beneficial in the attribution of different meaning to analogous clothing. However, Barthes becomes inapplicable in his positioning of the meaning of clothing before its form. This is perhaps the problem with all purely functional explanations of fashion. Modernity in Japanese clothing was something performed, not just a means of communicating something else. The understanding of modernity and the misunderstanding of it were not mutually exclusive. Modernity was immutable, and Japanese clothing did not have to represent modernity: it was modernity. Its performance was aesthetic and, by definition, did not have to have a function other than itself.

Dynamic Theories of Fashion

Dynamic theories focus on fashion as a pattern of change, and thus, dynamic explanations address a set of questions that are different from those addressed by functional explanations. Theories that fall into the functional category explore the questions of the individual and social consequences of fashion, and of the motivations to be fashionable. Theories that fall into the category of dynamic explanation explore the problem of how fashion changes, or why it changes in a particular way. The very structure of the present book necessitates that its satisfactory conclusions be, at least in some way, dynamic, as it seeks to elucidate how and why Japanese fashion changed over the modern period.

Diffusion in Fashion

In the attempt to explain the workings of fashion, anthropology and sociology have a long history of examining the phenomenon of diffusion. A pioneering work on imitation was written by French sociologist Gabriel Tarde in 1890.[80] By imitation, Tarde meant the adoption of innovations. Although Tarde attempted to establish the laws by which innovations diffuse and are adopted, a more definitive study of the diffusion and adoption of innovations was compiled by Everett Rogers some seventy years later, in his review and synthesis of over five hundred publications on the subject.[81] Rogers defined an innovation as any idea or any thing that was perceived as new. He identified four crucial elements in the process of diffusion and innovation: the innovation itself, the communication of the innovation, the social system in which the process occurs and certain temporal aspects—in particular, the fact that different kinds of people adopt an innovation at different stages of the process.

Rogers stated that adopters of any new innovation or idea could be categorized as innovators (2.5 per cent), early adopters (13.5 per cent), early majority (34 per cent), late majority (34 per cent) and laggards (16 per cent), based on a bell curve. Each adopter's willingness and ability to adopt an innovation would depend on awareness, interest, evaluation, trial and adoption. Rogers's research suggested that innovations would spread through society in an S curve, as the early adopters select the technology first, followed by the majority, until a technology or innovation or fashion is common.[82]

Clothing fashions may be analyzed as innovations, and the dissemination of fashion throughout a population may be examined using the various concepts employed in the study of the diffusion and adoption of innovations. The trickle-down theory could be interpreted as a form of diffusion theory, for it posits the spread of fashion as occurring from the upper to the lower classes. However, the principal focus of trickle-down theory is a functional aspect of fashion, rather than the pattern of change. The trickle-down theorist emphasizes the functions of fashion in the struggle for status. It has become generally accepted that diffusion theory is more applicable to clothing fashions than is trickle-down theory.[83] Fashions are not adopted or rejected solely on the basis of the way people in the upper socioeconomic strata respond to them.

The analysis of clothing fashions in terms of innovations is a useful mechanism, but perhaps not really applicable to the level of fashion change which is the focus of this book. The adoption of sartorial modernity by Japan is not simply an innovation but an adjustment in the relations of practices, styles, institutions and hermeneutic structures of clothing and indeed is about all interpretive judgements concerning how things should look. While the research in the present book lacks the statistical sophistication of Rogers, mainly because data on the scale required to see the patterns Rogers identifies does not exist for something as broad in scope as all the fashion choices over the whole early modern period of Japanese history, it is clear from the available information that the larger story of Japanese clothing did not follow Rogers's template of innovation adoption. Shiseidō's survey of people walking in Ginza in 1927, for example, shows that the scope and salience attributed to sartorial modernity by the media and in the popular imagination was in no way proportionate to its actual manifestation on the streets. Furthermore, the abandonment of certain innovations, particularly by late Meiji era women, is also unaccounted for by Rogers's innovation schema. The complexity of factors involved, such as gender and national identity, means that it is not really feasible to consider modernity as a single innovation. Further, the motility and multiplicity of flows of information and barriers to it are perhaps the characterizing features of modernity in clothing. Thus, part of the phenomenon the present study examines is the coming into being of something Rogers presupposes to exist.

To adopt Rogers's interpretation of the way in which things change would be, in the case of such a large subject as Japanese sartorial modernity, to fall for the illusion that modernity had a linear narrative and that all its elements developed evenly and in concert. Harootunian argues that 'modernism was the historical watermark of uneven development, its signature, even though it sought to efface and repress this historical condition of production.' He contends that 'capitalism has no really normal, balanced state even though it claims one in an indeterminate future.'[84] One of the pleasant illusions of modernity is that it has an even and purposeful development. Rogers's understanding of an innovation implies that it is part of a development and transformation for the better, when in matters of fashion this is not necessarily the case.

To analyze modernity in Japanese clothing in terms of diffusion and adoption means to treat it like any other innovation and explore those factors that account for the spread, or lack of spread, of a new fashion. However, the implication of an innovation is a matter of technology—something that can get better at what it does. This is at the heart of the problem posed by the history of Japanese fashion. Almost all interpretations of fashion consider it to have a purpose and function over and above itself, and while this can certainly be the case, it can also exist as an end in itself. The logical extension of treating clothing as an art object of the everyday is that it can be construed to exist at a level beyond function.

Further, to see the underlying structure in patterns of change in terms of mathematical abstractions, such as an S curve, is only possible at a basic level. When examining not just the diffusion of one trend or object, as Rogers does, but the diffusion of an abstraction like modernity, if indeed it is a diffusion, the complexity of the necessary interpretive instruments increases exponentially. The usefulness of diffusion theory is thus very limited in explaining anything larger than the particular. To attempt to extend this analysis to something larger would be to fall into the methodological trap of the phylogenetic thinking which Barthes criticized; fashion is a social phenomenon and can't be understood by the sum of individual intentions and motivations; large patterns of change cannot be explained by the sum of individual changes. The pattern within the pattern is not just countless S curves seen together; it is an aesthetic with properties that exist in the whole which do not exist in the parts.

Cyclic Fashion

Another dynamic approach to the interpretation of fashion is the cyclic approach. One of the best-known exponents of the cyclic nature of fashion was anthropologist A. L. Kroeber. On the basis of his study of changing fashions in women's dress, Kroeber argued that not only clothing styles but civilization itself must be seen as a rhythmic phenomenon, one that has 'an existence, an order and a causality as objective and as determinable as those of the sub-psychic or inorganic'.[85] With respect to women's fashions in particular, Kroeber found cycles of change over a long period of time, in such things as the width and length of skirts, the diameter and length of waists and décolletage. He pointed out that the rhythms of change could not be explained as due to the actions of particular individuals, for when 'a swing of fashion requires a century for its satisfaction, a minimum of at least several personalities is involved'.[86] Like others who have identified cycles in social life, Kroeber viewed the social process as possessing a dynamic of its own that is independent of the will or the actions of particular individuals.[87] History, for Kroeber, does not create clothes, and it does interact analogically with them. Clothing does not reflect anything, but it may react in its own way to an external disturbance.

The way in which sartorial modernity was adopted in Japan, at least through the methodology with which this book has approached it, renders Kroeber's conclusions inapplicable. Barthes argued that 'clothes live in close symbiosis with their historical context, much more than language; violent historical episodes (wars, exoduses, revolutions) can rapidly smash a system: but also in contrast to language, the recasting of the system is much quicker.'[88] The present study examines a period of extreme upheaval, and any attempt to separate Japanese clothing from Japan's encounter and reengagement with the world would certainly neglect the empirical evidence. Japan's relationship with the models for its modernization was the governing factor in its clothing adoption and rejection. Dialectics between foreign and indigenous and modern and traditional are central to clothing fashions because of this. These fashions are incontestably and inextricably linked to history.

General form, as well as measurement, has been used as an instrument to identify cycles in female dress fashions. Agnes Young examined the form of skirts from 1760 to 1937.[89] Young categorized all skirts into three fundamental types: the bell-shaped skirt was represented by the hoop skirt; the back-fullness contour was most strikingly represented by the bustle; and the tubular contour was prominent in the flapper dress of the 1920s. After examining silhouettes of changing styles over a 179-year period, Young concluded that women's fashions move through a series of recurring cycles. Each cycle lasts for about a third of a century. Young argued that during a particular cycle, there will be annual changes, but the changes will represent variations of a fundamental type. And in the period of her study, there were only the three basic types 'which have succeeded one another in unchanging sequence over the past two centuries'.[90] In Japan, the relationship with foreign clothing was linear rather than cyclical—such clothing was gradually adopted. While Young's conclusions may have been relevant for European and American women's dress, the historical circumstances of the Japanese experience were different, because their modernity was mediated and judged by comparison with an imagined monolithic West.

Fashions other than those in female dress have been analyzed in cyclic terms. Dwight Robinson found a cyclical pattern in the changing fashions in shaving and trimming beards among English men from 1842 to 1972.[91] Robinson found a close correlation between the cycles of skirt width measured by Kroeber and the cycles of beard frequency or the percentage of men with beards. In a manner similar to that of Kroeber, he interpreted fashion as a process that operates in accord with its own dynamic: ' . . . fashion cycles display a regularity that puts them effectively outside the influence of external events. World War I had no discernible effect on the skirt width cycle; neither did that war disrupt the mode of shaving popular among men. Once a new fashion trend is set in motion, there is little—whether it be technological innovation, political edict, functional change, even basic economics—that can be done to stop it or change its course.'[92] While this may have been true for Europe and America, Japan in the early modern period was an exception, in which one very large event—modernity—was in discourse with clothing fashions and fashions of personal adornment.

One final cyclical model is that linking economic prosperity and experimentation and austerity. The model claims that during good economic times, hemlines rise and women are more experimental in dress, while in periods of recession, austerity and modesty prevail. In early modernity, the periods of greatest experimentation in women's clothing tended to be linked to politically destabilizing events more than to economic events. The early enthusiasm for modern clothing at the Restoration was replaced with a movement towards more traditional women's dress in periods of nationalism and war. Other events, such as the great earthquake, might causally link clothing with its environment. The gradual economic enrichment of Japan led to a conservative samuraization of clothing taste. In the Japanese example, factors in the relationship between clothing and modernity were perhaps more important as instruments of change than the economy.

Hermann Bahr argued that one thing which distinguished modernity from all that is past, and gave it its particular character, was knowledge of the eternal creation and disappearance of all things in ceaseless flight. It also depended on insight into the connectedness of all things, and on the dependency of each thing upon every other in the unending chain of existence.[93] The knowledge of cycles of forms was perhaps a defining factor in clothing consciousness in modernity. Recognition of fashion as a dynamic form of self- and national actualization, far superior to static forms, was more important than any particular form that fashion took at any particular moment.

The problem with all cyclical interpretations of fashion is that sartorial modernity was linear. Clothing and the hermeneutic structures pertaining to it were entirely different after modernity from the way they were before it. Japanese sartorial modernity was a change in clothing that was irreversible and therefore incapable of being interpreted in accordance with a cyclical model. While part of modernity is reflexive—a continual reappraisal which destroys certainty—and this creates a formless regret and means that modernity repeatedly clothes itself in reconstructions of the past, the very fact that it does so is unprecedentedly new. It is not part of a cycle but a new means of using the past in the formulation of the present.

Erotics in Fashion

James Laver, long-serving curator at the Victoria and Albert Museum in London, asserted that there were three governing principles of dress. The first was the hierarchical principle—people dress for status. The second was the utility principle—people use dress for functional purposes like warmth and protection. And the third was the seduction principle—individuals dress in order to attract the opposite sex. Laver argued that for certain social reasons, women's fashions primarily follow the seduction principle and that, particularly in women's clothing, 'modesty is not the cause of clothing but its effect.'[94] For instance, a woman does not cover her breasts because she is modest. Rather, she is modest because she has covered her breasts. Laver reasoned that since there are societies in which the breasts are never covered, and the people in those societies are neither less moral nor less modest than the societies they exist in, there must be a certain relativity with regard to considerations of clothing and immodesty.

Initially, Laver's analysis of the erotic nature of fashion appears to provide a functional rather than a dynamic explanation. This means that the consequence of a particular fashion is that some portion of the female anatomy is defined as seductive. The explanation becomes dynamic, however, because it maintains that the part of the anatomy defined as erotic changes over time. Psychologists have called this the 'shifting erogenous zone' theory of fashion. As psychoanalyst Edmund Bergler put it, fashion is basically a 'series of permutations of seven basic themes, each theme being a part of the female body . . . Parts of the body "appear" and "disappear" as the theme of fashion changes.'[95] At one time, fashions may emphasize and partially expose the breasts. At another time, the breasts will be covered and the fashion will focus attention on the legs. And so forth.

It is necessary to keep shifting the focus of attention, according to Bergler, as a woman is a desirable sexual object for a man, but he cannot focus his attention on the entire person. In order to maximize sexual attraction, the woman dresses in such a way as to focus the man's attention on one part of her body. But in time the effect of a particular part diminishes, so she must shift the erogenous zone. As with anything else, novelty maximizes the appeal. Laver argued that at one time it was appropriate for a woman to expose her breasts but not her ankles. At other times she might expose her ankles but not her breasts. Some fashions have emphasized breasts (the 'sweater girl' look) or the buttocks (the bustle), while others have de-emphasized them (the flapper). Bare legs, bare shoulders and bare breasts have all been considered indecent at some times and fashionable at other times. Thus, fashion may be likened to 'a game of hide-and-seek between seduction and prudery, and nothing is more astonishing than the things prudery finds itself able to accept, once it has grown used to them.'[96]

Empirical support for this theory in the Japanese context is somewhat insufficient. Once again, the preoccupation with women's clothing is with the choice between foreign and native styles and between modern and traditional styles, not between emphases on differing erogenous zone. Japan certainly encountered many of the forms discussed, including the bustle and the flapper dress, and the revues performed in city theatres acknowledged the role of sexual freedom that was expressed in clothing in modernity. However, the shifting of erogenous zones as a source of women's clothing change in Japan is less easy to discern. The patterns which are perceivable seem much more closely related to a modern aesthetic within women's clothing gradually manifesting itself and to several conservative reactions to it which are overcome. Naturalism in clothing—following the body rather than covering it—was the larger trend of modernity in Japan, and this and general emancipation perhaps provide a better explanation for any particular sexual emphasis in clothing.

The *Zeitgeist* in Fashion

The final dynamic interpretation of fashion is that the idea that it, like every facet of culture, is a reflection of the *Zeitgeist*—the spirit of the times. The theory maintains that in order to understand the changing fashions it is necessary to understand the changing society. For the clothes of a period are 'significant expressions of the inter-relation' of the various elements of culture, including 'the social and religious phi-losophies (as dress serves to symbolize them), the taste of an age, the economic and industrial progress, the development of dressmaking as a craft'.[97]

If clothing expresses the spirit of the age, it follows that we can use changing fashions as an indication of a changing society. Thus, one way to identify the point at which significant change is occurring is to note the important changes in fashion. As Pierre Clerget argues, 'a new style of dress is the visible sign that a transformation is taking place in the intellect, customs, and business of a people.'[98] Clerget gives the example of the adoption of European costume and the rejection of plaited hair during the rise of the Chinese Republic. Clerget also quotes Hippolyte Taine's obser-vation that the advent of trousers marked the greatest change in history, the passing of Greek and Roman civilization into the modern. Clerget's argument is premised on the assumption that nothing is more resistant to change than daily custom. In order to produce a radical change in customary dress, there must be a fundamental change in people. Therefore, the transition from the robes of the classical world to the trousers of the modern world represents a basic change, both in civilization and in the people who comprise that civilization.

In the Japanese experience this was certainly the case; the transition from robed kimono to clothing systems of interchangeable parts was a reflection of the same types of processes occurring throughout Japanese culture. As Japanese culture started to question traditional epistemologies, and began a continual reappraisal of all cultural forms, as demanded by science and reason, so too its sartorial forms were questioned and continually reshaped, beginning a system of fashion. National and individual identity then became manifested within the dynamic rather than within the static, in existential recognition that selfhood and nationhood were processes of becoming. All clothing fashions were, throughout the early modern period in Japan, a reflection of and a performance of modernity—and thus causally linked, in gen-eral, to their environment via adjustments in their structure mediated by the flow of information. While Clerget and Taine argue that clothing fashions are a reflection of the *Zeitgeist*, in the Japanese context, and perhaps more widely in the characteriza-tion of fashion, clothing was part of the performance of the *Zeitgeist* and not just a mirror held up to it.

The idea that clothing fashions are causally linked to the spirit of the times consti-tutes a very broad dynamic theory. It is possible to amalgamate it with another theory without any inconsistency. For instance, although Flügel placed emphasis on social and sexual competition as the basis for any particular fashion, he also agreed that clothing fashions show certain parallels with such other fashions as architecture and interior decoration. Flügel argued that new fashions, whether in clothing or anything else, 'if they are to be successful, must be in accordance with certain ideals current at the time that they are launched'.[99] Social and sexual competition, for Flügel, ought to be interpreted as operating within the broader framework of ideals, and any particular fashion is the outcome of both the ideals and the competition.

Similarly, Laver's work tended towards the affirmation of the *Zeitgeist* as a broader framework within which the hierarchical, utility and seduction principles work: 'In every period costume has some essential line, and when we look back over the fashions of the past we can see quite clearly what it is, and can see what is surely very strange, that the forms of dresses, apparently so haphazard, so dependent on the whim of the designer, have an extraordinary relevance to the spirit of the age. The aristocratic stiffness of the old regime in France is completely mirrored in the brocaded gowns of the eighteenth century . . . Victorian modesty expressed itself in a multitude of petticoats, the emancipation of the post-war flapper in short hair and short skirts. We touch here something very mysterious, as if the Time Spirit were a reality, clothing itself ever in the most suitable garments and rejecting all others.'[100]

Laver's argument is perhaps formulated in reverse: clothing only seems eminently suitable to a time in hindsight because we attribute meaning to both social and sartorial forms from the same vantage point and so a parallel appears obvious. Japan is somewhat problematic even with regard to this, however, as its sartorial modernity was an avant-garde phenomenon and was defined by nonrepresentative extremes. The bustle dress was, both in its Euro-American context of origin and in Japan, extremely unsuited to the aesthetic dictates of modernity. It was a violent reaction against modernity. And yet it is such drastic counter-aesthetics which so often represent sartorial modernity.

It is easy, however, to construct a case in support of the argument that the changes in Japanese clothing fashions reflect and perform changes in Japanese society. Indeed, in the early modern Japanese context, it would be very difficult to dispute the interrelation of clothing and society that creates and reflects the age, in the way that Kroeber postulated. Both as part of the broad sweep of Japanese modern history and at a more micro level, fashion changes accompany basic social changes.[101] What is in accord with the spirit of one age is completely discordant with the spirit of a new age. A mode of dress that is outrageous at one point in time may be considered typical at a later time. Or, as Laver put it in his oft-quoted formula, '. . . the same dress is indecent ten years before its time, daring one year before its time, chic (chic being defined as contemporary seductiveness) in its time, dowdy three years after its time, hideous twenty years after its time, amusing thirty years after its time, romantic a hundred years after its time and beautiful a hundred and fifty years after its time.'[102]

Hirano Ken'ichirō argues that, in Japan, 'clothes have the function, among others, of symbolizing the world-view of the group of people who wear them.'[103] While Hirano still positions the role of clothing as merely reflective rather than participatory within the *Zeitgeist*, he does see clothing as being linked to history. Russian semiologist P. G. Bogatyrev goes further to assert that clothes, 'among other signs, express the aesthetic, moral, and national outlook—in short the will of the people wearing them'.[104] This expression of will is a much less passive characterization of the role of clothing. Not all of the elements that govern clothing operate at the same time; however, the relationship to the *Zeitgeist* is imperative in modernity. Alexandre Kojève interpreted Marx and Hegel as correct in predicting that history was inexorably progressing towards the emergence of a universal and homogeneous state—though liberal, not socialist.[105] This has implications for cultural objects such as clothes. Modernity, for Kojève, was an inevitable trend in one direction. The *Zeitgeist* was the progression to the completion of the dialectic between irrational and rational forms.

Modernity, Weber said, was the progressive disenchantment of the world. Superstitions disappeared; cultures grew more homogeneous; life became increasingly rational. The trend was steadily in one direction. Reactionary political movements— fascism and Bolshevism—and atavistic cultural differences when they appear— constitute a backlash against the general historical tendency, just as clothing styles that do not conform to the principles of modernity are antibodies generated within modernity and not external to it. This is the general shape of the *Zeitgeist* in the Japanese context; though many reactionary forms dominated much of clothing history in the early modern period, the progress of sartorial modernity was inevitable and indomitable.

Fashion as Aesthetics

Several major criticisms can be levelled against the application of functional and dynamic theories in the Japanese context. First, many theories confuse the part with the whole. Barthes called this the phylogenetic model, the tendency among theorists to see fashion as a collection of individual traits, each with its own evolutionary pathway to the present. This criticism has been levelled against the cyclic theory espoused by Kroeber. It has been argued that 'style consists of the total effect rather than single elements.'[106] Indeed, Kroeber's own evidence reveals differing rhythms for different parts or dimensions of dress. Moreover, 'specific embellishments are added or eliminated in irregular sequence,' and 'there is seldom a total repetition of style.'[107] While cycles of change may be identified in such things as skirt lengths or the general form of the skirt, we cannot say that fashion is a cyclical affair in the sense of providing precise repetitions. Such things as skirt length may be inherently cyclical—what else can skirt length do except go up or down? Wherever there is a finite number of alternatives, it is not surprising to find some rhythm of change among these alternatives. Furthermore, in Japan, modernity was a change in the nature of life that was both linear and irreversible. Once change had begun, it was an inexorable trend towards rationalism in form.

A second problem with most existing theories is their failure to account for all of the evidence. Fashion is a massive and largely unknowable event. What is knowable, to follow Derrida, is the history of meaning rather than an actual history of clothing, and therefore theories of clothing fashion are largely theories composed of adjustments to other theories rather than to empirical evidence. There is simply too much evidence to be encompassed, and the patterns that theorists choose to identify have often been arbitrarily selected because of the way they fit into other branches of knowledge. The convenience of certain evidence in favor of an argument will always mean that the majority of clothing will be ignored. This is not a problem that is easily overcome. The Japanese example illustrates the fact that most clothing behaviour and choices were actually against the trend being proclaimed. The majority of members of the population dressed against the general forms of modernity until well after the Second World War.

The argument that individuals employ fashion in the pursuit of meaning or identity or to experience a more fulfilling life does not explain why they will accept uncomfortable or unhealthy fashions. However, to argue that all fashion involves only status-striving or class-conventional behaviour is to overlook individual non-pecuniary aspects of clothing behaviour. This is an example of the attempt to fit fashion into other—economic or materialist—areas of knowledge and interpretation. Fashion can have differing elements that operate at different moments. The problems with all class-based or status-related theory are exemplified in the Japanese case. The different formation of class and evolution of individualism in Japan, in comparison with the West, meant that the role of clothing in these structures was also radically different. These theories are thus largely inapplicable.

This leads to the third general criticism: theories tend to focus on only a portion of the total process of fashion, while it is clear from the Japanese example that not all facets operate concurrently. Functional explanations tend to ignore fashion as a process, or at least they tend to ignore important aspects of the process. To interpret fashion in terms of individual or national identity and meaning is to recognize important elements in clothing behaviour, but it also overlooks the social structure required for the pursuit of identity and meaning to occur. The individual's sartorial actions must take place in the context of limited alternatives, and these alternatives exist prior to the individual.

A fourth problem with the existing theories is the ambiguous or unrealistic linkage they make between the structural and the social–psychological levels of social life. It has been noted that the problem with theories of individual identity and meaning is that the significance of the social structure is ambiguous at best. In the cyclic theories, the significance of the social–psychological level is ignored. Fashion is a supra-individual process that is external to, and coercive upon, the individual. Fashion exists as a social fact, but its traits are still manifested in individual objects, which contain features that are like a metaphoric DNA of the interpretation of fashion. Some interpretations hold that each element can reconstitute the whole. Yet theories in which ontogeny recapitulates phylogeny do not satisfactorily reconcile the individual and collective aspects of fashion.

A final problem is the generally ignored aesthetic component of fashion's governing dynamics. But this deficiency also provides the possibility of a coherent and engirding interpretation of modern Japanese clothing, and goes towards some manner of synthesis between the dynamic and functional interpretations of fashion. Ōtsuka Yasuji argued that the pivot of aesthetic experience was the experience of art and that

> Since creation and reception are at the centre of the work of art, and they develop in absolutely opposite directions, even the theory of empathy . . . while being appropriate to reception, is inadequate to explain the act of creation.[108]

Ōtsuka understood aesthetics to be limited by the assumption of its application only to the reception of an object. Fashions and aesthetics can be conceived as patterns of forms or tastes—at the level of the individual creation or the collective reception. Ōtsuka gave a lecture on the 'Artistic Value of Japan Clothes' in 1903, in which he argued that items of clothing could be understood as aesthetic objects on the level of artistic expression, both as a medium of self-actualization and at the level of collective judgement.[109] Ōtsuka highlighted the aesthetic differences between premodern Japanese clothing and modern clothes, mentioning the adherence to the body of modern tailored clothing and the fact that indigenous wrapped clothing allowed movement and posture to be seen. Using clothing, Ōtsuka differentiated between premodern and modern aesthetics; however, the real innovation from the point of view of fashion theory was that he regarded clothes unconditionally as aesthetic objects. Interestingly, modernism in clothing becomes more like the body, while modernism in objects rejects it as the primary source of form.

It was the aim of this book to assess the canon of fashion theory within the context of the Japanese experience of modernity. In the pursuit of this aim, it became clear that aesthetics and the treatment of clothes as aesthetic objects would be required to satisfactorily account for the motivations and the course of Japanese clothing history. Certain central assumptions about the governing dynamics of fashion were simply not applicable in the Japanese case. However, what was applicable, and probably had wider application than just in Japanese clothing history, was that fashion operated with a sui generis quality, in that it didn't merely represent or symbolize social conditions but was a means of performing and affecting the social. Furthermore, it was an activity engaged in and for itself—an aesthetic activity in that it had no greater purpose than itself. At some level at least, it was artistic practice and had the characteristics of artistic practice.

What was universal about the Japanese experience of sartorial modernity was that rationalism led to individualism, because individual experience was no longer mediated through the religio-ceremonial dimension of life. Thus the self and aesthetic experience became more important, because in a condition of disappearing supernaturalism there was nothing else. This facet of modernity was not a Western structure imposed upon Japan, as some aesthetics theory argues, but a universal reaction to the universal conditions of modernity. The self becomes an aesthetic expression— nonfunctional, existing in the Platonic sense of pleasure in itself, not through a lack or completion of a purpose. At the heart of fashion is this purely decorative motivation. Thus far, there have been dynamic or diachronic and functional or synchronic aspects of fashion theory. The *economics of aesthetics*, which this book has attempted to employ to explain modern Japanese fashion motivations, seeks to synthesize these two levels of explanation and demonstrate their concurrent functioning through an aesthetic framework.

In Japan, modernity, preference for the new—neophilia—because of the instability of constant rational questioning of epistemological authority was an idea of progress with an ill-defined destination, and it existed as a concept long before it existed as an actuality. This stylistic questioning naturally continually sought the reinstatement of earlier sartorial conditions. While modernity often appears to have a linear narrative of progress, it is actually characterized by uneven development. However, the trend of modernity is, despite multiple reactions against the general tendency, an irrepressible movement. Disenchantment is almost impossible to reverse. Traditionalism in Japanese clothing was an antibody generated by modernity, not a virus indigenous to Japan. Clothing modernity in Japan was at the heart of Japan's particular national trauma of late entry into the modern world. The replacement of supernaturalism with aesthetics shaped the Japanese discourse of sartorial modernity, perhaps to a unique degree. The problem of causation in fashion is deepened in the Japanese context by the extra dimension of a foreign/native dialectic that amplifies the traditional/modern dialectic. Yet Japan's responses were aesthetic—new ways of being, not just reflections of new ways of being. Clothing performed aesthetic modernity; it didn't just reflect it.

Notes

Chapter 1

1. Foucault argues that modernity created a new individual subject through discipline and the internalization of surveillance. See Michel Foucault, *Discipline and Punish: The Birth of the Prison*, trans. Alan Sheridan (New York: Pantheon, 1977).
2. This consideration, that social relations ontologically preceded individual consciousness, has its origins in Karl Marx's criticism of the conception of a conscious subject as an ideological conception on which political liberalism was founded. Karl Marx, *The Eighteenth Brumaire of Louis Bonaparte* (Moscow: Progress Publishers, 1954).
3. Anne Hollander, *Sex and Suits* (New York: A. A. Knopf, New York, 1994).
4. Michael Carter, *Fashion Classics* (Oxford: Berg, 2004).
5. Elizabeth Wilson, 'Fashion and Modernity', in Christopher Breward and Carline Evans, eds, *Fashion and Modernity* (Oxford: Berg, 2005). p. 9.
6. François-Louis Ganshof, *Feudalism*, trans. Philip Grierson (New York: Harper & Row, 1964).
7. Mark Bloch, *Feudal Society*, trans. L. A. Manyon (Chicago: University of Chicago Press, 1961).
8. Perry Anderson, *Lineages of the Absolutist State* (London: Verso, 1974). See Appendix on Japanese Feudalism, p. 435.
9. T. Fujitani, *Splendid Monarchy: Power and Pageantry in Modern Japan* (Berkeley: University of California Press, 1996), p. 19.
10. 'Enlightened times will only enlighten a small number of honest men—the common people will always be fanatical.' Quotation from Voltaire, *Candide* (London: Oxford University Press, 1968).
11. Susan Sontag, *Where the Stress Falls* (New York: Farrar Straus Giroux, 2001).
12. Arno Mayer, *The Persistence of the Old Regime: Europe to the Great War* (London: Croom Helm, 1981).
13. Clement Greenberg, 'Abstract and Representational', in *Works: The Collected Essays and Criticism* (Chicago: University of Chicago Press, 1986).
14. John Clark, 'What Modern and Contemporary Asian Art Is (Or Is Not): The View from MOMA and the View from Asia', lecture given at the symposium,

'The Modern in Asia', held 13 June 2004 at the Mori Art Museum in Tokyo. The symposium was held in connection with the exhibition 'Modern Means: Continuity and Change in Art, 1880 to the Present, Highlights from the Museum of Modern Art, New York', Mori Art Museum, Roppongi Hills, Tokyo. It was a critique of the general narrative of how modern art evolved in the American context and by extension how it will evolve in non-American contexts established and promulgated by Alfred H. Barr and the Museum of Modern Art in New York. See also John Clark, 'What Modern and Contemporary Asian Art Is (Or Is Not): The View from MOMA and the View from Asia', in John Clark, Maurizio Pelleggi and Kanaga Sabapathy, eds, *Eye of the Beholder* (Sydney, Australia: Wild Peony, 2006), pp. 297–319.

15. Charles Baudelaire, 'The Painter of Modern Life', in *The Painter of Modern Life and Other Essays*, trans. J. Mayne (London: Phaidon Press, 1964), p. 12.

16. Georg Simmel, 'The Metropolis and Mental Life', in *On Individuality and Social Forms* (Chicago: University of Chicago Press, 1971), pp. 324–39.

17. Walter Benjamin, 'On Some Motifs in Baudelaire', in Benjamin, *Illuminations*, trans. H. Zohn (London: Fontana/Collins, 1973).

18. Monet and impressionism were clearly influenced by Japan, as architecture and minimalism were influenced by Zen aesthetics. See Gary Hickey and Virginia Spate, *Monet and Japan* (Canberra: National Gallery of Australia, 2001).

19. Jean Baudrillard, paraphrased in an article by Wilson, 'Fashion and Modernity', p. 13.

20. Jean Baudrillard, *Symbolic Exchange and Death* (London: Sage, 1993), p. 95.

21. Jean Baudrillard, 'After the Orgy', in Baudrillard, *Symbolic Exchange and Death*.

22. For a summary and critique of James Laver's work, see Carter, *Fashion Classics*, Chapter 7.

23. Alfred Kroeber and J. Richardson, 'Three Centuries of Women's Dress Fashions: A Quantitative Analysis',' in A, L. Kroeber, *The Nature of Culture* (Chicago: University of Chicago Press, 1952).

24. Marx, *Eighteenth Brumaire*, p. 10.

25. See Zygmunt Bauman, *Hermeneutics and the Social Sciences: Approaches to Understanding* (London: Hutchinson, 1978); Meyer Schapiro, 'Style', in Sol Tax, ed., *Anthropology Today* (Chicago: University of Chicago Press, 1943); Georg Simmel, 'The Problem of Style', *Theory, Culture and Society* 8/3 (August 1991); and Susan Sontag, 'On Style', in Sontag, *Against Interpretation, and Other Essays* (New York: Octagon Books, 1978).

26. See exhibition catalogue, Tokyo National Museum, *Arts of East and West from World Expositions: 1855–1900: Paris, Vienna and Chicago* (Tokyo: NHK, 2004).

27. David Aram Kaiser and Marilyn Butler, *Romanticism, Aesthetics and Nationalism* (Cambridge: Cambridge University Press, 1999).

28. Simmel, 'The Problem of Style', p. 63.
29. This is essentially Georg Simmel's characterization. The more aesthetically autonomous the adorning object, he argues, the more it approaches the work of art. 'The work of art cannot, in principle, be incorporated into another life—it is a self-sufficient world, The essence of stylization is precisely the dilution of this individual poignancy, this generalization beyond the uniqueness of the personality.' Georg Simmel, 'Adornment', in David Frisby and Mike Featherstone, *Simmel on Culture* (London: Sage, 1997), p. 209. See also Michael Carter, *Putting a Face on Things* (Sydney, Australia: Power, 1997); and Tag Gronberg, 'Decoration: Modernism's Other', *Art History* 15 (December 1992).
30. See Donald Keene, *Dawn to the West*, vol. 3, *Japanese Literature of the Modern Era: Fiction* (New York: Columbia University Press, 1998), especially with reference to those authors who deal with Japan's engagement with modernity: Natsume Sōseki, Tanizaki Jun'ichirō, Kawabata Yasunari, Mori Ōgai and Nagai Kafū.
31. This use of *Zeitgeist* is very much James Laver's fashion-specific use of the term. 'It [fashion] all seems very wasteful and almost meaningless, this discarding of old clothes in order to conform to the whim of half a dozen French designers, but the matter is not quite so simple as that. The designers are not their own masters. They can only introduce an innovation if it happens to be in accordance with the spirit of the age.' James Laver, 'The Triumph of Time', in Sylva Norman, ed., *Contemporary Essays* (London: Elkin Mathews and Marrot, 1933).
32. Laver, 'The Triumph of Time'.
33. James Laver, *Taste and Fashion: From the French Revolution until To-day* (London: Harrap & Company, 1937), p. 255.
34. Maynard, *Out of Line: Australian Women and Style* (Sydney, Australia: University of New South Wales Press, 2001), p. 2.
35. Roland Barthes, *Oeuvres Complètes*, vol. 1 (Paris: Seuil, 1993), p. 743.
36. Georg Simmel, 'The Philosophy of Fashion', in D. Frisby and M. Featherstone, eds, *Simmel on Culture* (London: Sage, 1997), p. 205.
37. Georg Simmel, 'Sociological Aesthetics', quoted in David Frisby, *Fragments of Modernity* (Cambridge: Polity, 1985), p. 57.
38. Simmel, 'Philosophy of Fashion', p. 187.
39. Ibid., p. 192.
40. Kishida Ryūsei, 'Modaanjo—Short-haired Missy', trans. John Clark, in *Modern Boy Modern Girl: Modernity in Japanese Art 1910–1935* (Sydney, Australia: Art Gallery of New South Wales, 1998).
41. Max Weber, *The Protestant Ethic and the Spirit of Capitalism*, trans. Talcott Parsons (London: Unwin University Books, 1930).
42. Ibid.

43. See Harry Harootunian, *Overcome by Modernity: History, Culture and Community in Interwar Japan* (Princeton, NJ: Princeton University Press, 2000), pp. 95–101.

44. Kon Wajirō, *Gendai fuzoku* (Tokyo: Yusankaku, 1929).

45. Kawazoe Noboru, 'Kon Wajirō', in *Nihon minzoku bunka taikei* (Tokyo: Kondansha, 1978), p. 245.

46. Ibid., pp. 282–3.

47. John Clark, unpublished manuscript lent to the author, 2004.

48. Herbert Spencer, *The Principles of Sociology* (London: Williams and Norgate, 1896), p. 203. Originally published 1879.

49. Georg Simmel, 'Die ästhetische Bedautung des Gesichts', in *Brücke und Tür: Essays des Philosophen zur Geschichte, Religion, Kunst und Gesellschaft*, trans. Lore Ferguson (K. F. Koehler: Stuttgart, 1957), pp. 153–9.

Chapter 2

1. J. Edward Kidder, *Jomon Pottery: Prehistoric Japanese Arts, Contributions by Teruya Esaka* (Tokyo: Kodansha International, 1968).

2. Wm. Theodore de Bary, Donald Keene, George Tanabe and Paul Varley, *Sources of Japanese Tradition*, vol. 1, *From the Earliest Times to 1600* (New York: Columbia University Press, 2002).

3. Katsuhisa Takahashi, *Haniwa no seiki* (Tokyo: Kodansha, 1996).

4. Donald Keene, *Yoshimasa and the Silver Pavilion* (New York: Columbia University Press, 2003).

5. D. Jenkins, *The Floating World Revisited* (Portland, OR: Portland Art Museum, 1993).

6. T. Screech, *The Shogun's Painted Culture: Fear and Creativity in Japanese States, 1760–1829* (London: Reaktion Books, 2000).

7. D. Shively, 'Sumptuary Regulations and Status in early Tokugawa Japan', *Harvard Journal of Asiatic Studies* 25 (1965), pp. 123–34.

8. S. Thompson and H. Harootunian, *Undercurrents in the Floating World: Censorship and Japanese Prints* (New York: Asia Society, 1991).

9. Yoshikazu Hayashi, *Edo no niyuyojikan* (Tokyo: Kawade Shobo Shinsha, 1989).

10. Matsumiya Saburō, *Edo kabuki to kōkoku* (Tokyo: Tōhō Shobō, 1973).

11. Karl Marx and Frederick Engels, *The Communist Manifesto* (London: Penguin Classics, 2002).

12. Louis Menand, 'Foreword', in Edmund Wilson, *To the Finland Station* (New York: New York Review of Books, 2003).

13. Christopher Breward and Caroline Evans, *Fashion and Modernity* (Oxford: Berg, 2005).

14. Hannah Arendt, *The Origins of Totalitarianism* (New Haven, CT: Meridian, 1960).

15. Jordan Sand, 'The Cultured Life as Contested Space: Dwelling and Discourse in the 1920s', in Elise K. Tipton and John Clark, eds, *Being Modern in Japan* (Honolulu: University of Hawai'i Press, 2000), p. 99.

16. See William Jay Rathbun, *Beyond the Tanabata Bridge: Traditional Japanese Textiles* (Seattle, WA: Seattle Art Museum, 1993); Helen Minnich, *Japanese Costume and the Makers of its Elegant Tradition* (Rutland, VT: Tuttle, 1963); and Sanpei Takako, *Nihon kigyō-shi* (History of Textile Manufactures in Japan) (Tokyo: Yuzan-kaku, 1961).

17. Hirano Ken'ichirō, 'The Westernisation of Clothes and the State in Meiji Japan', in Hirano Ken'ichirō, ed., *The State and Cultural Transformation: Perspectives from East Asia* (Tokyo: United Nations University Press, 1993).

18. Ernst Haeckel, much like Herbert Spencer, was always quotable, even when wrong. His most famous theory, 'ontogeny recapitulates phylogeny', claims that the development of the embryo of every species repeats the evolutionary development of that species in full. Or otherwise put: each successive stage in the development of an individual represents one of the adult forms that appeared in its evolutionary history. This structure is repeated across social science, such as fashion, as well, leading to the conclusion that fashion, writ large, is a reproduction of individual sartorial actions and motivations. See Ernst Haeckel, *The Riddle of the Universe at the Close of the Nineteenth Century*, trans. J. McCabe (London: Watts, 1901). Originally published 1899.

19. The characterization of the mechanisms of fashion as superorganic will be taken up in Chapter 5 in relation to the theory of A. L. Kroeber, 'On the Principle of Order in Civilization as Exemplified by Changes of Fashion,' *American Anthropologist* 21 (July 1919).

20. For Edo culture with regard to free choice and social restriction in dress, see Nishiyama Matsunosuke, *Edo Culture: Daily Life and Diversions in Urban Japan, 1600–1868*, trans. Gerald Groemer (Honolulu: University of Hawai'i Press, 1997).

21. Even today, conceptions of Japanese fashion tend towards nonrepresentative extremes. Publications such as Aoki Shaoichi, *Fruits* (London: Phaidon Press, 2001), and Louise Mitchell, *The Cutting Edge: Fashion from Japan* (Sydney, Australia: Powerhouse Publishing, 2005), describe minority fashion cultures, which they then use to attempt to define a Japanese essence.

22. See Takamatsu Mari, 'Ethics of Exhibitions: A Study on Representation of the Female Nude in the Last Decade of the 19th Century in Japan', in *Studies in Aesthetics and Art History*, vol. 21 (Kyoto: Department of Aesthetics and Art History, Kyoto University, 2000).

23. *The Voyage of the Beagle*, published in 1839, is Charles Darwin's memoir of his five-year voyage on the ship HMS *Beagle*, beginning in 1831, when he was twenty-two. *The Voyage of the Beagle* is a detailed scientific field journal, covering biology, geology and anthropology, that demonstrates Darwin's keen

power of observation, at a time when Westerners were still discovering much
of the rest of the world. It also hints at ideas that Darwin would later develop
into the theory of evolution. Thus it is not exactly accurate to say that Darwin
assumed the Patagonian Indians were at the lowest stage of evolution as his
theory of evolution was not yet complete. In Patagonian culture there were
quite complex clothing customs, and it just happened that the highest level of
formality was in fact being naked. Therefore, even intertextually, where clothing is seen as a hierarchical indicator of civilization, Darwin's conclusions were
incorrect, as he had not observed the entire range of dress customs of the Patagonian Indians; nor did he account for the possibility that nakedness could
be part of a system rather than the absence of one. If all that was observed of
Western culture of the nineteenth century was nude painting, then that too could
be misunderstood as a clothing norm rather than a specific pictorial, supremely
intimate, level of formality. See E. Janet Browne, *Charles Darwin: Voyaging*
(Princeton, NJ: Princeton University Press, 1996).
24. This purely political approach to early Japanese clothing modernity is common amongst the more politically focused of historians, especially in Marius
B. Jansen, ed., *The Nineteenth Century*, vol. 5 of *The Cambridge History of
Japan*, ed. Marius B. Jansen, John W. Hall, Madoka Kanai and Denis Twitchett
(Cambridge: Cambridge University Press, 1989).
25. Fujitani, *Splendid Monarchy*, p. 19.
26. This where Fujitani's thesis differs from what Foucault might have argued. Foucault, in the Western context, would perhaps have drawn the opposite conclusion: the common people were *available* for regulation as the material through
which a society's norms could be demonstrably created.
27. Fujitani, *Splendid Monarchy*.
28. Foucault, *Discipline and Punish*.
29. Edward Seidensticker, *Low City, High City* (London: Allen Lane, 1983), p. 43.
30. The Western comparison is of course imperfect in such general terms, and a
specificity of consideration of Japanese fashion and modernity is still required
because there is no simple comparison to contemporary Western models. For
an examination of the French Revolution with regard to the body and morality,
see Lynn Hunt, ed., The *Invention of Pornography: Obscenity and the Origins
of Modernity, 1500–1800* (New York: Zone Books, 1993).
31. Fujitani, *Splendid Monarchy*, pp. 20–21.
32. Adam Smith, *An Inquiry into the Nature and Causes of the Wealth of Nations*
(Oxford: Clarendon Press, 1976).
33. Ibid.
34. Emile Durkheim, *The Division of Labor in Society* (New York; Free Press,
1964).
35. Roland Barthes, *Barthes, Selected Writings*, ed. and with an introduction by
Susan Sontag (London: Fortuna, 1983).

36. This point is illustrated in Yasunari Kawabata, *Asakusa kurenaidan (The Scarlet Gang of Asakusa)*, trans. Alisa Freedman (Berkeley: University of California Press, 2005), especially Ronald Richie's Foreword to the text.

37. Barthes, *Barthes, Selected Writings*.

38. Roland Barthes, 'The Striptease', in *Barthes, Selected Writings*.

39. Paul Derval, *The Folies Bergère*, trans. Lucienne Hill (London: Methuen, 1955); and Charles Castle, *The Folies Bergère* (London: Methuen, 1982).

40. Ian Burma, 'Virtual Violence', *New York Review of Books* 52/11 (23 June 2005).

41. For a description of those days and the times of the Casino Folies, see Edward Seidensticker, *Tokyo Rising: The City since the Great Earthquake* (New York: Knopf, 1990); and Seidensticker, *Low City, High City*.

42. Seidensticker, *Tokyo Rising*, p. 76.

43. Isozaki Arata, 'Of City, Nation and Style', in Masao Miyoshi and H. D. Harootunian, eds, *Postmodernism in Japan: Post-Contemporary Interventions* (Durham, NC: Duke University Press; 1989).

44. Kendall H. Brown and Sharon A. Minichiello, *Taishō Chic: Japanese Modernity, Nostalgia and Deco* (Honolulu: Honolulu Academy of Arts, 2002), p. 18. For a work of large scope, see Shuji Takanashi, ed., *Yoga to Nihonga: Kindai no bijutsu II* (Tokyo: Kodansha, 1992).

45. See Timothy Clark, *Kitagawa Utamaro* (Tokyo: Asahi Shinbunsha, 1995). This is the catalogue of an exhibition held at the British Museum, London, August–October 1995, and at Chiba City Art Museum, November–December 1995.

46. An obvious example is provided by Ishii Hakutei and the Sasaku Hanga artists. See Chiaki Ajioka, Noriko Kuwahara and Junko Nishiyama, *Hanga: Japanese Creative Prints* (Sydney, Australia: Art Gallery of New South Wales, 2000).

47. Barbara Sato, *The New Japanese Woman: Modernity, Media and Women in Interwar Japan* (Durham, NC: Duke University Press, 2003).

48. Vera Mackie, 'Modern Selves and Modern Spaces', in Elise K. Tipton and John Clark, eds, *Being Modern in Japan* (Honolulu: University of Hawai'i Press, 2000), p. 194.

49. For discussions of the *moga*, see Miriam Silverberg, 'The Modern Girl as Militant', in Gail Lee Bernstein, ed., *Recreating Japanese Women: 1600–1945* (Berkeley: University of California Press, 1991); Silverberg, 'The Café Waitress Serving Modern Japan', in Stephen Vlastos, ed., *Mirror of Modernity: Invented Traditions of Modern Japan* (Berkeley: University of California Press, 1991); and Elise K. Tipton, 'The Café, Contested Space of Modernity in Interwar Japan', in Elise K. Tipton and John Clark, eds, *Being Modern in Japan* (Honolulu: University of Hawai'i Press, 2000).

50. 'Modern Girl', *Shiseidō geppō*, June 1926. Available in Shiseidō Corporate Museum.

51. Thorstein Veblen, *The Theory of the Leisure Class* (New York: Mentor Books, 1953). Originally published 1899.

52. Louis Vuitton opened a luggage shop in Paris in 1854. A century and a half later, Vuitton's handbags and luggage are a status symbol around the world. Hata Kyōjirō, the CEO of Louis Vuitton Japan, claims that 44 per cent of Japanese women own at least one Louis Vuitton product, signalling perhaps a democratization of luxury in which the item itself signals the luxury, not its scarcity or exclusiveness. Hata Kyōjirō, *Louis Vuitton Japan: The Building of Luxury* (Tokyo: Nikkei, 2003).

53. The terms sadism and masochism were first used consistently to describe these behaviours by the German psychoanalyst Richard Freiherr von Krafft-Ebing in his 1886 book *Psychopathia Sexualis*, a famous study of sexual perversity. Sigmund Freud, a contemporary of Krafft-Ebing, noted that both were often found in the same individuals, and combined the two into a single dichotomous entity known as sadomasochism (often abbreviated as S&M or S/M).

54. Richard Martin and Harold Koda, *Infra-apparel* (New York: Metropolitan Museum of Art, 1993).

55. Sanpei Takako, *Nihon kigyō-shi*, pp. 107, 115, 124, 143–6, 150, 197–291.

56. Chihō-shi Kenkyū Kyōgikai (Local History Society), *Nihon sangyō-shi taikei* (History of Manufactures in Japan) (Tokyo: University of Tokyo Press, 1961), vol. 1, p. 271.

57. Thomas Carlyle Smith mentions that in the Bunka era (1804–1818), some sheep were imported from China to provide wool for the Tokugawa family. See *Political Change and Industrial Development in Japan: Government Enterprise, 1868–1880* (Stanford, CA: Stanford University Press, 1955), p. 63. In terms of output, this could not have amounted to much.

58. Nihon Orimono Shimbunsha (Japan Textile News Co.), *Dai Nihon orimono 2600-nen shi* (A 2600-Year History of Textiles in Greater Japan) (Tokyo: Nihon Orimono Shimbunsha, 1940), vol. 1, pp. 220–3; vol. 2, p. 266. Some wool was imported as early as the Ashikaga period (1392–1568). See Smith, *Political Change and Industrial Development in Japan*, p. 63.

59. Osaka Yōfuku Sho-Dōgyō Kumiai (Osaka Association of Merchants and Tailors of Western Suits), *Nihon yōfuku enkaku-shi* (The History of Western Suits in Japan) (Osaka: Osaka Yōfuku Sho-Dōgyō Kumiai, 1930), pp. 26–8.

60. Between 1859 and 1868, imports of woollen fabrics for the army and navy amounted to between 20 and 40 per cent of total imports. Japan Statistical Association, *Historical Statistics of Japan* (Tokyo: Japan Statistical Association, 1987), vols 1 and 3.

61. Osaka Yōfuku Sho-Dōgyō Kumiai, *Nihon yōfuku enkaku-shi*, pp. 26–8.

62. See Tokyo Yōfuku Shokogyo Dogyo Kumiai Kanda-ku bu, *Tōkyō yōfuku shokogyō dōgyō kumiai enkaku-shi* (The History of the Tokyo Association

of Merchants and Manufacturers of Western Suits) (Tokyo: Tokyo Yōfuku Shokogyo Dogyo Kumiai Kanda-ku bu, 1920), pp. 53–72.

63. Osaka Yōfuku Sho-Dōgyō Kumiai, *Nihon yōfuku enkaku-shi*, p. 134.

64. D. C. Bissell, *The First Conglomerate: 145 Years of the Singer Sewing Machine Company* (New York: Audenreed Press, 1999).

65. Osaka Yōfuku Sho-Dōgyō Kumiai, *Nihon yōfuku enkaku-shi*, pp. 65–88.

66. Meirion Harries, *Soldiers of the Sun: The Rise and Fall of the Imperial Japanese Army* (New York: Random House, 1991).

67. Osaka Yōfuku Sho-Dōgyō Kumiai, *Nihon yōfuku enkaku-shi*, pp. 65–88.

68. Irokawa Daikichi, *The Culture of the Meiji Period*, translation edited by Marius B. Jansen (Princeton, NJ: Princeton University Press, 1985). Originally published as *Meiji no bunka*.

69. Hirano Ken'ichirō, 'The Westernisation of Clothes and the State in Meiji Japan'.

70. Osaka Yōfuku Sho-Dōgyō Kumiai *Nihon yōfuku enkaku-shi*, pp. 80–1.

71. The differences in dress during the rebellion can be seen in the contemporary paintings contained in Fudō Kenji, ed., *Gahō kindai 100-nenshi*, (A Hundred-year Pictorial History of Modern Japan) (Tokyo: Nihon Kindai-shi Kenkyu-kai, Kokusai bunka Jōhō-sha, 1951), vol. 4, pp. 316–19.

72. Hirano Ken'ichirō, 'The Westernisation of Clothes and the State in Meiji Japan'.

73. See Tōkyō Fujin-Kodomo Fuku Seizō Oroshi Kyōdō Kumiai (The Cooperative Society of the Manufacturers and Wholesalers of Ladies' and Children's Suits in Tokyo), *Tōkyō fujin-kodomo fuku gyōkai 30-nenshi* (A Thirty Year History of the Ladies' and Children's Suits Traders of Tōkyō) (Tokyo: Tokyo Fujin-Kodomo Fuku Seizō Oroshi Kyōdō Kumiai, 1960), pp. 9–12.

74. Shirokiya Co., *Shirokiya 300-nenshi* (A Three Hundred Year History of the Shirokiya) (Tokyo: Shirokiya Co., 1957), p. 252.

75. Osaka Yōfuku Sho-Dōgyō Kumiai *Nihon yōfuku enkaku-shi*, pp. 113–14. Obviously these transformations took quite some time. In Reischauer's essay on the Japanologist Serge Elisséeff, we read that after Elisséeff was admitted to Tokyo Imperial University in 1908, he 'soon shifted from the student uniform to a kimono and hakama, the formal double skirt, then worn by the more old-fashioned students and men of education.' Edwin O. Reischauer, 'Serge Elisséeff', *Harvard Journal of Asiatic Studies* 20 (June 1957), p. 11.

76. Ishibashi Tanzan, *Nihon bōeki shoran* (Foreign Trade of Japan: A Statistical Survey) (Tokyo: Tōyō Keizai Shimpō-sha, the Oriental Economist, 1935), p. 243.

77. Setsuo Uenoda, *Japan, Yesterday and Today: Sketches and Essays on Japanese City Life*, 2nd edn (Tokyo: Tokyo News Service, 1956).

78. Susan B. Hanley, *Everyday Things in Premodern Japan: The Hidden Legacy of Material Culture* (Berkeley: University of California Press, 1997), pp. 69–71.

79. Itō Yoshiichi, *Edo no Yumenoshima* (Tokyo: Yoshikawa Kōbunkan, 1982) pp. 26–8.

80. Mackie, 'Modern Selves and Modern Spaces.'

81. Marius B. Jansen, *The Making of Modern Japan* (Cambridge, MA: Harvard University Press, 2000), p. 569.
82. For the Great Kanto Earthquake, see Seidensticker, *Tokyo Rising*.
83. On the rise of the conductress, see Nakagawa Kōichi, *Basu no Bunkashi* (The Cultural History of the Bus) (Tokyo: Chikuma-shobō, 1986), pp. 151–5.
84. Seidensticker, *Tokyo Rising*, pp. 33–5.
85. Ibid.
86. Nitobe Inazo, *Bushido: The Soul of Japan* (New York: G. P. Putnam's Sons, 2001), p. 135. Originally published 1905.
87. Seidensticker, *Tokyo Rising*, pp. 33–5.
88. Seidensticker, *Tokyo Rising*.
89. 'Japanese Ministry of Education: School Health Statistics', in Japan Statistical Association, *Historical Statistics of Japan*, vols 1 and 3 (Tokyo: Japan Statistical Association, 1987).
90. Michael Smitka, *The Textile Industry and the Rise of the Japanese Economy*, Japanese Economic History 1600–1960, no. 4 (New York: Garland, 1998).
91. Osaka Yōfuku Sho-Dōgyō Kumiai, *Nihon yōfuku enkaku-shi*.
92. Hirano Ken'ichirō, 'The Westernisation of Clothes and the State in Meiji Japan'.
93. Ibid.
94. According to Jackie Hogan, 'The Social Significance of English Usage in Japan', *Japanese Studies* 23/1 (May 2003), pp. 43–58, English-derived vocabulary in Japan serves both referential and pragmatic functions. It is used to label the world and to shape it in particular ways. Hogan's article examines the ways in which speakers in one rural community in Japan use English-derived lexical items to manage personal impressions and social distance, to negotiate socially sensitive topics and to express subtle approval or disapproval of the West and Western cultural influences in Japan.
95. Hanley, *Everyday Things in Premodern Japan*; and Nihon Orimono Shimbunsha, *Dai Nihon orimono 2600-nen shi.*
96. Kozo Yamamura and Susan B. Hanley, *Economic and Demographic Change in Preindustrial Japan 1600–1868* (Princeton, NJ: Princeton University Press, 1977).
97. Hanley, *Everyday Things in Premodern Japan*, pp. 174–8.
98. For an analysis of Kabuki and its dynamic role in society, see Seidensticker, *Low City, High City*; and Toshio Kawatake, *Kabuki: Baroque Fusion of the Arts*, trans. Frank and Jean Connell Hoff (Tokyo: International House of Japan, 2003).
99. John G. Roberts, *Mitsui: Three Centuries of Japanese Business* New York: Art Media Resources, 1989).
100. Ibid.
101. Seidensticker, *Low City, High City*, gives a history of the development of department stores and their role in the changing acquisitive patterns of Japan.

102. Seidensticker, *Low City, High City*, pp. 108–13.
103. Ibid., p. 112.
104. Ibid., p. 113.
105. Ibid.
106. The survey is quoted but unreferenced in Seidensticker, *Tokyo Rising*, pp. 40–2.
107. Survey quoted but unreferenced in Seidensticker, *Tokyo Rising*, pp. 40–2.
108. Churchill was referring to warfare, but his point can be taken more universally as referring to a major difference in time. From Paul Virilio and Sylvère Lotringer, *Pure War* (New York: Semiotext(e), 1997), p. 19.

Chapter 3

1. Carol Gluck, *Japan's Modern Myths: Ideology in the Late Meiji Period* (Princeton, NJ: Princeton University Press, 1985). See also Jansen, *The Nineteenth Century*.
2. See especially James Laver, *The Age of Optimism: Manners and Morals, 1848–1914* (London: Weidenfeld & Nicolson, 1966). Also see James Laver, *British Military Uniforms* (London: Penguin, 1948).
3. See Harries, *Soldiers of the Sun*; and Emiko Ohnuki-Tierney, *Kamikaze, Cherry Blossoms, and Nationalisms: The Militarization of Aesthetics in Japanese History* (Chicago: University of Chicago Press, 2001).
4. Jordan Sand, *House and Home in Modern Japan: Architecture, Domestic Space, and Bourgeois Culture 1880–1930* (Cambridge, MA: Harvard University Press, 2003).
5. At the end of the eighteenth century, the bourgeois male underwent what has been called the 'great masculine renunciation'. J. C. Flügel, *The Psychology of Clothes* (London: Hogarth, 1930), p. 111.
6. Julia Meech-Pekarik, *The World of the Meiji Print* New York and Tokyo: Weatherhill, 1986). p. 102.
7. Fujitani, *Splendid Monarchy*.
8. William Elliot Griffis, *The Mikado: Institution and Person* (Princeton, NJ: Princeton University Press, 1915), p. 308.
9. See Taki Kōji, *Tennō no shōzō* (Tokyo: Iwanami Shoten, 1988).
10. Luke Gartlan, 'With Argus Eyes: The Early Life and Work of Baron von Stillfried-Ratenicz (1939–1911)', unpublished thesis, Department of Art History and Theory, University of Sydney, Australia, 2004, discusses an earlier photograph which was actually the first photograph taken of the Emperor. The photograph, by Raimund von Stillfried-Ratenicz, 'His Imperial Majesty the Tenno of Japan and Suite, 1872', can be seen as plate 59 in John Clark, *Japanese Exchanges in Art 1850s–1930s with Britain, Continental Europe and the USA* (Sydney, Australia: Power Publications, 2001).

11. Joshua S. Mostow, Norman Bryson and Maribeth Graybill, *Gender and Power in the Japanese Visual Field* (Honolulu: University of Hawai'i Press, 2003).

12. Laver, *British Military Uniforms*.

13. Ota Rinichiro, *Nihon kindai gunpuku shi* (Tokyo: Yūzankaku Shuppan, 1972), pp. 7–10.

14. One of those orders is found as the entry of 1 July 1861 in Kuroita Katsumi, *Zoku Tokugawa jikki* (The True Record of the Tokugawa Continued) (Tokyo: Kokushi Taikei Henshu-kai, 1976). See also Ienaga Saburō, *Nihonjin no yōfuku kan no hensen* (Tokyo: Domesu Shuppan, 1976), p. 22.

15. Ota Rinichiro, *Nihon kindai gunpuku shi*, pp. 12–16.

16. Tanno Iku, ed., *Sōgō fukushoku-shi jitem* (General Clothing History Encyclopedia) (Tokyo: Yūzankaku, 1980), p. 134.

17. Ota Rinichiro, 'Kindai Nihon gunpuku shi', *Hifuku bunka*, Bunka Fukusō Gakuin, Tokyo, no. 68 (October 1961), p. 17.

18. Laver, *British Military Uniforms*.

19. Tanno Iku, ed., *Sōgō fukushoku-shi jitem*, pp. 240–3.

20. Shōwa Joshi Daigaku Hifukugaku Kenkyūshitsu, *Kindai Nihon fukusō-shi* (Tokyo: Kindai Bunka Kenkyujo, 1971), p. 53.

21. Ibid., pp. 326–7.

22. Tanno Iku, ed., *Sōgō fukushoku-shi jitem*, pp. 240–3.

23. Theodore F. Cook, 'Soldiers in Meiji Society and State: Japan Joins the World', in Banno Junji, ed., *Nihon kin-gendai shi* (Tokyo: Iwanami Shoten, 993).

24. Jansen, *The Making of Modern Japan*; and Jansen, *The Nineteenth Century*.

25. Jansen, *The Making of Modern Japan*, pp. 396–7.

26. Foucault, *Discipline and Punish*.

27. Fujitani, *Splendid Monarchy*, p. 25.

28. Taki Kōji, *Tennō no Shōzō*.

29. Fujitani, *Splendid Monarchy*, p. 177.

30. Jason G. Karlin, 'The Gender of Nationalism: Competing Masculinities in Meiji Japan', in *Journal of Japanese Studies* 28/1 (Winter 2002).

31. Fujitani, *Splendid Monarchy*, p. 192.

32. Albert Altman, 'Shimbunshi: The Early Meiji Adaptation of the Western Style Newspaper', in W. G. Beasley, ed., *Modern Japan: Aspects of History, Literature and Society* (Berkeley: University of California Press, 1975), p. 64.

33. Meech-Pekarik, *The World of the Meiji Print*, p. 105.

34. *The Far East* (16 January 1872).

35. Meech-Pekarik, *The World of the Meiji Print*, p. 105.

36. *The Far East* (16 January 1872).

37. Meech-Pekarik, *The World of the Meiji Print*, p. 106.

38. Tsuda Mamichi, 'An Official Insignia,' in *Meiroku Zasshi: Journal of the Japanese Enlightenment*, trans. William Reynolds Braisted (Cambridge, MA:

Harvard University Press, 1976). For the Emperor's visit to Kyoto in 1872, see *The Far East* (1 August 1872).

39. Laver, *British Military Uniforms*, p. 23.
40. Marius B. Jansen, *China in the Tokugawa World* (Cambridge, MA: Harvard University Press, 1992), pp. 116–18.
41. Hollander, *Sex and Suits*.
42. Flügel, *The Psychology of Clothes*.
43. This orthodox account of the development of the suit and the bourgeoisie is seen in Hollander, *Sex and Suits*. See also John Harvey, *Men in Black* (Chicago: University of Chicago Press, 1995).
44. Anderson, *Lineages of the Absolutist State*, p. 450.
45. C. D. Sheldon, *The Rise of the Merchant Class in Tokugawa Japan 1600–1868*, (New York: J. J. Augustin Inc., 1958), pp. 33–6.
46. Anderson, *Lineages of the Absolutist State*, pp. 451–2.
47. Toshio George Tsukahira, *Feudal Control in Tokugawa Japan: The Sankin-kōtai System* (Cambridge, MA: Harvard University Press, 1966), pp. 96–102.
48. John Whitney Hall, *Japan from Prehistory to Modern Times* (New York: Dell, 1970), p. 210.
49. Vladimir Lenin emphasized that 'It is impossible to conceive a capitalist nation without foreign trade, nor is there any such nation' See *Collected Works*, vol. 3, (London: Martin Lawrence, 1927), p. 65. The shogunal policy of seclusion, in effect, precluded any possibility of transition to the capitalist mode of production proper within the Tokugawa framework.
50. Nishiyama Matsunosuke, *Edo Culture*.
51. Kozo Yamamura and Hanley, *Economic and Demographic Change in Preindustrial Japan 1600–1868*.
52. Hanley, *Everyday Things in Premodern Japan*, p. 2.
53. Allen C. Kelley and Jeffery G. Williamson, *Lessons from Japanese Development: An Analytical Economic History* (Chicago: University of Chicago Press, 1974), pp. 22–3.
54. Hanley, *Everyday Things in Premodern Japan*, p. 95.
55. Joan Thirsk, *Economic Policy and Projects: The Development of a Consumer Society in Early Modern England* (Oxford: Clarendon Press, 1978).
56. Charles Baudelaire, *Selected Writings on Art and Artists*, trans. P. E. Charvet (London: Penguin Books, 1972), p. 105.
57. Robert Hughes, *American Visions* (London: Random House, 1997), pp. 69–137.
58. Johann Joachim Winckelmann, *Selections*, trans. David Irwin (London: Phaidon Press, 1972).
59. Hollander, *Sex and Suits*.
60. Alain de Botton, *On Seeing and Noticing* (London: Penguin, 2005), p. 29.
61. Weber, *The Protestant Ethic*.

62. The idea of a civilized centre came from Michael Carter at the University of Sydney in a series of lectures on 'Costume, Clothing and Fashion' given in 1998.
63. Nakaano Hajiimu, 'Introduction to the Work of Kuki Shūzō', in Kuki Shūzō, *Iki no kōzō* (Reflections on Japanese Taste: the Structure of Iki), trans. John Clark (Sydney, Australia: Power Publications, 1997), p. 10.
64. Kuki Shūzō, *Iki no kōzō*, p. 38.
65. Susan Sontag, 'Notes on Camp', in Susan Sontag, *Against Interpretation, and Other Essays* (New York: Octagon Books, 1978).
66. Nakaano Hajiimu, 'Introduction to the Work of Kuki Shūzō', p. 12.
67. Kuki Shūzō, *Iki no kōzō*, pp. 39–40.
68. Jimbō, *Ukiyo-buro*, p. 206. Quoted in Kuki Shūzō, *Iki no kōzō*, p. 76.
69. Kuki Shūzō, *Iki no kōzō*, p. 76.
70. See Adam Gopnik, 'Shining Tree of Life: What the Shakers Did', *New Yorker* (13 and 20 February 2006).
71. Kuki Shūzō, *Iki no kōzō*, p. 87.
72. Terry Smith, *Making the Modern: Industry, Art and Design in America* (Chicago: Chicago University Press, 1993).
73. Jean-Jacques Rousseau, *The Social Contract*, trans. Maurice Cranston (London: Penguin books, 1968), p. 59.
74. Laver, *Taste and Fashion*.
75. David Givens, a research anthropologist, quoted in Robert Wright, *The Moral Animal* (London: Vintage, 1994).
76. Jansen, *The Nineteenth Century*.
77. Jansen, *The Making of Modern Japan*.
78. Fukuzawa Yūkichi, *Autobiography*, trans. Eiichi Kiyooka (New York: Columbia University Press, 1960).
79. Ibid.
80. Carmen Blacker, *The Japanese Enlightenment: A Study of the Writings of Fukuzawa Yūkichi* (Cambridge: Cambridge University Press, 1964).
81. George Sanson, *The Western World and Japan* (New York: A. A. Knopf, 1951), p. 428.
82. Henry T. Finck, *Lotos-Time in Japan* (New York: Charles Scribner's Sons, 1895), p. 112.
83. Isabella Bird, *Unbeaten Tracks in Japan* (New York: G. P. Putnam's, 1880), p. 11.
84. Translated in the *Japan Weekly Mail* (7 November 1885).
85. *Japan Weekly Mail* (7 November 1885).
86. Meech-Pekarik, *The World of the Meiji Print*, p. 144.
87. Erwin Baelz, *Awakening Japan: The Diary of a German Doctor*, ed. Toku Baelz (Bloomington: Indiana University Press, 1974), pp. 30–1.
88. Inoue's document on the empire of the Eastern Sea is quoted in Donald Shively, 'The Japanization of the Middle Meiji', in Donald Shively, ed., *Tradition and*

Modernization in Japanese Culture (Princeton, NJ: Princeton University Press, 1971), pp. 77–119. Erwin Baelz writes about Inoue in *Awakening Japan,*. p. 66.

89. See the Rokumeikan menu for 3 June 1885, illustrated in Asukai Masamichi, ed., *Meiji*, vol. 11 of Kodama Kōta, Hayashiya Tatsusaburō and Higuchi Kiyoyuki, eds., *Zusetsu Nihon bunka no rekishi* (Pictorial History of Japanese Culture) (Tokyo: Shōgakukan, 1981), p. 156.

Chapter 4

1. Meech-Pekarik, *The World of the Meiji Print*, p. 137.
2. These stages are suggested by Meech-Pekarik in *The World of the Meiji Print*, p. 137.
3. Stella Blum, 'Evolution of Fashion: 1835–1895', in Blum et al., *Rōman ishōten* (Exhibition of Romantic Clothing) (Kyoto: Kyoto Costume Institute, 1980).
4. Stella Blum, *Victorian Fashions and Costumes from Harper's Bazaar, 1867–1898* (New York: Dover Publications, 1974).
5. Hanley, *Everyday Things in Premodern Japan*, pp. 166–7.
6. Rula Razek, *Dress Codes: Reading Nineteenth Century Fashion* (Stanford, CA: Stanford University Press, 1999).
7. Meech-Pekarik, *The World of the Meiji Print*.
8. Ibid.
9. Ienaga Saburō, *Nihonjin no yōfuku kan no hensen*, pp. 27–9.
10. Lacadio Hearn, *The Japanese Letters of Lacadio Hearn*, ed. Elizabeth Bisland (Wilmington, DE: Scholarly Resources, 1973), p. 233.
11. Brown and Minichiello, *Taishō Chic*, p. 32.
12. *Josei* was a women's magazine originally published monthly in Osaka and Tokyo by Purantonsha from May 1922 to May 1928. Reprinted with a supplement under the title *Zasshi Josei*, by Turumi Shunsuke (Tokyo: Nihon Tosho Centre, 1991–1993).
13. Known in the English translation as *Naomi*. Tanizaki Jun'ichirō, *Naomi*, trans. Anthony Chambers (Tokyo: Charles E. Tuttle, 1985).
14. Satō, *The New Japanese Woman*.
15. Barbara Satō, 'An Alternate Informant: Middle Class Women and Mass Magazines in 1920s Japan', in Elise K. Tipton and John Clark, eds, *Being Modern in Japan* (Sydney: Australian Humanities Research Foundation, 2000).
16. Yamakawa Kikue, *Yamakawa Kikue Shū*, vol. 5 (Tokyo: Iwanami Shoten, 1982), p. 290.
17. The argument is made with regard to pens, photography, sound recording and other things in Tanizaki Jun'ichirō, *In Praise of Shadows*, trans. Thomas J. Harper and Edward G. Seidensticker (New Haven, CT: Leete's Island Books, 1977), pp. 7–9.

18. F. Scott Fitzgerald, *The Great Gatsby* (New York: C. Scribner's Sons, 1925).

19. Aloïs Riegl argued that in art, while classicist aesthetics tacitly assumed only one type of beauty or perfect form, there was actually a dialectic between two types of beauty or intrinsic formal perfection, and he set out two comprehensive principles of form in art: the animate organic and the inanimate, symmetrical crystalline. He argues that this dialectic is played out in the history of art, with different ages and cultures valuing either more organic (Classical Greece, High Renaissance) or more crystalline (Egyptian and Byzantine) aesthetics. Aloïs Riegl, *Problems of Style: Foundations for a History of Ornament*, trans. Evelyn Kain (Princeton, NJ: Princeton University Press, 1992).

20. Tanizaki Jun'ichirō, quoted in Seidensticker, *Tokyo Rising*, pp. 25–26.

21. Nagai Kafū, *During the Rains and Flowers in the Shade: Two Novellas*, trans. Lane Dunlop (Stanford, CA: Stanford University Press, 1994).

22. Akagi Shunsuke, 'Hitomi Kinue', in Tsubota Itsuō, ed., *Taisho no josei gunzō, Nihon josei no rekishi 12* (History of Japanese Women, vol. 12, A Group Portrait of Taishō Period Women) (Tokyo: Akatsuki kyōiku tosho, 1981), pp. 64–5.

23. *Bijingaku* (A Study of Beautiful Women), published by Fujin sekai (Woman's World Magazine) company, Tokyo, 1927.

24. Tanizaki Jun'ichirō, *Naomi*, pp. 29–30.

25. The story, reported originally in *Miyako shinbun*, was published in the *Japan Times* (22 January 1941). See also 'Kenkō yakudōbi kinsei, yokusan bijin ni kagakuteki kentō', in *Bijutsu Nippon* 7/2 (February 1941). The committee was made up of several doctors, dancer Ishii Baku, yōga painter Nakamura Ken'ichi and nihonga painter Itō Shinsui. Part of the committee's mandate was to determine and then disseminate the characteristics of a new Shōwa beauty, or 'New Structure beauty' (*shintaisei bijin*) in line with the New Structure (*shintaisei*) being promulgated by the government.

26. Kishida Ryūsei, 'Modaanjo—Short-haired Missy'.

27. *The Shiseidō Story: A History of Shiseidō: 1872–1972* (Tokyo: Shiseidō Public Relations Department, 2003).

28. Murata Takako, *Female Beauty in Modern Japan: Makeup and Coiffure* Tokyo: Pola Research Institute of Beauty and Culture, 2003), p. 63.

29. *Seitō* (Bluestocking) magazine, reprinted by Meiji Bunken, Tokyo, 1967–1970. Originally published monthly, Seitōsha, 1911–1916.

30. Information from the Pola Museum and its publication, *Female Beauty in Modern Japan: Makeup and Coiffure*, ed. Murata Takako, trans. Komada Makiko (Tokyo: Pola Research Institute of Beauty and Culture, 2003), and from conversations with Satō Michiko, Associate Curator at the Pola Art Foundation.

31. Simmel, 'Adornment'.

32. Desmond Morris, *People Watching: Guide to Body Language* (London: Vintage, 2002), p. 365.

33. Friedrich Wilhelm Nietzsche, 'AntiChrist', in *The Complete Works*, trans. Oscar Levy (New York: Gordon, 1974).

34. Siegfried Kracauer, 'Propaganda and the Nazi War Film', in Krackauer, *From Caligari to Hitler: a Psychological History of the German Film* (Princeton, NJ: Princeton University Press, 1947).

35. Kishida Ryusei, 'Modaanjo—Short-haired Missy'.

36. Tanizaki Jun'ichirō, *Naomi*.

37. Seidensticker, *Low City, High City*, p. 91.

38. Tanaziki Jun'ichirō, *In Praise of Shadows*.

39. Newspaper unreferenced in Seidensticker, *Low City, High City*, p. 93.

40. Seidensticker, *Low City, High City*, p. 93.

41. Ibid.

42. Murata Takako, *Female Beauty in Modern Japan*.

43. Hirosawa Ei, *Kurokami to keshō no Shōwashi* (History of Shōwa in Women's Hair and Make-up) (Tokyo: Iwanami shoten, 1993), pp. 136–54.

44. F. Scott Fitzgerald, 'Bernice Bobs Her Hair', in *5 Short Stories: Bernice Bobs Her Hair and Other Stories* (London: Bodley Head, 1963).

45. The essay footnote states: 'Written in characters the title of this piece literally means "girl with her hair cut", a pun on *modaan gaaru*, modern girl, which is transcribed phonetically in the Japanese. It is taken from Kishida Ryūsei, *Shinko Zaiku Renga no Michisuji*, "Guide to old and new things in Ginza brick-town", completed on 4 May 1927, and published in the evening edition of *Tokyo Hibi Shinbum*, between 24 May and 10 June 1927. It was republished in Sakai Tadayasu, ed., *Kishida Ryūsei Zuihitsushō* (Tokyo: Iwanami Shoten, 1996), pp. 29–40.' Kishida Ryūsei, 'Modaanjo—Short-haired Missy'.

46. Kishida Ryūsei, 'Modaanjo—Short-haired Missy'.

47. Peter Dale, *The Myth of Japanese Uniqueness* (London: Routledge and Nissan Institute for Japanese Studies, University of Oxford, 1986).

48. Irokawa Daikichi, *The Culture of the Meiji Period*.

49. Yanagida Kunio, *Japanese Manners and Customs in the Meiji Era*, trans. Charles S. Terry (Tokyo: Obunsha, 1957), p. 18.

50. The Empress's proclamation was published in *Chōya shimbun* on 17 January 1887.

Chapter 5

1. Natsume Sōseki, *Wagahai wa neko de aru*, Chapter 7 in Natsume Sōseki, *Sōseki zenshū* (Complete Works), vol. 2 (Tokyo: Iwanami Shoten, 1956), pp. 20–3.

2. Jacques Derrida, 'Cogito and the History of Madness', in *Writing and Difference*, trans. Alan Bass (Chicago: University of Chicago Press, 1978), p. 308.

3. Roland Barthes, 'The Discourse of History', in E. S. Schaffer, ed., *Comparative Criticism*, vol. 3, *A Year Book*, trans. S. Bann (Cambridge: Cambridge University Press, 1981), pp. 3–20.

4. Irokawa Daikichi, *The Culture of the Meiji Period*, p. 51.

5. Kon Wajirō, *Nihon fukushoku shōshi*, in his *Kon Wajirō shū* (Complete Works), vol. 7 (Tokyo: Domesu Shuppan, 1972), p. 324.

6. H. Suganami, 'Japan's Entry into International Society', in Headley Bull and A. Watson, eds, *The Expansion of International Society* (Oxford: Clarendon Press, 1984), pp. 185–99.

7. Mori Arinori, *Mori Arinori zenshū*, vol. 1 (Tokyo: Senbundō Shoten, 1972), p. 162.

8. Hirano Ken'ichirō, 'The Westernisation of Clothes and the State in Meiji Japan', p. 122.

9. H. D. Harootunian, 'A Sense of an Ending and the Problem of Taishō', in B. S. Silberman and H. D. Harootunian, eds, *Japan in Crisis: Essays on Taishō Democracy* (Princeton, NJ: Princeton University Press, 1974), pp. 3–28.

10. Irokawa Daikichi, *The Culture of the Meiji Period*, pp. 68–9.

11. Hirano Ken'ichirō, 'The Westernisation of Clothes and the State in Meiji Japan', p. 130.

12. A. J. Toynbee, *Rekishi no kyōkun* (Can We Learn Lessons from History?), trans. and ed. Matsumoto Shigeharu (Tokyo: Iwanami Shoten, 1957), pp. 86–9.

13. Ernst Bloch, *Heritage of Our Times*, trans. Neville and Stephen Plaice (Berkeley: University of California Press, 1991), pp. 37–185. Quoted in Harootunian, *Overcome by Modernity*, p. xvii.

14. Hirano Ken'ichirō, 'The Westernisation of Clothes and the State in Meiji Japan', p. 129.

15. Seidensticker, *Tokyo Rising*, p. 242.

16. S. H. Nolte and S. A. Hastings, 'The Meiji State's Policy Toward Women 1890–1910', in Gail Lee Berstein, ed., *Recreating Japanese Women, 1600–1945* (Berkeley: University of California Press, 1991), pp. 151–74.

17. In a survey near Asagaya station in the western suburbs of Tokyo, Kon Wajirō judged 20 per cent of the 588 houses he counted to be 'culture style' (*bunka shiki*), while only 5 per cent were 'eclectic'. Kon Wajirō, 'Kōgai fūzoku zakkei', reprinted in Kon Wajirō and Yoshida Kenkichi, *Modernorojio 'Kōgengaku'* (Tokyo: Gakuyō Shobō, 1996), p. 115.

18. Sand, 'The Cultured Life as Contested Space'.

19. Hirano Ken'ichirō, 'The Westernisation of Clothes and the State in Meiji Japan', p. 122.

20. For example, in 1900 the average twenty-year-old male was 160 cm tall and the average female was 147.9 cm tall. By 1940, they were 164.5 and 152.7 cm tall, respectively. Keichirō Nakagawa and Henry Rosovsky, 'The Case of the Dying Kimono: The Influence of Changing Fashions on the Development of the Japanese Woolen Industry', in *Business History Review* 37 (Spring–Summer 1963), pp. 59–68.

21. Harootunian, 'A Sense of an Ending and the Problem of Taishō', pp. 3–28.
22. Nishitani Kenji, *Nishida Kitarō*, trans. Yamamoto Seisaku and James W. Heisig (Berkeley: University of California Press, 1991).
23. Kuki Shūzō, *Iki no kōzō*.
24. Harootunian, 'A Sense of an Ending and the Problem of Taishō', pp. 3–28.
25. Ibid.
26. Takamura Kōtarō, quoted in Harootunian, 'A Sense of an Ending and the Problem of Taishō', in Peter Francis Kornicki, ed., *Meiji Japan: Political, Economic and Social History, 1868–1912* (New York: Routledge, 1998), p. 95.
27. Harootunian, 'A Sense of an Ending and the Problem of Taishō', pp. 3–28.
28. Quoted by Isamu Fukuchi, 'Kokoro and the Spirit of Meiji', in *Monumenta Nipponica* 48/4 (1993), p. 469.
29. Ienaga Saburō, *Nihonjin no yōfuku kan no hensen*, p. 27.
30. Fukuzawa Yūkichi, quoted in Irokawa Daikichi, *The Culture of the Meiji Period*, p. 59.
31. Ienaga Saburō, *Nihonjin no yōfuku kan no hensen*, pp. 11–13, 32–3.
32. Dale, *The Myth of Japanese Uniqueness*.
33. Tetsuo Najita and H. D. Harootunian, 'Japan's Revolt against the West', in Bob Tadashi Wakabayashi, ed., *Modern Japanese Thought* (Cambridge: Cambridge University Press, 1998), p. 207.
34. Michele Marra, *Modern Japanese Aesthetics: A Reader* (Honolulu: University of Hawai'i Press, 1999), p. 1
35. G.W.F. Hegel, *Introductory Lectures on Aesthetics*, trans. Bernard Bosanquet (London: Penguin, 1933), p. 3.
36. Marra, *Modern Japanese Aesthetics*, p. 4.
37. Tetsuo Najita and Harootunian, 'Japan's Revolt Against the West', p. 232.
38. René König, *The Restless Image: A Sociology of Fashion*, trans. F. Bradley (London: George Allen and Unwin, 1973), p. 77.
39. Roland Barthes, *The Fashion System*, trans. M. Ward and R. Howard (Berkeley and Los Angeles: University of California Press, 1990).
40. Herbert Blumer, 'Fashion: From Class Differentiation to Collective Selection', *Sociological Quarterly* 10/3 (1969), pp. 275–91.
41. Gilles Lipovetsky, *The Empire of Fashion*, trans. Catherine Porter (Princeton, NJ: Princeton University Press, 1994).
42. Jean Baudrillard, *For a Critique of the Political Economy of the Sign*, trans. Charles Levin (St. Louis, MO: Telos Press, 1981), p. 78.
43. Blumer, 'Fashion: From Class Differentiation to Collective Selection', p. 290.
44. Tsuji Zennosuke, *Nihon bunkahi* (Tokyo: Shunjusha, 1950), vol. 7, p. 18.
45. Hirakawa Sukehiro, 'Japan's Turn to the West', trans. Bob Tadashi Wakabayahi, in Bob Tadashi Wakabayashi, ed., *Modern Japanese Thought* (Cambridge: Cambridge University Press, 1998), p. 61.

46. Orrin E. Klapp, *Collective Search for Identity* (New York; Holt, Rinehart and Winston, 1969), p. 73; and Klapp, *Currents of Unrest* (New York: Holt, Rinehart and Winston, 1972), p. 325.

47. Klapp, *Collective Search for Identity*, p. 114.

48. Kamishima Jirō, 'Meiji no shūen', in Hashikawa Bunzō and Matsumoto Sannosuke, eds, *Kindai Nihon seiji shisōshi* (Tokyo: Yuhikaku, 1971), pp. 384–6.

49. Georg Simmel, 'Fashion', *International Quarterly* 10 (October 1904), pp. 130–55.

50. Georg Simmel, 'Fashion', *American Journal of Sociology* 62/6 (May 1957), pp. 545–6.

51. Edward Sapir, 'Fashion', in *Encyclopedia of the Social Sciences*, vol. 6 (New York: Macmillan, 1931), pp. 139–44.

52. René König, *À La Mode: On the Social Psychology of Fashion*, trans. F. Fradley (New York: Seabury Press, 1973.)

53. König, *The Restless Image*, p. 76.

54. Barthes, *Oeuvres Complètes*, vol. 1 p. 744.

55. Allan G. Johnson, *The Blackwell Dictionary of Sociology*, 2nd edn (Oxford: Blackwell, 2000), p. 290.

56. Flügel, *The Psychology of Clothes*, p. 138.

57. Ibid., p. 138.

58. Ibid.. p. 139.

59. Yanagita [Yanagida] Kunio, *Meiji-Taishō shi, Sesō hen* (History of Meiji and Taishō Social Phenomena) (Tokyo: Kōdansha, 1931).

60. Flügel, *The Psychology of Clothes*.

61. Herbert Spencer, *The Principles of Sociology,* vol. 2 (Westport, CT: Greenwood Press, 1975).

62. Ibid., p. 210.

63. Herbert Spencer, *The Principles of Sociology*, vol. 2, (New York: D. Appleton and Co., 1896).

64. Thorstein Veblen, 'The Economic Theory of Woman's Dress', *Popular Science Monthly* 46 (December 1894), p. 200.

65. Thorstein Veblen, *Imperial Germany and the Industrial Revolution* (New York: Viking Press, 1954); and Veblen, 'The Opportunity of Japan', in *Essays in Our Changing Order* (New York: Viking Press, 1934). For additional remarks on Veblen's discussion of Germany and Japan, see Reinhard Bendix, *Nation-Building and Citizenship* (New York: John Wiley and Sons, 1964), pp. 6–7, 210–11.

66. Yuniya Kawamura, *Fashion-ology: An Introduction to Fashion Studies* (New York: Berg, 2005), p. 37.

67. Philippe Perrot, *Fashioning the Bourgeoisie: A History of Clothing in the Nineteenth Century*, trans. Richard Bienvenu (Princeton, NJ: Princeton University Press, 1994).

68. Werner Sombart, *Luxury and Capitalism*, trans. W. R. Ditmar (Ann Arbor: University of Michigan Press, 1902).
69. Thorstein Veblen, *The Theory of the Leisure Class* (New York: Mentor Books, 1953), pp. 120–1. Originally published 1899.
70. Flügel, *The Psychology of Clothes*, p. 111.
71. Veblen, *The Theory of the Leisure Class*, p. 127.
72. Dwight E. Robinson, 'The Economics of Fashion Demand', *Quarterly Journal of Economics* 75 (August 1969), p. 376.
73. Ibid., p. 392.
74. König, *The Restless Image*, p. 76.
75. John Maynard Keynes, *The General Theory of Employment, Interest, and Money* (London: Macmillan, 1936), p. 158.
76. Adam Smith, *The Theory of Moral Sentiments* (New York: Augustus M. Kelley, 1966).
77. Keynes, *The General Theory of Employment, Interest, and Money*, Chapter 12.
78. Barthes, *The Fashion System*.
79. Barthes, *Oeuvres Complètes*, vol. 1, p. 743.
80. Gabriel de Tarde, *The Laws of Imitation*, trans. E. G. Parsons from the 2nd French edition (New York: H. Holt and Company, 1903).
81. Everett M. Rogers, *Diffusion of Innovations* (New York: Free Press, 1962).
82. Ibid.
83. Fred D. Reynolds and William R. Darden, 'Why the Midi Failed', *Journal of Advertising Research* 12 (August 1972) pp. 39–44; and Reynolds and Darden, 'Fashion Theory and Pragmatics: The Case of the Midi', *Journal of Retailing* 49 (Spring 1973), pp. 51–62.
84. Harootunian, *Overcome by Modernity*, p. xxi.
85. A. L. Kroeber, 'On the Principle of Order in Civilization as Exemplified by Changes of Fashion', *American Anthropologist* 21 (July 1919), p. 263.
86. Ibid., p. 260.
87. Robert H. Lauer, *Perspectives on Social Change*, 2nd edn (Boston: Allyn & Bacon, 1977), Chapter 2.
88. Barthes, *Oeuvres Complètes*, vol. 1, p. 749.
89. Agnes Brooks Young, *Recurring Cycles of Fashion, 1760–1937* (New York: Cooper Square Publishers, 1966).
90. Ibid., p. 3.
91. Dwight E. Robinson, 'Style Changes: Cyclical, Inexorable, and Foreseeable', *Harvard Business Review* 53 (November 1975), pp. 121–31; and Robinson, 'Fashions in Shaving and Trimming of the Beard,' in *American Journal of Sociology* 81 (March 1976), pp. 1133–9.
92. Robinson, 'Style Changes', p. 126.
93. Hermann Bahr, *Prophet der Moderne: Tagebücher, 1888–1904* (Vienna: Böhlau, 1987).

94. James Laver, *Clothes* (London: Burke, 1952), p. 3.
95. Edmund Bergler, 'A Psychoanalyst Looks at Women's Clothes', *Cosmopolitan* (February 1960), p. 52.
96. James Laver, *Modesty in Dress* (London: William Heinemann, 1969), p. 38.
97. Elsie M. Frost, 'Fashion—A Reflection of a Way of Life', *Journal of Home Economics* 40 (May 1948), p. 245.
98. Pierre Clerget, 'The Economic and Social Role of Fashion', *Annual Report of the Smithsonian Institute* (1913), p. 763.
99. Flügel, *The Psychology of Clothes*, p. 152.
100. James Laver, *Taste and Fashion: From the French Revolution until To-day* (London: Harrap & Company, 1937), p. 250.
101. George Bush and Perry London use the case of the disappearance of knickers to argue that fundamental changes in mode of dress indicate changing social roles and self-concepts within a particular society. This argument could be used and debated with regard to the changes in Japanese underwear that accompanied the Shirokiwa fire. See George Bush and Perry London 'On the Disappearance of Knickers: Hypothesis for the Functional Analysis of the Psychology of Clothing', in Mary Ellen Roach and Joanne Bubolz Eicher, eds, *Dress, Adornment and the Social Order* (New York: John Wiley & Sons, 1965).
102. Laver, *Modesty in Dress*, p. 40.
103. Hirano Ken'ichirō, 'The Westernisation of Clothes and the State in Meiji Japan', p. 121.
104. P. G. Bogatyrev, *The Functions of Folk Costume in Moravian Slovakia*, trans. Richard G. Crum (The Hague: Mouton, 1971). Also see Kuwano Takashi, *Minshū bunka no kigōgaku: Senkakusha Bogatyrev no shigoto* (Tōkyo: Tokai Daigaku Shuppankai, 1981).
105. Alexandre Kojève, *Introduction à la Lecture de Hegel, Lectures on the Phenomenology of Spirit*, trans. James H. Nichols Jr. (Ithaca, NY: Cornell University Press, 1980).
106. Ralph H. Turner and Lewis M. Killian, *Collective Behaviour*, 2nd edn (Englewood Cliffs, NJ: Prentice-Hall, 1972), p. 153.
107. Ibid.
108. Ōtsuka Yasuji, *Collected Lectures*, vol. 1 (Tokyo: Iwanami-shoten, 1931), pp. 241–5. Quoted in Imamichi Tomonobu, 'Bigakusha Hyōden: Ōtsuka Yasuji' (Biographies of Aestheticians: Otsuka Yasuji), in *Nihon no Bigaku* (The Aesthetics of Japan) Tokyo: Kōdansha, 1986), pp. 83–90.
109. Otsuka Yasuji's lecture was entitled 'Nihonfuku no Bijutsuteki Kachi' (The Artistic Value of Japanese Clothes), and it was presented in 1903 to the Society of Bamboo and Oak Trees (Chikuhaku-Kai). See Otsuka Yasuji, *Collected Lectures*, vol. 1, p. 161. Quoted in Imamichi Tomonobu, 'Bigakusha Hyoden: Otsuka Yasuji', pp. 83–90.

Select Bibliography

Akagi Shunsuke, 'Hitomi Kinue', in Tsubota Itsuo, ed., *Taishō no josei gunzō, Nihon josei no rekishi 12* (History of Japanese Women, vol. 12, A Group Portrait of Taishō Period Women), Tokyo: Akatsuki kyōiku tosho, 1981.

Altman, Albert, 'Shimbunshi: The Early Meiji Adaptation of the Western Style Newspaper' in W. G. Beasley, ed., *Modern Japan: Aspects of History, Literature and Society*, Berkeley: University of California Press, 1975.

Anderson, Perry, *Lineages of the Absolutist State*, London: Verso, 1974.

Anesaki, A., *Life, Art, and Nature in Japan*, Tokyo: Tuttle, 1973.

Asukai Masamichi, ed., *Meiji*, vol. 11, *Zusetsu Nihon bunka no rekishi* (Pictorial History of Japanese Culture), ed. Kodama Kōta, Hayashiya Tatsusaburō and Higuchi Kiyoyuki, Tokyo: Shōgakukan, 1981.

Awakawa, Y., *Zen Painting*, Tokyo: Kodansha, 1970.

Bacon, Alice Mabel, *Japanese Girls and Women*, Houghton, New York, 1891.

Bacon, Alice Mabel, *A Japanese Interior*, Boston: Houghton Mifflin and Co., 1893.

Baelz, Erwin, *Awakening Japan: The Diary of a German Doctor*, ed. Toku Baelz, Bloomington: Indiana University Press, 1974.

Barthes, Roland, *Empire of Signs*, trans. Richard Howard, New York: Hill and Wang, 2000.

Barthes, Roland, *The Fashion System*, trans. Matthew Ward and Richard Howard, Berkeley and Los Angeles: University of California Press, 1990.

Baudelaire, Charles, 'The Painter of Modern Life', in *The Painter of Modern Life and Other Essays*, trans. J. Mayne, London: Phaidon Press, 1964.

Baudrillard, Jean, *The System of Objects*, trans. James Benedict, London: Verso, 1968.

Bauman, Zygmunt, *Hermeneutics and the Social Sciences: Approaches to Understanding*, London: Hutchinson, 1978.

Bellah, R. N., 'Japan's Cultural Identity: Some Reflections on the Work of Watsuji Tetsurō', *Journal of Asian Studies* 24/4 (August 1965).

Benjamin, Walter, *The Arcades Project*, trans. Howard Eiland and Kevin McLaughlin, Cambridge, MA: Harvard University Press, 1999.

Benjamin, Walter, *Illuminations*, trans. Harry Zohn, New York; Harcourt, Brace and World, 1968.

Bergler, Edmund, 'A Psychoanalyst Looks at Women's Clothes', *Cosmopolitan* (February 1960).

Bernstein, Gail Lee, ed., *Recreating Japanese Women: 1600–1945*, Berkeley: University of California Press, 1991.

Bird, Isabella, *Unbeaten Tracks in Japan*, New York: G. P. Putnam's, 1880.

Bissell, D. C., *The First Conglomerate: 145 Years of the Singer Sewing Machine Company*, New York: Audenreed Press, 1999.

Bix, Herbert, P., *Hirohito and the Making of Modern Japan*, New York: HarperCollins, 2000.

Blacker, Carmen, *The Japanese Enlightenment: A Study of the Writings of Fūkuzawa Yukichi*, Cambridge: Cambridge University Press, 1964.

Bloch, Mark, *Feudal Society,* trans. L. A. Manyon, Chicago: University of Chicago Press, 1961.

Blum, Stella, 'Evolution of Fashion: 1835–1895', in Stella Blum et al., *Rōman ishōten* (Exhibition of Romantic Clothing), Kyoto: Kyoto Costume Institute, 1980.

Blum, Stella, *Victorian Fashions and Costumes from Harper's Bazaar, 1867–1898*, New York: Dover Publications, 1974.

Blumer, Herbert, 'Fashion: From Class Differentiation to Collective Selection', *Sociological Quarterly* 10/3 (1969).

Bowring, R. J., *Mori Ōgai and the Modernization of Japanese Culture*, Cambridge: Cambridge University Press, 1979.

Breward, Christopher, and Evans, Caroline, *Fashion and Modernity*, Oxford: Berg, 2005.

Brown, Kendall H., *Light in Darkness: Women in Japanese Prints of Early Shōwa (1926–1945)*, Los Angeles: Fisher Gallery, University of Southern California, 1996.

Brown, Kendall H., and Minichiello, Sharon A., *Taishō Chic: Japanese Modernity, Nostalgia and Deco*, Honolulu: Honolulu Academy of Arts, 2002.

Buruma, Ian, *A Japanese Mirror*, London: Jonathan Cape, 1984.

Bush, George, and London, Perry, 'On the Disappearance of Knickers: Hypothesis for the Functional Analysis of the Psychology of Clothing', in Mary Ellen Roach and Joanne Bubolz Eicher, eds, *Dress, Adornment and the Social Order*, New York: John Wiley & Sons, 1965.

Carter, Michael, *Fashion Classics*, Oxford: Berg, 2004.

Clark, John, *Japanese Exchanges in Art 1850s–1930s with Britain, Continental Europe and the USA*, Sydney, Australia: Power Publications, 2001.

Clark, John, *Modern Asian Art*, Sydney, Australia: Craftsman House, 1998.

Clark, John, 'What Modern and Contemporary Asian Art Is (Or Is Not): The View from MOMA and the View from Asia', in John Clark, Maurizio Pelleggi and Kanaga Sabapathy, eds, *Eye of the Beholder*, Sydney, Australia: Wild Peony, 2006.

Clark, Timothy, *Kitagawa Utamaro*, Tokyo: Asahi Shinbunsha, 1995.

Conrad, Peter, *Modern Times, Modern Places: Life and Art in the 20th Century*, London: Thames and Hudson, 1998.

Crossick, Geoffrey, *Cathedrals of Consumption: The European Department Store 1850–1939*, London: Ashgate, 1999.

Cunningham, M., et al., *The Triumph of Japanese Style: 16th Century Art in Japan*, Cleveland, OH: Cleveland Museum of Art and Indiana University Press, 1991.

Dalby, Lisa, *Kimono: Fashioning Culture*, New Haven, CT: Yale University Press, 1993.

Dale, Peter, *The Myth of Japanese Uniqueness*, London: Routledge and Nissan Institute for Japanese Studies, University of Oxford, 1986.

Derval, Paul, *The Folies Bergère*, trans. Lucienne Hill, London: Methuen, 1955.

De Tarde, Gabriel, *The Laws of Imitation,* translated from the 2nd French edition by E. G. Parsons, New York: H. Holt and Company, 1903.

Dobson, Sebastian, and Bennett, Terry, *Images of Anglo-Japanese Relations*, Tokyo: Jardine Fleming, 1999.

Doi, L. T., *The Anatomy of Self: Individual versus Society*, Tokyo: Kodansha International, 1986.

Dorson, R. M., ed., *Studies in Japanese Folklore*, Bloomington: Indiana University Press, 1962.

Durkheim, Emile, *The Division of Labor in Society*, New York: Free Press, 1964.

Duus, Peter, ed., *The Twentieth Century*, vol. 6, *The Cambridge History of Japan*, Cambridge: Cambridge University Press, 1988.

Eisenstadt, S. N., *Japanese Civilization: A Comparative View*, Chicago: University of Chicago Press, 1996.

Ema Tsutomu, *Nihon fukushoku shiyō* (Outline of the History of Japanese Fashions), Kyoto: Hoshino-shoten, 1944.

Field, N., *The Splendour of Longing in the Tale of Genji*, Princeton, NJ: Princeton University Press, 1987.

Fitzgerald, F. Scott, 'Bernice Bobs Her Hair', in *5 Short Stories: Bernice Bobs Her Hair and Other Stories*, London: Bodley Head, 1963.

Fitzgerald, F. Scott, *The Great Gatsby,* New York: C. Scribner's Sons, 1925.

Flügel, J. C., *The Psychology of Clothes*, London: Hogarth, 1930.

Foucault, Michel, *Discipline and Punish: The Birth of the Prison,* trans. Alan Sheridan, New York: Pantheon Books, 1977.

Foucault, Michel, *The Order of Things: An Archaeology of the Human Sciences*, New York: Vintage Books, 1966.

Frisby, David, *Cityscapes of Modernity*, Cambridge: Polity Press, 2001.

Fujino Shozaburo, Fujino Shiro and Ono Akira, *Textiles*, vol. 11, *Estimates of Long-Term Economic Statistics of Japan since 1868*, Tokyo: Toyo Keizai Shinposha, 1979.

Fujitani, T., *Splendid Monarchy: Power and Pageantry in Modern Japan*, Berkeley: University of California Press, 1996.

Fukai Akiko, *Fashion: A History from the 18th to the 20th Century*, Kyoto: Kyoto Costume Institute, Taschen, 2002.

Fukushoku Hakubutsukan, ed., *Kindai no yōsō* (Modern Western-style Dress), Tokyo: Bunka Gakuen, 1983.

Fukuzawa Yūkichi, *Autobiography*, trans. Eiichi Kiyooka, New York: Columbia University Press, 1960.

Ganshof, François-Louis, *Feudalism*, trans. Philip Grierson, New York: Harper & Row, 1964.

Gartlan, Luke, *With Argus Eyes: The Early Life and Work of Baron von Stillfried-Ratenicz (1939–1911)*, unpublished thesis, Department of Art History and Theory, University of Sydney, Australia, 2004.

Gluck, Carol, *Japan's Modern Myths: Ideology in the Late Meiji Period*, Princeton, NJ: Princeton University Press, 1985.

Goodman, R., and Reesing, K., *Ideology and Practice in Modern Japan*, London: Routledge, 1992.

Griffis, William Elliot, *The Mikado: Institution and Person*, Princeton, NJ: Princeton University Press, 1915.

Guest, R., *A Compendious History of Cotton Manufacture*, Library of Industrial Classics, London: Frank Cass, 1968.

Guth, Christine, *Art of Edo Japan: The Artist and the City 1615–1868*, New York: Harry N. Abrams, 1996.

Habu Kiyo, *Yosō koto, Seikiru koto: Josei tachino nihon kindai* (Dressing up Life: Modern Times for Japanese Women), Tokyo: Keiso Shobo, 2004.

Hall, John Whitney, *Japan from Prehistory to Modern Times*, New York: Dell, 1970.

Hane Mikiso, *Peasants, Rebels, and Outcasts: The Underside of Modern Japan*, New York: Pantheon Books, 1982.

Hanley, Susan B., *Everyday Things in Premodern Japan: the Hidden Legacy of Material Culture*, Berkeley: University of California Press, 1997.

Harootunian, Harry, *Overcome by Modernity: History, Culture and Community in Interwar Japan*, Princeton, NJ: Princeton University Press, 2000.

Harootunian, Harry, 'A Sense of an Ending and the Problem of Taishō', in B. S. Silberman and H. D. Harootunian, eds, *Japan in Crisis: Essays on Taishō Democracy*, Princeton, NJ: Princeton University Press, 1974.

Harries, Meirion, *Soldiers of the Sun: The Rise and Fall of the Imperial Japanese Army*, New York: Random House, 1991.

Harvey, John, *Men in Black*, Chicago: University of Chicago Press: 1995.

Hasegawa, M., '*Karagokoro*, The Paradox That Shaped Japanese Culture', *Japan Echo* 12/2 (1985).

Hashiyama Takashi, *Bakumatsu Meiji bummei kaika* (Civilization and Enlightenment in the Late Edo and Meiji Periods), Nagoya: Maspro Denkō Kabushiki Kaisha, 1979.

Hata Kyōjirō, *Louis Vuitton Japan: The Building of Luxury*, Tokyo: Nikkei, 2003.

Hatsuda Tōru, *Hyakkaten no tanjō*, Tokyo: Sanseidō, 1993.

Hearn, Lacadio, *The Japanese Letters of Lacadio Hearn*, ed. Elizabeth Bisland, Wilmington, DE: Scholarly Resources, 1973.

Hendry, J., *Wrapping Culture*, Oxford: Clarendon Press, 1993.

Hendry, J., and Webber, J., eds, *Interpreting Japanese Society: Anthropological Approaches*, *Journal of the Anthropological Society of Oxford*, Occasional Papers, no. 5, 1986.

Hirakawa Sukehiro, 'Japan's Turn to the West', trans. Bob Tadashi Wakabayahi, in Bob Tadashi Wakabayahi, ed., *Modern Japanese Thought*, Cambridge: Cambridge University Press, 1998.

Hirano Ken'ichirō, 'The Westernization of Clothes and the State in Meiji Japan', in Hirano Ken'ichirō, ed., *The State and Cultural Transformation: Perspectives from East Asia*, Tokyo: United Nations University Press, 1993.

Hirosawa Ei, *Kurokami to keshō no Shōwashi* (History of Shōwa in Women's Hair and Make-up), Tokyo: Iwanami shoten, 1993.

Hisamatsu, S., *The Vocabulary of Japanese Literary Aesthetics*, Tokyo: Center for East Asian Cultural Studies, 1963.

Hobsbawm, Eric J., and Ranger, Terence, *The Invention of Tradition*, Cambridge: Cambridge University Press, 1983.

Hogan, Jackie, 'The Social Significance of English Usage in Japan', *Japanese Studies* 23/1 (May 2003).

Hollander, Anne, *Seeing through Clothes*, Berkeley: University of California Press, 1993.

Hollander, Anne, *Sex and Suits*, New York: A. A. Knopf, 1994.

Hori, I., *Japanese Folk Religion*, Chicago: University of Chicago Press, 1968.

Howell, David L., *Geographies of Identity in Nineteenth Century Japan*, Berkeley: University of California Press, 2005.

Huber, Richard, 'Effect on Prices of Japan's Entry into World Commerce after 1858', *Journal of Political Economy* 79/3 (May–June 1971).

Huffman, James L., *Politics of the Meiji Press: The Life of Fukuchi Gen'ichirō*, Honolulu: University Press of Hawaii, 1980.

Hume, Nancy, G., *Japanese Aesthetics and Culture: A Reader*, Albany: State University of New York Press, 1995.

Hunt, Alan, *Governance of the Consuming Passions: A History of Sumptuary Law*, New York: Palgrave Macmillan, 1996.

Ienaga Saburō, *Nihonjin no yōfuku kan no hensen*, Tokyo: Domesu Shuppan, 1976.

Imamichi Tomonobu, 'Bigakusha Hyōden: Otsuka Yasuji' (Biographies of Aestheticians: Ōtsuka Yasuji), in *Nihon no Bigaku* (The Aesthetics of Japan), Tokyo: Kōdansha, 1986.

Inoue Masahito, *Nihonjin yōfuku to* (The Japanese and Western Style Clothing), Tokyo: Kasaido, 2001.

Irokawa Daikichi, *The Culture of the Meiji Period*, translation edited by Marius B. Jansen, Princeton, NJ: Princeton University Press, 1970. Originally published as *Meiji no bunka*.

Isamu Fukuchi, 'Kokoro and the Spirit of Meiji', *Monumenta Nipponica* 48/4 (1993).

Isozaki Arata, 'Of City, Nation and Style', in *Postmodernism in Japan: Post-Contemporary Interventions*, ed. Masao Miyoshi and H. D. Harootunian, Durham, NC: Duke University Press, 1989.

Ivy, Marilyn, *Discourses of the Vanishing: Modernity, Phantasm, Japan*, Chicago: Chicago University Press, 1995.

Jansen, Marius B., *China in the Tokugawa World*, Cambridge, MA: Harvard University Press, 1992.

Jansen, Marius B., *The Making of Modern Japan*, Cambridge, MA: Harvard University Press, Cambridge, 2000.

Jansen, Marius B., ed., *The Nineteenth Century*, vol. 5, *The Cambridge History of Japan*, ed. Marius B. Jansen, John W. Hall, Madoka Kanai and Denis Twitchett, Cambridge: Cambridge University Press, 1989.

Japan Statistical Association, *Historical Statistics of Japan*, vols 1 and 3, Tokyo: Japan Statistical Association, 1987.

Johnson, Kim K. P., Torntore, Susan J. and Eicher, Joanne B., *Fashion Foundations: Early Writings on Fashion and Dress*, Oxford: Berg, 2003.

Kafū Nagai, *Selections*, Tokyo: Chikuma Shobō, 2001.

Kageyama, H., *The Arts of Shinto*, New York: Weatherhill, 1973.

Kamishima Jirō, 'Meiji no shuen', in Hashikawa Bunzo and Matsumoto Sannosuke, eds, *Kindai Nihon seiji shisoshi*, Tokyo: Yuhikaku, 1971.

Karlin, Jason G., 'The Gender of Nationalism: Competing Masculinities in Meiji Japan', *Journal of Japanese Studies* 28/1 (Winter 2002).

Kato, S., *Form, Style and Tradition*, Tokyo: Kodansha, 1966.

Kawabata Yasunari, *The Scarlet Gang of Asakusa*, trans. Alisa Freedman, Berkeley: University of California Press, 2005.

Kawamura, Yuniya, *Fashion-ology: An Introduction to Fashion Studies*, New York: Berg, 2005.

Kawazoe Noboru, 'Kon Wajirō', in *Nihon minzoku bunka taikei*, Tokyo: Kondansha, 1978.

Keene, Donald, *Dawn to the West*, vol. 3, *Japanese Literature of the Modern Era: Fiction*, New York: Columbia University Press, 1998.

Keene, Donald, *Dawn to the West*, vol. 4, *Japanese Literature of the Modern Era: Poetry, Drama, Criticism*, New York: Columbia University Press, 1999.

Keene, Donald, *Yoshimasa and the Silver Pavilion*, New York; Columbia University Press, 2003.

Keichirō Nakagawa, and Rosovsky, Henry, 'The Case of the Dying Kimono: The Influence of Changing Fashions on the Development of the Japanese Woolen Industry', *Business History Review* 37 (Spring–Summer 1963).

Kelley, Allen C., and Williamson, Jeffery G., *Lessons from Japanese Development: An Analytical Economic History*, Chicago: University of Chicago Press, 1974.

Kishida Ryūsei, 'Modaanjo—Short-haired Missy', trans. John Clark, in *Modern Boy Modern Girl: Modernity in Japanese Art 1910–1935*, Sydney, Australia: Art Gallery of New South Wales, 1998.

Kishida Ryūsei, *Shinko Zaiku Renga no Michisuji*, "Guide to Old and New Things in Ginza Brick-town", completed on 4 May 1927, published in the evening edition of *Tokyo Hibi Shinbum*, between 24 May and 10 June 1927. Republished in Sakai Tadayasu, ed., *Kishida Ryūsei Zuihitsushō*, Tokyo: Iwanami Shoten, 1996.

Koike Mitsue, 'Ifuku no imi', in Yabe Akihiko, ed., *Seikatsu no naka no ifuku*, Tokyo: Ōbunsha, 1983.

Kojève, Alexandre, *Introduction à la Lecture de Hegel, Lectures on the Phenomenology of Spirit*, trans. James H. Nichols, Jr., Ithaca, NY: Cornell University Press, 1980.

Kōjin, Karatani, 'The Discursive Space of Modern Japan,' in *Boundary 2* 18/3 (1991).

Kondō Tomie, 'Meiji fukusō dangi' (A Lesson in Meiji Clothing), in Sekine Masaru and Kikuchi Jōrō, eds, *Hakubutsukan Meiji Mura: Meiji no tatazumai* (Meiji Village Museum: The Look of Meiji), vol. 7, *Nihon no hakubutsukan* (Japanese Museums), Tokyo: Kondansha, 1980.

Kon Wajirō, *Nihon fukushoku shōshi*, in Kon Wajirō, *Kon Wajirō shū* (Complete Works), vol. 7, Tokyo: Domesu Shuppan, 1972.

Kon Wajirō and Yoshida Kenkichi, *Moderunorojio 'Kōgengaku'*, Tokyo: Gakuyō Shobō, 1996.

König, René, *The Restless Image: A Sociology of Fashion*, trans. F. Bradley, London: George Allen and Unwin, 1973.

Konishi, J., *A History of Japanese Literature*, Princeton, NJ: Princeton University Press, 1984.

Koyama Shizuko, *Ryōsai kenbo to iu kihan*, Tokyo: Keisō Shobō, 1991.

Kozo Yamamura and Hanley, Susan B., *Economic and Demographic Change in Preindustrial Japan 1600–1868*, Princeton, NJ: Princeton University Press, 1977.

Kroeber, A. L., 'On the Principle of Order in Civilization as Exemplified by Changes of Fashion', *American Anthropologist* 21 (July 1919).

Kroeber, Alfred., and Richardson, J., 'Three Centuries of Women's Dress Fashions: A Quantitative Analysis', in A. L. Kroeber, *The Nature of Culture*, Chicago: University of Chicago Press, 1952.

Kuki Shūzō, *Iki no kōzō* (Reflections on Japanese Taste: The Structure of *Iki*), trans. John Clark, Sydney, Australia: Power Publications, 1997.

Kuwabara Takeo, *Japan and Western Civilization: Essays on Comparative Culture*, Tokyo: University of Tokyo Press, 1983.

Kuwano Takashi, *Minshū bunka no kigōgaku: Senkakusha Bogatyrev no shigoto*, Tokyo: Tōkai Daigaku Shuppankai, 1981.

Lane, Richard, *Images from the Floating World: The Japanese Print*, Oxford: Oxford University Press, 1978.

Laver, James, *British Military Uniforms*, London: Penguin Books, 1948.

Laver, James, *Clothes*, London: Burke, 1952.

Laver, James, *A Letter to a Girl on the Future of Clothes*, London: Home & Van Thal, 1946.

Laver, James, *Modesty in Dress*, London: William Heinemann Ltd., 1969.

Laver, James, *Style in Costume*, Oxford: Oxford University Press, 1949.

Laver, James, *Taste and Fashion: From the French Revolution until To-day*, London: Harrap & Company, 1937.

Laver, James, 'The Triumph of Time', in Sylva Norman, ed., *Contemporary Essays*, London: Elkin Mathews and Marrot, 1933.

Levy, I., *Hitomaro and the Birth of Japanese Lyricism*, Princeton, NJ: Princeton University Press, 1984.

Lipovetsky, Gilles, *The Empire of Fashion*, trans. Catherine Porter, Princeton, NJ: Princeton University Press, 1994.

Lippit, Seiji. M., *Topographies of Japanese Modernism*, New York: Columbia University Press, 2002.

Loti, Pierre, *Japoneries d'automne*, Paris: Calmann-Lévy, 1889.

Mackie, Vera, 'Modern Selves and Modern Spaces', in Elise K. Tipton and John Clark, eds, *Being Modern in Japan*, Honolulu: University of Hawai'i Press, 2000.

MacPherson, Kerrie L., *Asian Department Stores*, Honolulu: University of Hawai'i Press, 1998.

Maeda Ali, *Text and the City: Essays on Japanese Modernity*, Durham, NC: Duke University Press, 2004.

Marra, Michael, *A History of Modern Japanese Aesthetics*, Honolulu: University of Hawai'i Press, 2001.

Marra, Michele, *The Aesthetics of Discontent: Politics and Reclusion in Medieval Japanese Literature*, Honolulu: University of Hawai'i Press, 1991.

Marra, Michele, *Modern Japanese Aesthetics: A Reader*, Honolulu: University of Hawai'i Press, 1999.

Martin, Richard, and Koda, Harold, *Intra Apparel*, New York: Metropolitan Museum of Art, 1993.

Mashimo Yoshiyuki, *Samurai: Dandyism in Japan*, Tokyo: Tokyo Metropolitan Museum of Photography, 2003.

Matsunaga, A., *The Buddhist Philosophy of Assimilation (Honji-suijaku)*, Tokyo: Sophia University, 1969.

Mayer, Arno, *The Persistence of the Old Regime: Europe to the Great War*, London: Croom Helm, 1981.

Maynard, Margaret, *Out of Line: Australian Women and Style*, Sydney, Australia: University of New South Wales Press, 2001.

McClain, James L., and Hall, John Whitney., *Early Modern Japan*, vol. 4, *The Cambridge History of Japan*, Cambridge: Cambridge University Press, 1991.

McClain, James L., Merriman, John M., and Ugawa Kaoru, *Edo and Paris: Urban Life and the State in the Early Modern Era*, Ithaca, NY: Cornell University Press, 1994.

McNeil, P., 'Myths of Modernism: Japanese Architecture, Interior Design and the West c. 1920–1940', *Journal of Design History* 5/4 (1992).

McVeigh, Brian J., *Nationalisms of Japan, Managing and Mystifying Identity*, Oxford: Rowman & Littlefield, 2004.

Meech-Pekarik, Julia, *The World of the Meiji Print*, New York and Tokyo: Weatherhill, 1986.

Miner, E., Odagiri, H., and Morrell, R. E., *The Princeton Companion to Classical Japanese Literature*, Princeton, NJ: Princeton University Press, Princeton, 1985.

Mitchell, Louise, *The Cutting Edge: Fashion from Japan*, Sydney, Australia: Powerhouse Publishing, 2005.

Mitchell, R. H., *Censorship in Imperial Japan*, Princeton, NJ: Princeton University Press, 1983.

Mitsuda Kiyoko, 'Kindaiteki boseikan no juyō to henka—"kyōiku suru hahaoya" kara "ryōsai kenbo" e,' in Wakita Haruko, *Bosei o tou—rekishiteki hensen*, vol. 2, Tokyo: Jinbun Shoin, 1985.

Miyoshi Masao, *Accomplices of Silence*, Berkeley: University of California Press, 1974.

Miyoshi Masao and Harootunian, H. D., eds, *Japan in the World*, Durham, NC: Duke University Press, 1993.

Mokyr, Joel, *The British Industrial Revolution: An Economic Perspective*, London: Westview Press, 1998.

Mori Arinori, *Mori Arinori zenshū*, vol. 1, Tokyo: Senbundō Shoten, 1972.

Morrow, Carol, 'Kimono', unpublished manuscript, Power Library, Sydney University, Australia, 1998.

Mostow, Joshua S., Bryson, Norman, and Graybill, Maribeth, *Gender and Power in the Japanese Visual Field*, Honolulu: University of Hawai'i Press, 2003.

Murata Takako, *Female Beauty in Modern Japan: Makeup and Coiffure*, trans. Komada Makiko, Tokyo: Pola Research Institute of Beauty and Culture, 2003.

Nagai Kafū, *During the Rains and Flowers in the Shade: Two Novellas*, trans. Lane Dunlop, Stanford, CA: Stanford University Press, 1994.

Najita, T., and Scheiner, I., eds, *Japanese Thought in the Tokugawa Period*, Chicago: Chicago University Press, 1978.

Nakaano Hajiimu, 'Introduction to the Work of Kuki Shūzō,' in Kuki Shūzō, *Iki no kōzō* (Reflections on Japanese Taste: The Structure of Iki), trans. John Clark, Sydney, Australia: Power Publications, 1997.

Nakabayashi, Masaki, *Kindai Shihon Shugi No Soushiki* (Organization in Modern Capitalism: Governance of Trade and Production in the Silk Reeling Industry), Tokyo: University of Tokyo Press, 2003.

Nakamura, H., *A History of the Development of Japanese Thought*, Tokyo: Kokusai Bunka Shinkokai, 1967.

Nakane Chie, *Human Relations in Japan*, a summary translation of *Tateshakai no Ningen Kankei* (Personal Relations in a Vertical Society), Tokyo: Ministry of Foreign Affairs, 1972.

Nakane Chie, *Kinship and Economic Organization in Rural Japan*, London: Athlone Press, 1967.

Napier, Susan, *The Fantastic in Modern Japanese Literature: The Subversion of Modernity*, London: Routledge, 1996.

Natsume Sōseki, *Complete Works* (Sōseki zenshū), vol. 2, Tokyo: Iwanami Shoten, 1956.

Nihon Orimono Shimbunsha (Japan Textile News Co.), *Dai Nihon orimono 2600-nen shi* (A 2600 Year History of Textiles in Greater Japan), Tokyo: Nihon Orimono Shimbunsha, 1940.

Nisbett, Richard E., *The Geography of Thought*, New York: Free Press, 2003.

Nishitani Kenji, *Nishida Kitarō*, trans. Yamamoto Seisaku and James W. Heisig, Berkeley: University of California Press, 1991.

Nishiyama Matsunosuke, *Edo Culture: Daily Life and Diversions in Urban Japan, 1600–1868*, trans. Gerald Groemer, Honolulu: University of Hawaii Press, 1997.

Nitobe Inazo, *Bushido: The Soul of Japan*, New York: G. P. Putnam's Sons, 2001. Originally published 1905.

Nolte, S. H., and Hastings, S. A., 'The Meiji State's Policy toward Women 1890–1910', in Gail Lee Berstein, ed., *Recreating Japanese Women, 1600–1945*, Berkeley: University of California Press, 1991.

Oë Kenzaburō, 'Japan's Dual Identity: A Writer's Dilemma', in Masao Miyoshi and H. D. Harootunian, eds, *Postmodernism and Japan*, Durham, NC: Duke University Press, 1989.

Ohnuki-Tierney, Emiko, *Kamikaze, Cherry Blossoms, and Nationalisms: The Militarization of Aesthetics in Japanese History*, Chicago: University of Chicago Press, 2001.

Ohnuki-Tierney, Emiko, *Rice as Self: Japanese Identities through Time*, Princeton, NJ: Princeton University Press, 1993.

Okakura Kakuzo, *The Awakening of Japan*, New York: Century Co., 1905.

Okakura, Kakuzo, *The Ideals of the East*, London: John Murray, 1904.

Osaka Yōfuku-sho Dōgyō Kumiai (Osaka Association of Merchants and Tailors of Western Suits), *Nihon yōfuku enkaku-shi* (The History of Western Suits in Japan), Osaka: Osaka Yōfuku-sho Dōgyō Kumiai, 1930.

Ota Rinichiro, 'Kindai Nihon gunpuku shi', *Hifuku bunka*, Bunka Fukusō Gakuin, Tokyo, no. 68 (October 1961).

Ōtsuka Yasuji, *Collected Lectures*, vol. 1, Tokyo: Iwanami-shoten, 1933.

Otten, C. M., ed., *Anthropology and Art: Readings in Cross-cultural Aesthetics* New York: Natural History Press, 1971.

Perrot, Philippe, *Fashioning the Bourgeoisie: A History of Clothing in the Nineteenth Century*, trans. Richard Bienvenu, Princeton, NJ: Princeton University Press, 1994.

Pyle, K. B., *The New Generation in Meiji Japan: Problems of Cultural Identity 1885–1895*, Stanford, CA: Stanford University Press, 1969.

Rathbun, William Jay, *Beyond the Tanabata Bridge: Traditional Japanese Textiles*, Seattle, WA: Seattle Art Museum, 1993.

Razek, Rula, *Dress Codes: Reading Nineteenth Century Fashion*, Stanford, CA: Stanford University Press, 1999.

Reischaurer, Edwin O., 'Serge Elisséeff', *Harvard Journal of Asiatic Studies* 20 (June 1957).

Richie, Donald, *The Image Factory: Fads and Fashions in Japan*, London: Reaktion, 2003.

Richie, Donald, and Buruma, I., *The Japanese Tattoo*, New York: Weatherhill, 1980.

Rimer, J. Thomas, *Culture and Identity: Japanese Intellectuals during the Inter-war Years*, Princeton, NJ: Princeton University Press, 1990.

Roberts, John G., *Mitsui: Three Centuries of Japanese Business*, New York: Art Media Resources, 1989.

Robertson, Jennifer, *Takarazuke: Sexual Politics and Popular Culture in Modern Japan*, Berkeley: University of California Press, 1998.

Robinson, Dwight E., 'The Economics of Fashion Demand', *Quarterly Journal of Economics* 75 (August 1969).

Robinson, Dwight E., 'Style Changes: Cyclical, Inexorable, and Foreseeable', *Harvard Business Review* 53 (November 1975).

Roden, D., *Schooldays in Imperial Japan: A Study in the Culture of a Student Elite*, Los Angeles: University of California Press, 1980.

Rogers, Everett M., *Diffusion of Innovations*, New York: Free Press, 1962.

Rosovsky, Henry, and Kazushi Ohkawa, *Japanese Economic Growth: Trend Acceleration in the Twentieth Century*, Stanford, CA: Stanford University Press, 1973.

Sakai Tadayasu, ed., *Kishida Ryūsei Zuihitsushō*, Tokyo: Iwanami Shoten, 1996.

Sand, Jordan, 'The Cultured Life as Contested Space: Dwelling and Discourse in the 1920s', in Elise K. Tipton and John Clark, eds, *Being Modern in Japan*, Honolulu: University of Hawai'i Press, 2000.

Sand, Jordan, *House and Home in Modern Japan: Architecture, Domestic Space, and Bourgeois Culture 1880–1930*, Cambridge, MA: Harvard University Press, 2003.

Sanpei Takako, *Nihon kigyō-shi* (History of Textile Manufactures in Japan), Tokyo: Yuzan-kaku, 1961.

Sanson, George, *The Western World and Japan*, New York: A. A. Knopf, 1951.

Sapir, Edward, 'Fashion', in *Encyclopedia of the Social Sciences*, vol. 6, New York: Macmillan, 1931.

Satō, Barbara, 'An Alternate Informant: Middle Class Women and Mass Magazines in 1920s Japan', in Elise K. Tipton and John Clark, eds, *Being Modern in Japan*, Sydney: Australian Humanities Research Foundation, 2000.

Satō, Barbara, 'Middle-Class Women and Mass Magazines in 1920s Japan', unpublished manuscript.

Satō, Barbara, *The New Japanese Woman: Modernity, Media and Women in Interwar Japan*, Durham, NC: Duke University Press, 2003.

Seidensticker, Edward, *Low City, High City*, London: Allen Lane, 1983.

Seidensticker, Edward, *Tokyo Rising: The City since the Great Earthquake*, New York: Knopf, 1990.

Setsuo Uenoda, *Japan, Yesterday and Today: Sketches and Essays on Japanese City Life*, 2nd edn, Tokyo: Tokyo News Service, 1956.

Shiga Shigetaka, *Nihon fūkei ron* (On Landscape), Tokyo: Iwanami Shoten, 1995.

Shively, Donald, 'The Japanization of the Middle Meiji' in Donald Shively, ed., *Tradition and Modernization in Japanese Culture*, Princeton, NJ: Princeton University Press, 1971.

Shively, Donald, *Tradition and Modernization in Japanese Culture*, Princeton, NJ: Princeton University Press, 1971.

Shōwa Joshi Daigaku Hifukugaku Kenkyūshitsu (Shōwa Women's University Clothing Studies Laboratory), *Kindai Nihon fukusō-shi* (A History of Clothing in Modern Japan), Tokyo: Kindai Bunka Kenkyujo, 1971.

Shü, Kishida, and Butler, K. D., *Kurobune gensö*, Tokyo: Seidosha, 1992.

Sievers, Sharon L., *Flowers in Salt: The Beginnings of Feminist Consciousness in Modern Japan*, Stanford, CA: Stanford University Press, 1983.

Silverberg, Miriam, 'The Café Waitress Serving Modern Japan', in Stephen Vlastos, ed., *Mirror of Modernity: Invented Traditions of Modern Japan*, Berkeley: University of California Press, 1991.

Simmel, Georg, 'Adornment', in D. Frisby and M. Featherstone, eds, *Simmel on Culture*, London: Sage, 1997.

Simmel, Georg, 'The Philosophy of Fashion', in D. Frisby and M. Featherstone, eds, *Simmel on Culture*, London: Sage, 1997.

Simmel, Georg, 'The Problem of Style', trans. Mark Ritter, *Theory, Culture and Society* 8/3 (August 1991).

Smith, Thomas Carlyle, *Political Change and Industrial Development in Japan: Government Enterprise, 1868–1880*, Stanford, CA: Stanford University Press, 1955.

Smitka, Michael, *The Japanese Economy in the Tokugawa Era: 1600–1868*, Japanese Economic History 1600–1960, no. 6, New York: Garland, 1998.

Smitka, Michael, *The Textile Industry and the Rise of the Japanese Economy*, Japanese Economic History 1600–1960, no. 4, New York: Garland, 1998.

Sombart, Werner, *Luxury and Capitalism*, trans. W. R. Ditmar, Ann Arbor: University of Michigan Press, 1902.

Suganami, H., 'Japan's Entry into International Society', in Headley Bull and A. Watson, eds, *The Expansion of International Society*, Oxford: Clarendon Press, 1984.

Suzuki, D. T., *Zen and Japanese Culture*, Princeton, NJ: Princeton University Press, 1970.

Takamatsu Mari, 'Ethics of Exhibitions: A Study on Representation of the Female Nude in the Last Decade of the 19th Century in Japan', in *Studies in Aesthetics and Art History*, vol. 21, Kyoto: Department of Aesthetics and Art History, Kyoto University, 2000.

Takashina, S., 'The Japanese Aesthetic Sense', *Japan Echo* 11/3 (1984).

Taki Kōji, *Tennō no shōzō*, Tokyo: Iwanami Shoten, 1988.

Tanaka, Stefan, *Japan's Orient: Rendering Pasts into History*, Berkeley: University of California Press, 1993.

Tanaka, Stefan, *New Times in Modern Japan*, Princeton, NJ: Princeton University Press, 2004.

Tanaka, T., 'The Acceptance of Western Civilization in Japan (Meiji Period)', *East Asian Cultural Studies* 6 (March 1967).

Tanizaki Jun'ichirō, *In Praise of Shadows*, trans. Thomas J. Harper and Edward G. Seidensticker, New Haven, CT: Leete's Island Books, 1977.

Tanizaki Jun'ichirō, *Naomi*, trans. Anthony Chambers, Tokyo: Charles E. Tuttle, 1985.

Tanno Iku, ed., *Sōgō fukushoku-shi jitem* (General Clothing History Encyclopedia), Tokyo: Yūzankaku, 1980.

Tetsuo Najita and Harootunian, H. D., 'Japan's Revolt against the West', in Bob Tadashi Wakabayashi, ed., *Modern Japanese Thought*, Cambridge: Cambridge University Press, 1998.

Tetsurō Watsuji, *Climate*, trans. Geoffrey Bownas, Tokyo: Hokuseido Press, 1961.

Thompson, James Matthew, *Louis Napoleon and the Second Empire*, Oxford: Blackwell, 1965.

Tipton, Elise K., 'The Café, Contested Space of Modernity in Interwar Japan', in Elise K. Tipton and John Clark, eds, *Being Modern in Japan*, Honolulu: University of Hawaii Press, 2000.

Tobin, Joseph, 'Introduction', in Joseph J. Tobin, ed., *Re-made in Japan: Everyday Life and Consumer Taste in a Changing Society*, New Haven, CT: Yale University Press, 1992.

Toshio Kawatake, *Kabuki: Baroque Fusion of the Arts*, trans. Frank and Jean Connell Hoff, Tokyo: International House of Japan, 2003.

Totman, Conrad, *Early Modern Japan*, Berkeley: University of California Press, 1993.

Toynbee, A. J., *Rekishi no kyōkun* (Can We Learn Lessons from History?), trans. and ed. Matsumoto Shigeharu, Tokyo: Iwanami Shoten, 1957.

Tsubota Itsuo, ed., *Taishō no josei gunzō, Nihon josei no rekishi 12* (History of Japanese Women, vol. 12, A Group Portrait of Taishō Period Women), Tokyo: Akatsuki kyōiku tosho, 1981.

Tsuda Mamichi, 'An Official Insignia', in *Meiroku Zasshi: Journal of the Japanese Enlightenment,* trans. William Reynolds Braisted, Cambridge, MA: Harvard University Press, 1976.

Tsuji Zennosuke, *Nihon bunkahi,* Tokyo: Shunjusha, 1950, vol. 7.

Tsukahira, Toshio George, *Feudal Control in Tokugawa Japan: The Sankin-kōtai System,* Cambridge, MA: Harvard University Press, 1966.

Tsurumi, E. Patricia, *Factory Girls: Women in the Thread Mills of Meiji Japan,* Princeton, NJ: Princeton University Press, 1990.

Turner, Ralph H., and Killian, Lewis M., *Collective Behaviour,* 2nd edn, Englewood Cliffs, NJ: Prentice-Hall, 1972.

Turumi Shunsuke, *Zasshi Josei,* Tokyo: Nihon Tosho Centre, 1991–1993.

Ueda Makoto, *Literary and Art Theories in Japan,* Cleveland, OH: Press of Case Western Reserve University, 1991.

Umetani, N., *The Role of Foreign Employees in the Meiji Era in Japan,* Tokyo: Institute for the Developing Economies, 1971.

Uno, Kathleen, 'The Origins of "Good Wife, Wise Mother" in Modern Japan', in Erich Pauer and Regine Mathias, eds, *Japanische Frauengeschichte(n),* Marburg, Germany: Forderverein Marburger Japan-Reiche, 1995.

Veblen, Thorstein, 'The Opportunity of Japan', in Thorstein Veblen, *Essays in Our Changing Order,* New York: Viking Press, 1934.

Veblen, Thorstein, *The Theory of the Leisure Class,* New York: Mentor Books, 1953. Originally published 1899.

Vlastos, Stephen, *Mirror of Modernity: Invented Traditions of Modern Japan,* Berkeley: University of California Press, 1998.

Wakabayashi, Bob Tadashi, *Modern Japanese Thought,* Cambridge: Cambridge University Press, 1998.

Weisenfeld, Gennifer, *Mavo: Japanese Artists and the Avant-garde 1905–1931,* Berkeley: University of California Press, 2002.

Wiley, Peter Booth, *Yankees in the Land of the Gods: Commodore Perry and the Opening of Japan,* New York: Penguin, 1990.

Wilson, Elizabeth, 'Fashion and Modernity', in Christopher Breward and Carline Evans, eds, *Fashion and Modernity,* Oxford: Berg, 2005.

Worringer, W., *Abstraction and Empathy,* London: Routledge & Kegan Paul, 1967.

Yamakawa Kikue, *Yamakawa Kikue Shū,* vol. 5, Tokyo: Iwanami Shoten, 1982.

Yanagita [Yanagida] Kunio, *Japanese Manners and Customs in the Meiji Era,* trans. Charles S. Terry, Tokyo: Obunsha, 1957.

Yanagita [Yanagida] Kunio, *Meiji-Taishō shi, Sesō hen* (History of Meiji and Taishō Social Phenomena), Tokyo: Kōdansha, 1931.

Yasue Aoki Kidd, *Women Workers in the Japanese Cotton Mills: 1880–1920*, Ithaca, NY: Cornell University Press, 1978.

Yasutaka, T., 'Pleasure Quarters and Tokugawa Culture', in A. C. Gerstle, ed., *18th Century Japan*, Sydney, Australia: Allen & Unwin, 1989.

Young, Agnes Brooks, *Recurring Cycles of Fashion, 1760–1937*, New York; Cooper Square Publishers, 1966.

Yuasa, Y., *The Body: Toward an Eastern Mind-Body Theory*, trans. Nagatomo Shigenori and T. P. Kasulis, Albany: State University of New York Press, 1987.

Zennosuke, Tsuji, *Nihon bunkashi*, Tokyo: Shunjōsha, 1950.

Index